D1564735

# BALKAN BREAKTHROUGH

TWENTIETH-CENTURY BATTLES

Spencer C. Tucker, editor

# BALKAN
# BREAKTHROUGH

## THE
## BATTLE
## OF
## DOBRO POLE
## 1918

### RICHARD C. HALL

Indiana University Press
Bloomington | Indianapolis

This book is a publication of

Indiana University Press
601 North Morton Street
Bloomington, Indiana 47404-3797 USA

www.iupress.indiana.edu

Telephone orders    800-842-6796
Fax orders              812-855-7931
Orders by e-mail    iuporder@indiana.edu

© 2010 by Richard C. Hall
All rights reserved

No part of this book may be reproduced or utilized in any form or by any means, elec-
tronic or mechanical, including photocopying and recording, or by any information
storage and retrieval system, without permission in writing from the publisher. The
Association of American University Presses' Resolution on Permissions constitutes
the only exception to this prohibition.

⊗ The paper used in this publication meets the minimum requirements of the American National Standard for Information Sciences—Permanence of Paper for Printed
Library Materials, ANSI Z39.48-1992.

Manufactured in the United States of America

Library of Congress Cataloging-in-Publication Data

Hall, Richard C. (Richard Cooper), [date]
  Balkan breakthrough : the Battle of Dobro Pole 1918 / Richard C. Hall.
     p. cm. — (Twentieth-century battles)
  Includes bibliographical references and index.
  ISBN 978-0-253-35452-5 (cloth : alk. paper)
  1. Dobro Pole, Battle of, Serbia, 1918. 2. World War, 1914–1918—Campaigns—
Serbia. I. Title.

  D562.D63H35 2010
  940.4'37—dc22

                                                                          2009031095

1 2 3 4 5 15 14 13 12 11 10

# Contents

# Maps

# Acknowledgments

This book is result of work that began in the library of the Air War College. I am grateful for all the assistance the staff there gave me. Also, the help of Vasil Zagarov at Bibliotelescope in Sofia was critical to the completion of the study. My colleagues at Georgia Southwestern State University were supportive and helpful. And as ever, my wife, Audrey, gave me the sympathy and encouragement to pursue my goals.

# Introduction

The mountainous southeastern corner of Europe is bordered on three sides by substantial bodies of water. The Adriatic Sea in the west, the Black Sea in the east, and the Aegean or White Sea in the south form this region into the peninsula. This entire region is often called the Balkan Peninsula, after the Turkish name for the central mountain range in Bulgaria. Mountains throughout much of the region hinder advancement overland. River valleys offer the main means of access into the hinterland. Chief among these is the Danube, which empties into the Black Sea. In the west, a high mountain chain impedes access from the Adriatic. In the south, several rivers break through the mountains and afford a connection to the interior. These include the Vardar and the Struma, which cut through the rocky mountain ridges of southeastern Europe. In several locations these rivers pass through narrow defiles, with only limited level land on one or both sides of the river. The Vardar, combined with the Morava River flowing to the north, offers a relatively easy passage between the Aegean and the Danube. Several cities on the Balkan periphery provide commercial access into the interior. On the Adriatic these include Dubrovnik (It: Ragusa) and Split (It: Spaleto). On the Black Sea these commercial outlets are Burgas and Varna in Bulgaria and Constanța in Romania. The largest and most important of these port cities is located in the south on an arm of the Aegean Sea. This is Salonika (Eng), Thessaloniki (Gk), Solun (Bg). Here a cosmopolitan population and an active economy combine to form one of the most important urban areas in southeastern Europe.[1] This port was the major maritime access point for much of the central Balkan Peninsula, including the large mixed ethnic region of Macedonia. One railroad line linked Salonika with Athens to the south and Constantinople to the east. Another extended up into Macedonia, connecting Salonika with the main city of central Macedonia, Skopie, and then on up to the Serbian capital, Belgrade.

The term *Balkan* has come to be associated with obscure and complex conflict in southeastern Europe. Often such conflicts lack resolution. This was not always the case. The establishment of Ottoman Turkish rule by the mid fifteenth century began a relatively peaceful era in the region. The introduction of the western European concept of nationalism into southeastern Europe at the end of the eighteenth century and the beginning of the nineteenth century, however, brought about a series of conflicts caused by the efforts of the inhabitants of southeastern Europe, also known as the Balkan Peninsula or simply as the Balkans, to emulate the western Europeans and establish nationalist states. In these conflicts, the peoples of this region initially directed their political and military efforts primarily against the Ottoman Empire. As these efforts achieved some success in throwing off Ottoman rule and establishing national states, the Balkan peoples increasingly came into conflict among themselves over Ottoman spoils. The inherent instability caused by these conflicts inevitably attracted the attention of the Great European Powers. These included Austria (Austria-Hungary after the *Ausgleich* of 1867), France, Italy, Germany, Great Britain, and Russia. Especially interested in these issues were the two Great Powers most proximate to this region, Austria-Hungary and Russia. At Berlin in 1878, the Great Powers sought to impose an overall settlement on the region that would maintain their interests. In their efforts to preserve the Berlin settlement, they were only partly successful. By the beginning of the twentieth century, the settlement was coming undone.

The consequence of the Great Powers' inability to preserve stability in Southeastern Europe was a prolonged conflict beginning in 1912. At first the Balkan states attempted to realize their nationalist objects by the final expulsion of Ottoman authority from Europe in the First Balkan War. Before this was achieved, the Balkan states fell to fighting among themselves over the Ottoman legacy in the Second Balkan War. The enhanced status of the Bulgarians after the First Balkan War antagonized all of their Balkan neighbors and led to the Second Balkan War and the defeat of Bulgaria.

The ensuing Treaty of Bucharest failed to impose a final settlement on the region. The defeated Bulgarians were vengeful. They sought an opportunity to attain the nationalist goals denied them by their former allies. The triumphant Greeks and Serbs were not sated. They wanted additional nationalist goals. In the case of the Greeks, these largely were at the expense of the Ottomans. In the case of the Serbs, these were in Austria-Hungary.

This study focuses on the continuation of this struggle during the First World War mainly from the Bulgarian perspective. In this struggle they sought to establish a large national state corresponding to perceived ethnic and historic frontiers. For Bulgaria, the renewed fighting in Southeastern Europe during the First World War represented an opportunity to redress the verdict of Bucharest. Bulgaria's eventual entry into the war on the side of Austria-Hungary, Germany, and the erstwhile Ottoman enemy was based purely on self interest. Unlike the militaries of the other Central Powers, Bulgarian soldiers did not fight on fronts away from their frontiers. Bulgarian soldiers fought only on the Macedonian Front in the south, often referred to in Bulgarian sources as the "Southern Front," and the Dobrudzha Front in Romania. In both of these regions they fought only for Bulgarian national interests. The commander in chief of the Bulgarian army, General Nikola Zhekov, emphasized this to the chief of the German General Staff, General Erich von Falkenhayn, soon after Bulgaria's entry in the war in 1915, when the Bulgarians found themselves fighting not only the Serbs, but to their great surprise the British and French: "*We* have committed our entire existence to this war, *we* have engaged in a bloody war and have sustained enormous losses."[2] The Bulgarians urged the elimination of the Macedonian Front from its inception. To their immense frustration, however, the Germans preferred to maintain it in order to concentrate Entente resources and manpower in a location remote from the decisive theaters of the war. Bulgarian military leaders warned that the Macedonian Front could become a potential problem. An Entente offensive in the summer and fall of 1916, which brought French and Serbian troops as far as Bitola, gave substance to the Bulgarian concerns. Their alarm became even more pronounced at the end of 1917 as German troops and equipment shifted to the Western Front for the great roll of the dice, and as the material and morale of the Bulgarian army deteriorated.

When Bulgaria entered the war, its material situation was bad. The Balkan Wars had already exhausted the country. The Bulgarians depended upon their German allies to provide them with most of their war equipment. Their expectations were never realized. The Germans could not meet their own demands. Nevertheless the Germans drew heavily upon Bulgaria's food resources. As a result, by 1917 morale in the ill-equipped and hungry Bulgarian army plummeted. The situation grew even worse the next year. Bulgaria could barely maintain its forces in the field. Its hope of victory in Macedonia depended upon the success of the Germans in the west.

The anticipated Entente offensive began at Dobro Pole on 14 September 1918 with a sustained artillery attack. At first the Bulgarians resisted to the extent of their ability. Only after the French and Serbian soldiers established a sustained presence in the forward Bulgarian positions did the Bulgarian army retreat. The Bulgarians could not maintain a successful defense in their secondary positions. At this point the years of material deprivation and the uncertainties about the war effort cause discipline to collapse in some units. Other Bulgarian divisions remained intact and even fought off British and Greek attacks. The damage was done, however. Due to the lack of reserves and the disorders in the Bulgarian ranks, the gap torn in the Bulgarian lines by the Entente attack grew larger. With the Entente front widening in Macedonia and with disaffected Bulgarian soldiers seizing Kyustendil and threatening Sofia, the Bulgarian government decided to seek an armistice on 25 September, just nine days after the offensive began. In the end, for the Bulgarians poor morale proved to be a stronger motivating factor than nationalist aspirations.

The collapse of the Bulgarian army following the Battle of Dobro Pole ended the cycle of fighting in Southeastern Europe for twenty years. It was one of the few overwhelmingly decisive battles of the First World War. Within two weeks of the beginning of the Battle of Dobro Pole, Bulgaria left the war. Two months later the First World War was over. For the third time since the end of Ottoman rule in 1878, Bulgaria had failed to achieve its nationalist agenda. For the second time in five years, Bulgaria had lost a nationalist-based war. The ensuing frustrations persisted throughout the interwar period. They undermined the development of parliamentary democracy in Bulgaria. They also led Bulgaria once again to seek redress on the side of Germany in the Second World War. Then it suffered yet another defeat. Forty-five years of Soviet domination ensued.

All dates are given according to the Gregorian calendar, although Bulgaria did not officially abandon the Julian calendar until 14 April 1916. In some cases in the footnotes, dates are given in both new style and old style, or only old style (os), and are marked accordingly. Place names are generally given according to the Bulgarian usage; Skopie instead of Skoplje. Where appropriate, alternatives are provided. Names of major locations are used according to common practice; Salonika instead of Thessaloniki or Solun, Belgrade instead of Beograd.

# Note on Transliteration

I have utilized the "Suggestions for the Transliteration of the Bulgarian Alphabet" proposed by J. F. Clarke and C. E. Black in C. E. Black, *The Establishment of Constitutional Government in Bulgaria* (Princeton, N.J.: Princeton University Press, 1943), pp. 321–23, for the transliteration of the Bulgarian alphabet, with three exceptions. I made no attempt to differentiate between the letters И and Й. Also, I have transliterated two letters now in disuse, Ѣ and Ж, according to the usage in T. Atanasov et al., *Bulgarsko-angleski rechnik* (Sofia, 1983).

# BALKAN BREAKTHROUGH

# BALKAN
## POLITICS
1

By the third quarter of the nineteenth century three national states had emerged in southeastern Europe from the non-national Ottoman Empire. These were Greece, Romania, and Serbia. All three sought to emulate the political and economic success of national states in western Europe. From the onset of their establishment none of these small southeastern European states considered their frontiers to be permanent. All sought to expand into neighboring territories to include greater numbers of their co-nationals in the same state or to conform to romantic notions of medieval predecessors. The Greeks sought all the Aegean Islands, Thessaly, Macedonia, and Thrace, then all under Ottoman control. The Romanians had claims to Habsburg Transylvania and Romanov Besserabia. The Montenegrins and Serbs contested Ottoman territories in Bosnia Hercegovina, Kosovo, and northern Albania. In addition both the Greeks and the Serbs claimed Macedonia as part of their national legacy. Not only were these small states eager to acquire territories from the large dynastic empires that bordered on southeastern Europe, they also increasingly advanced claims that overlapped each other's national aspirations. The only apparent means of maintaining and forwarding such claims was armed action. In this regard the peoples of southeastern Europe attempted to emulate the successes of the Italians in 1861 and the Germans ten years later. These countries had unified through conflict.

As national movements grew in southeastern Europe, they often cooperated with each other. The Serbian state aided the Bulgarian revolutionary movement through the initial three quarters of the nineteenth century. A series of intra-Balkan alliances developed in the 1860s. In 1867 Bulgarian revolutionary leaders even proposed a Bulgarian-Serbian state. Bulgarian revolutionaries also found refuge in Bucharest.

The national situation became more intense in southeastern Europe in the last quarter of the nineteenth century. In 1875, Orthodox and Muslim peasants in Hercegovina, the southwestern corner of Bosnia, rose against the Ottoman authorities. Both Montenegro and Serbia intervened in support of the insurrection. In the ensuing war the many Russian volunteers joined the Montenegrin and Serbian forces. A Russian general, Mikhail Chernyaev, assumed command of the Serbian army. Nevertheless the Serbs suffered defeat by the Ottomans in 1876. At the same time, Bulgarian revolutionaries mounted a national uprising against the Ottomans. The Bulgarians did not hesitate to slaughter the Turkish civilian population living there. The Ottoman authorities retaliated in kind. The result was the "Bulgarian Massacres," in which the Ottomans bore most if not all of the odium. Outraged populations elsewhere in Europe, especially in Great Britain, demanded action. The Russian government, however, used the opportunity to directly intervene on behalf of the beset Bulgarians. They did so in order to demonstrate the Pan-Slavist credentials of the tsarist regime. As the largest Slavic Orthodox power, the Russians perceived some leadership responsibility to other Slavic Orthodox peoples. They also acted to gain control over the strategic Straits passage between the Black Sea and the Mediterranean. The Straits consisted of three distinct bodies of war west to east, the narrow Dardanelles, the wide Sea of Marmara, and the narrow Bosporus. Control of this passage would ensure Russian access to year round maritime commerce and possession of the ancient imperial city of Constantinople, Tsarigrad in the Slavic languages.

In the aftermath of the defeat of the Serbian and Montenegrin efforts in Hercegovina, and with the intention of addressing Russia's inchoate sense of Slavic nationalism and Russia's much more concrete strategic goals in southeastern Europe, Tsar Alexander II declared war on the Ottoman Empire on 24 April 1877. A Russian force passed through Romania and crossed the Danube at Svishtov in June. It advanced to the Ottoman fortress of Pleven (Plevna). After failing to take the fortress, the Russians settled down for a siege. This lasted from July to December. After the Russians did not succeed on two occasions to take Pleven, a Romanian army reinforced them. Meanwhile in July, the Russians took control of the main north–south route across the Balkan Mountains at Shipka Pass. There they defeated Ottoman attempts to relieve Pleven in August and in September. Finally Pleven surrendered on 10 December 1877. The Russians then advanced south of the Balkan Mountains. They occupied Sofia on 4 January 1878. Ottoman resistance in Bulgaria collapsed as the Russian army reached Adrianople on 19 January 1878 and the final defensive positions in front of Constantinople, the Chataldzha lines, on 30 January. The next day the Ottomans sued for an armistice.

The ensuing peace negotiations were held at San Stefano, a suburb of Constantinople. On 3 March 1878 in the Treaty of San Stefano, the Ottomans acceded to a Russian demand for the establishment of a large independent Bulgaria. This state, which included Macedonia and most of Thrace, met the demands of the most expansive Bulgarian nationalists. Neither the other Great Powers nor the other Balkan states shared the Bulgarians' enthusiasm for the San Stefano Treaty. Greece, Romania, and Serbia all considered that the treaty had slighted their national demands. This did little to endear the new Bulgarian state to its neighbors.

Largely because of objections from Austria-Hungary and Great Britain that San Stefano Bulgaria would give the Russians a base from which they could dominate all of southeastern Europe and threaten Constantinople, the German chancellor, Otto von Bismarck, offered his services as an "honest broker" to revisit the settlement. A congress including representatives of all the Great Powers and the Ottoman Empire met at Berlin in the summer of 1878; they signed an agreement on 13 July 1878. Some of the Great Powers obtained direct benefit. Primary among these was Austria-Hungary, which gained the consent of the other Powers to occupy Bosnia-Hercegovina and the Sandjak of Novi Pazar, a small sliver of territory separating Montenegro from Serbia. Great Britain in turn occupied Cyprus.

This Treaty of Berlin also recognized the complete independence of Montenegro, Romania, and Serbia from the Ottoman Empire. All three countries received territorial augmentation. The Montenegrins obtained territory, although not as much as they would have under the San Stefano settlement. The Serbs got the area around Niš. The Romanians, although required to cede Besserabia to Russia, received a part of the territory south of the great bend of the Danube before it empties into the Black Sea, northern Dobrudzha, in return. This was small compensation for their efforts during the recent war. Greece got nothing.

The Treaty of Berlin dashed aspirations of Bulgarian nationalists. Bulgaria itself became a principality but remained under the sovereignty of the Ottoman sultan. The southeast around Plovdiv obtained special status as an Ottoman province with a Christian governor and received the name Eastern Rumelia. The western part of San Stefano Bulgaria, Macedonia, returned to direct Ottoman rule. This was a huge disappointment for most Bulgarians.

The Congress of Berlin attempted to establish a permanent settlement for the problems of southeastern Europe. It emphasized the role of the Great European Powers in questions arising from the development of Balkan nationalisms. Only they had the authority to consider future modifications of the settlement. Realization of the disparity between their own abilities and those of the Great Powers forced the Balkan nationalists to seek arrangements to continue their efforts.

After the Congress of Berlin, the states of southeastern Europe perceived each other as rivals for the remaining European territories of the Ottoman Empire. Montenegro and Serbia both sought territory in Albania and Hercegovina, Greece and Bulgaria in Thrace; and Bulgaria, Greece, and Serbia all claimed Macedonia. Their overlapping claims undermined their abilities to realize them.

The southeastern Europeans recognized that they stood little chance individually of contradicting the collective will of the Great Powers.

Therefore each state in southeastern Europe sought affiliation with either Austria-Hungary or Russia. Hohenzollern-ruled Romania resented the Russian intrusion of 1877 and the Russian confiscation of Besserabia the next year. The Bucharest government signed an alliance with Austria-Hungary in 1883, connecting Romania to the mighty Triple Alliance. Serbia, under the leadership of King Milan Obrenović, who had just assumed the royal title the previous year, likewise oriented its policy toward Vienna. Despite the disappointment of Berlin, the truncated Bulgarian principality remained pro-Russian. Alexander Battenberg, the Russian Tsar Alexander II's nephew, became prince of Bulgaria in 1879.

The first important breach of the Berlin settlement occurred in 1885. The Russian government had closely directed its Bulgarian satellite after 1878. In 1885, however, Bulgarian revolutionaries overthrew the Ottoman regime in Eastern Rumelia. Against the wishes of his cousin Tsar Alexander III, Prince Alexander of Bulgaria announced the annexation of Eastern Rumelia by Bulgaria.[1] Prince Alexander recognized that as a foreigner ruling Bulgaria, he needed to associate himself with the national inclinations of his principality. Tsar Alexander, already infuriated by his cousin's struggles against Russian control, ordered Russian officers and advisors home from Bulgaria. The tsar's personal inclinations seemed to supersede Russia's strategic interests.[2] The newly unified Bulgarian state lacked trained senior military officers and a Great Power patron. The Great Powers deadlocked over whether to permit the breach of the Berlin covenant.

In these circumstances, King Milan of Serbia perceived an opportunity. He did not want to see Bulgaria grow without compensation for Serbia. Accordingly, he declared war on Bulgaria on 13 November 1885. Serbian forces crossed the frontier and advanced toward Sofia. Most of the Bulgarian army was in the southeast to guard against Ottoman intervention. Furthermore, the withdrawal of Russian officers left in the Bulgarian army no higher rank than captain. Prince Alexander marched his troops to the northwest of the country and defeated the invaders at Slivnitsa 17–19 November. The Bulgarians then entered Serbian territory and moved toward Niš. At this point the Austro-Hungarians intervened to protect their Serbian client. They warned that further Bulgarian advance into Serbia would meet Austrian military resistance. The Treaty of Bucharest of 3 March 1886 prevented the Bulgarians from obtaining any advantage at the expense of the aggressors.[3] The Serbo-Bulgarian War had several important consequences. The Powers permitted the modification of the Berlin settlement with the minor condition that the Bulgarian prince assume the title of governor of Eastern Rumelia, to last for five years. The Bulgarian annexation of Eastern Rumelia stood. Nevertheless, this success did not save Prince Alexander. Bowing to his cousin's displeasure, he abdicated in 1886. Because of their unexpected success against the Serbs, the Bulgarians also gained a reputation as the military power in southeastern Europe. They became known as the "Prussians of the Balkans." Finally, possibility of unified Balkan action against the Ottomans, never strong after the Congress of Berlin, became even more remote.

This Great Power control received additional buttress by an accord between Austria-Hungary and Russia. In May 1897, in the aftermath of a visit of Emperor Francis Joseph to St. Petersburg, the Habsburg and Romanov states agreed to maintain the status quo in southeastern Europe.[4] This cooperation stabilized the situation there for the time being. The Balkan nationalities could achieve little success against the unity of the Powers determined to maintain the Berlin settlement.

This consensus compelled the national states in southeastern Europe to adjust their relations with the Great Powers. The Bulgarians returned to the Russian fold. Prince Ferdinand of Saxe-Coburg-Gotha, a Roman Catholic Austro-German prince who had replaced the unfortunate Alexander Battenberg in 1887, pursued a policy of détente with Russia. In 1894, his son and heir, Prince Boris, was baptized in the Bulgarian Orthodox Church. The next year, a Bulgarian delegation traveled to St. Petersburg and received a favorable welcome by Tsar Alexander III's son and successor, Tsar Nicholas II. These efforts greatly improved Bulgarian-Russian relations. Also during the period of Bulgarian-Russian estrangement, Russian strategic interests in the Straits remained strong. On 14 June 1902 the Bulgarians signed a military convention with their Great Power patrons.[5] This connection afforded Sofia a considerable sense of security against the neighboring Ottomans.

Much more dramatic events caused the change of direction in Belgrade. After failing to interest Austria-Hungary in the purchase of his patrimony, King Milan Obrenović abdicated in favor of his son Alexander in 1889. Alexander's continuation of his father's pro-Austrian policy did little endear him to an increasingly nationalist-minded population. The new king soon undercut his position further by his marriage to a woman many Serbs believed was an unsuitable connection. This was Draga Mašin, a widow of Czech origin. The unpopularity of the royal couple fueled a plot by Serbian army officers and some others. The plotters murdered the king and queen the night of 10 June 1903. Over manifestations of general European disapproval, the Karageorgević heir, Peter, became King Peter of Serbia. Under King Peter, Serbia oriented toward Russia. In 1905, Serbia became embroiled in a customs conflict with her chief trading partner, Austria-Hungary. This so-called Pig War lasted until the two countries signed an agreement 27 July 1910. By this time Serbia had found other markets for its mainly agricultural products. By the end of the Pig War Serbia had turned completely away from the old connection with the Dual Monarchy. Austria-Hungary's loss in this respect was Russia's gain.

Politics in Romania and Greece followed similar patterns. As in the Slavic states of southeastern Europe, national aspirations were a primary basis for politics. Variations in domestic and foreign politics depended upon perceptions as to which Great Power offered the best chance to realize these national goals. In Romania, the Conservatives supported the Hohenzollern king and the alliance with Austria-Hungary, while the Liberals looked westward to France. Neighboring Russia had little appeal for any Romanians. In Greece, the Danish Glücksberg dynasty and the army oriented toward Germany. The marriage of the German-educated Crown Prince Constantine to Princess Sophia Dorothea of Hohenzollern, the sister of Kaiser Wilhelm II, reinforced this connection. Activist nationalists lead by Eleutherios Venizelos, a native of Crete determined upon a strong nationalist program, looked to the British and French to support Greek national aims. Throughout southeastern Europe the political situation followed the growing division among the Great Powers. All the states of southeastern Europe maneuvered to obtain some advantage in this division. Only Serbia, after 1903, was clearly on the side of the Entente powers.

In 1903 nationalist tensions in Macedonia finally exploded. With its mixed population of Orthodox Slavs, Catholic and Islamic Albanians, Turks, Jews, Roma, Vlachs, and others, Macedonia became primary target of southeastern European nationalist aspiration during the last quarter of the nineteenth century. Bulgarian nationalists had focused on Macedonia every since the Berlin settlement had restored Ottoman sovereignty in July 1878. Greek and Serbian nationalists also considered Macedonia as theirs by cultural and historical right. Bulgarian, Greek, and Serbian armed bands roamed the more remote areas of Macedonia. Sometimes they fought the Ottoman authorities, other times each other. Even Romanian nationalists, claiming a kinship with the Vlachs, who spoke a similar Latin-based language, attempted to establish at least a cultural presence in Macedonia. In August 1903 a Bulgarian-inspired revolutionary organization called IMRO (Internal Macedonian Revolutionary Organization) began an armed uprising.[6] By September the Ottomans reasserted control throughout Macedonia. The insurrection failed.

This time the Berlin settlement held, largely because the Austro-Russian détente in the Balkans continued. An Austro-Russian agreement at Mürzteg in Austria on 2 October 1903 promised Austrian and Russian collusion in reforming Macedonia.[7] This Great Power intervention produced no real Ottoman reforms. The failure of the Bulgarian revolutionaries temporarily set back their cause in Macedonia, and increased the expectations of the Greeks and Serbs.

In 1908 a major upheaval in the Ottoman Empire initiated a series of events that led to the collapse of the Berlin settlement. During July a group of reform-minded nationalist Ottomans calling themselves the Committee for Union and Progress seized power. The committee, popularly known as the "Young Turks," had formed in the multiethnic port city of Salonika. The Young Turks were determined to force reforms to modernize the Ottoman Empire and to save it from further losses of power and territory. One focus of these reforms was the Ottoman military.

The possibility of any Ottoman reform that might preserve the empire immediately raised concerns among those countries whose policies aimed at a further weakening of Ottoman power. The first to react to the Young Turk Revolution were the Austrians and Russians. In August 1908 on Russian initiative, the Austro-Hungarian foreign minister, Alois von Aehrenthal, and the Russian foreign minister, Alexander Izvolsky, met at Aehrenthal's estate in Buchlau, Moravia. There Izvolsky agreed to accept the Austrian annexation of Bosnia and Hercegovina in return for Austria's endorsing Russian interest in the Straits.[8] Before Izvolsky could gain the

Balkan Peninsula — 1878

agreement of the other Great Powers to this alteration of the Berlin settlement, the Austrians announced the annexation on 6 October.

The previous day, the Bulgarian Prince Ferdinand, acting in collusion with the Habsburg monarchy, declared the full independence of Bulgaria from the Ottoman Empire. At the same time he assumed the title "tsar" in emulation of his medieval predecessors. Before the announcement, Izvolsky advised the Bulgarians not to associate themselves with the Austrian move. He suggested that they wait until after the Austrians acted. He promised that Russia then would support Bulgaria's breach of the Berlin settlement.[9] This precipitous Bulgarian action did not please their Russian patrons in St. Petersburg.

The Russians were furious that Austria had gained an advantage in the Balkans. To be sure, the advantage was slight, since the Austrians had managed Bosnia-Hercegovina as a virtual colony since 1878. The loss of the Russo-Japanese War in 1905 intensified the Russian sense of injury. The Serbian government shared the Russian outrage. Nationalist Serbs considered Bosnia-Hercegovina, with its large Serbian population, as a major aspiration. The withdrawal of Austro-Hungarian garrisons from the Sandjak of Novi Pazar did little to mollify the Serbs.

In this Bosnian Crisis the Great Power system still functioned. The Germans supported Austria, while the British and French did not back Russia. Under such circumstances there could be no question of war. Nevertheless, the Bosnian Crisis marked the end of the Austro-Russian détente in southeastern Europe. It also increased the antagonism between Austria-Hungary and Serbia.

The Young Turk Revolution caused great concerns in all the capitals of southeastern Europe. A strong Ottoman Empire would prevent the realization of nationalist aspirations by the Bulgarians, Greeks, Montenegrins, and Serbs. Just as the Bosnian crisis waned, the Young Turk revolt reverberated in Athens. In 1909 a group of nationalist Greek officers emulated their Ottoman counterparts and seized power. The next year Venizelos became Greek prime minister. He was sufficiently cautious to defer the announcement of the annexation of his native island at this time, but he awaited the opportunity. Despite the German connections of the Greek royal family, the Greek navy invited a British mission to assist its training in 1910. The mission arrived the next year.

Meanwhile the St. Petersburg foreign office sought a means to redress its defeat in the Bosnian affair. Russian ambassadors in Belgrade and Sofia prodded their South Slavic clients toward an accord that could block further Habsburg advance into the Balkans and could put pressure on Constantinople. In both southeastern European capitals politicians warmed to the idea of a Bulgarian-Serbian agreement that could act against the Ottomans with the apparent sanction of the Russians. Talks began in 1911. These resulted in a Bulgarian-Serbian agreement on 7 March 1912. This agreement promised military cooperation against both the Habsburg and Ottoman Empires and recognized Bulgarian interests in Thrace and Serbian interests in Albania and Kosovo.[10] The key provision, however, was a stipulation that if Macedonia could not become autonomous, it would be divided. Given the various Balkan claims to Macedonia, the inability to achieve autonomy was a foregone conclusion. Bulgaria would receive southern Macedonia, including the towns of Ohrid, Prilep, and Bitola (Monastir). The northern part of Macedonia became a "disputed zone," whose disposition would be arbitrated by the Russian tsar in the event that the Bulgarians and Serbs could not come to an agreement. This complicated arrangement satisfied the Bulgarians but disconcerted the Serbs. Nevertheless they prepared to abide by the agreement in anticipation of gains in Albania and Kosovo, and with the possibility of part of Macedonia.

Through the summer of 1912 diplomatic activity increased throughout southeastern Europe as diplomats in Athens, Belgrade, Cetinje, and Sofia worked to establish a loose Balkan League. This Balkan League was a loose confederation of bilateral agreements rather than a strong alliance. The Bulgarian-Serbian arrangement was by far the most specific. The Bulgarians and Greeks notably failed to stipulate the precise parameters of their claims in Macedonia. The Bulgarians in fact had little confidence in the Greeks and thought that they could realize their objectives in Macedonia without hindrance from the Greek army. By the fall of 1912 the arrangements, such as they were, were complete. The pending end of the war between the Italians and the Ottomans made action by the Balkan League imperative before Ottoman forces from North Africa could reinforce those in southeastern Europe.

The idea of nationalism did not originate in southeastern Europe. Nor was it particularly suited to the complex historical and cultural situations there. Nevertheless, the peoples of the region adopted it in the nineteenth century not only to free themselves from the faltering rule of the decrepit Ottoman Empire, but also as a means of development. Their aspirations for national states brought them into conflict both with the Ottoman authorities and among themselves. These Balkan aspirations also lead to efforts by individual Great Powers to use southeastern European nationalism to their own advantage. After 1878, the efforts of the Great Powers to preserve the Berlin settlement for southeastern Europe were mainly successful. All the southeastern European states then sought the patronage of the Great Powers to further their own aspirations.

The Young Turk coup of 1908 destabilized the Berlin settlement by introducing the possibility that the Ottoman regime, long considered to be the "sick man of Europe," was at last in recovery. A revived Ottoman Empire threatened many aspirations throughout Europe. In this situation the Great Powers, Austria-Hungary, and Russia looked to their own interests. At the same time the Bulgarians, the Greeks, the Montenegrins, and the Serbs overcame their own rivalries to combine against the threat of a revived Ottoman Empire. The consequence was the outbreak of a war in southeastern Europe that would last for six years. It eventually involved all of Europe.

# BALKAN
## WARS

**2**

The Balkan coalition decided to begin the war against the Ottoman Empire in the fall of 1912. The allies wanted to start the war before the Ottomans could end their war with Italy and bring additional troops to southeastern Europe. Each member of the Balkan coalition conducted a separate action against the Ottomans with particular aims. The Balkan allies had considerable forces at their disposal. The Bulgarians called upon 350,000 men, the Greeks 100,000, and the Serbs 230,000.[1] The Montenegrins had little more than a militia of around 50,000 men. The Greeks alone had a navy of some strength. The Ottomans also had a navy. Ground forces amounted to 280,000 men, but potential could grow to 450,000.[2]

The first of the Balkan allies to act was Montenegro. King Nikola opened the First Balkan War on 8 October 1912. The Montenegrin declaration of war alerted the Ottomans to the pending conflict in the Balkans.

They hurried to conclude the war with Italy. The Italians and Ottomans signed the Treaty of Ouchy, near Lausanne, Switzerland, on 15 October.

The other Balkan allies followed Montenegro's lead on 17 October. The Montenegrins sought the Sandjak of Novi Pazar and northern Albania, especially the largest city in the region, Scutari (Alb: Işkodra). The Serbs sent their forces into Macedonia, Novi Pazar, and Kosovo, and on into northern Albania. The Greeks advanced into Epirus and Macedonia. The chief objective of the Epirus force was the town of Janina (Gk: Ioannina), while the Macedonian force aimed at Salonika. Meanwhile the Greek fleet seized a number of the Aegean Islands and prevented the Ottoman fleet from transferring troops from Asia to Europe.

The Bulgarians faced a vexing strategic dilemma. The main Ottoman force in Europe was in Thrace, arrayed in front of Constantinople. This compelled the Bulgarians to sent most of their army into Thrace. By failing to do so, they risked the invasion of Bulgaria by a large Ottoman army. Many Bulgarians were old enough to remember the "Bulgarian Massacres" more than thirty years before. Bulgaria's main political goals, however, lay in the west. Most Bulgarians regarded Macedonia as a part of their national identity. Macedonia was the main goal of the Bulgarian effort against the Ottomans. A small Bulgarian force invaded Macedonia in conjunction with the Serbs, but this was not big enough to enforce Bulgarian claims to the area. In order to realize their aspirations in Macedonia, the Bulgarians had to depend on Serbian willingness to abide by the March agreement and on the goodwill of Russia in any arbitration settlement. Also a small Bulgarian detachment crossed the Rhodope Mountains and raced toward Salonika. Its purpose was to establish a Bulgarian presence in the most important Balkan port city ahead of the Greeks.

Because the bulk of the Ottoman forces in Europe were concentrated in front of their capital at Constantinople, the success of the Balkan coalition depended to a considerable degree upon the success of the Bulgarian army. The Bulgarians rapidly routed the Ottomans in Thrace. While the Second Bulgarian Army contained the large Ottoman fortress city of Adrianople, the First and Third Armies seized the other major fortress at Lozengrad (Tk: Kirklareli) on 24 October. They then advanced on into Thrace. At the Battle of Lyule Burgas–Buni Hisar (Tk: Kirklareli-Pinarhisar) the Bulgarians inflicted a major defeat on the Ottomans on

2 November. The Ottomans retreated in disorder to their final line of defense at Chataldzha (Tk: Çatalca) before their capital Constantinople. With the fall of Constantinople imminent, the Great Powers dispatched a flotilla to preserve order and maintain their interests. The Russians in particular were uncomfortable that the Bulgarian army, rather they their own, was poised to take the ancient imperial city. Bulgaria's victories also made her allies uneasy. Greece's Prime Minister Venizelos cabled the Greek military headquarters,

> After the annihilation of the Turks at Lozengrad, the Bulgarians are advancing unrestrained to Çatalca. It is believed that the Turks are incapable of offering serious resistance there, after their repeated defeats and the disintegration of their army. A European intervention being most likely imminent, our military operations must be hastened forthwith at all costs.[3]

On 17 November the Bulgarians attempted to force the Chataldzha lines, but failed due to exhaustion, epidemic disease, and effective supporting fire from Ottoman warships in the Sea of Marmara. After this both sides settled into trench warfare.

The Serbs won a big victory over the main Ottoman force in the western Balkans at Kumanovo in northern Macedonia on 24 October. Two subsequent encounters, at Prilep and Bitola, forced the surviving Ottomans to retreat to Albania. The withdrawal of the Ottomans opened the way for the Serbs to occupy all of the disputed zone of Macedonia as well as the unambiguously Bulgarian portion of Macedonia. Having cleared Macedonia of Ottoman forces, the Serbs moved on into Kosovo and from there into northern Albania. By the end of November, elements of the Serbian army had taken the Adriatic port of Durrës. This appearance of the Serbs on the Adriatic caused considerable alarm in Vienna. After the three Macedonian battles, the Serbs sent troops to assist the Bulgarians at Adrianople and the Montenegrins at Scutari. After overrunning Macedonia, the Serbs sent their Second Army to Adrianople to assist in the Bulgarian siege.

Meanwhile, after a victory over Ottoman forces at Giannitsa (Yanitsa), the Greeks reached Salonika on 8 November. There, in response to an Ottoman initiative, they entered into negotiations for the city. The next day, 9 November, the Ottomans agreed to terms. The next day, the Bulgarian

7th Rila Division entered the city over Greek protests. Upon entering the city, the commander of the Bulgarian division telegraphed Tsar Ferdinand, "From today Salonika is under the scepter of Your Majesty."[4] An uneasy co-dominium ensued. Both the Bulgarians and the Greeks perceived in Salonika the major port facilities necessary to develop the Macedonian hinterland. Meanwhile to the west, the other Greek force brought Janina under siege, but initially lacked the strength surround it, let alone to take it.

The Montenegrins succeeded in talking territories in Novi Pazar and northern Albania. Soon, however, the bulk of their forces became bogged down at Scutari. The lack of adequate Montenegrin tactical training and equipment as well as the determined leadership of the Ottoman commander prevented King Nikola from realizing his main goal in the Balkan War. Two determined Montenegrin attacks on the Ottoman defenses at Scutari failed.

After their defeat at Chataldzha, the Bulgarians agreed to an armistice the Ottomans had first proposed on 12 November. Armistice negotiations at the Chataldzha lines began on 25 November. The Bulgarians represented their Montenegrin and Serbian allies at the talks. The Greeks preferred to send their own representative. Both sides, exhausted from their recent efforts, quickly agreed to terms. According to these terms, all armies were to remain in their respective positions, the three besieged fortresses of Adrianople, Janina, and Scutari were to receive no provisions, the Bulgarians obtained use of the railroad running through Adrianople to provision their troops at Chataldzha, and the Ottomans lifted their naval blockade of Bulgarian Black Sea ports. The armistice terms favored the Balkan coalition. Only Serbia, however, had attained all of its goals. Bulgaria still sought the important Thracian city of Adrianople, Greece still wanted the town of Janina in northern Epirus, and Montenegro remained stuck in northern Albania outside of Scutari.

After armistice negotiations at Chataldzha, the Ottomans and the Balkan coalition agreed to conduct peace negotiations in London. Concurrently a conference of Great Power ambassadors met in the British capital. The Balkan states' swift victories surprised the Great Powers. Certain aspects of this success disconcerted the Powers. The Bulgarian advance on Constantinople alarmed the Russians; the country they had liberated in

1878 ungratefully threatened to deprive them of the goal they had sought since the days of Catherine the Great. The Serbian appearance on the Adriatic outraged the Austrians; they feared that the Serbs would grant Russia naval access to the Adriatic, and that the Serbs would cooperate with Italy to deny Austria egress from the Adriatic. To counter this they supported independence for Albania. Also, to indicate their determination on this issue to the Russians, they mobilized their military in Galicia. Clearly the Balkan War ended the Berlin settlement. The Powers, however, were disinclined to allow their issues to become a cause for conflict among themselves. As the Austro-Hungarian foreign minister, Leopold Berchtold, explained to a subordinate, "I could easily provoke a war in twenty four hours, but I do not want to do that."[5] The Great Power ambassadors' conference was an effort to coordinate their policies and to oversee the settlement of the Balkan War. While the Berlin settlement was gone, a new arrangement could stabilize the situation in the Balkans.

The peace talks between the Balkan allies soon broke down. In a proposal of 1 January 1913, the Ottomans conceded all their European territory west of Adrianople, but not Adrianople itself and not the Aegean Islands.[6] This was unacceptable to Bulgaria and Greece. Talks ceased after 6 January. On 23 January, a coup returned a bellicose cabal of Young Turks led by Enver Pasha to power in Constantinople. The new government made another effort to come to terms by offering to divide Adrianople with Bulgaria. The Balkan allies rejected the offer and denounced the armistice. The war resumed on 3 February.

By this time, the Bulgarians found themselves increasingly isolated. Disputes had arisen all around them. The problem between Bulgaria and Greece continued to grow. Both claimed Salonika. In London the Greeks were determined to secure recognition of their right to Salonika. One member of the Greek delegation, Stefanos Skouloudis, remarked, "If we do not bring back Salonika, we cannot return to Athens."[7] The Bulgarians, however, were in no mood to make any concessions to an ally they regarded as inferior. They rebuffed efforts to resolve the issue of Salonika and southern Macedonia. To a considerable degree the success of Bulgarian arms in the war against the Ottomans deluded them about their diplomatic prospects in its aftermath.

The Bulgarians also became involved in a quarrel with Romania. As the Balkan war drew near the Bulgarians sought to protect their northern frontier by reaching some kind of accommodation with their northern neighbor. Romania's alliance with Austria-Hungary and friendship with the Ottoman Empire were sources of concern. In response to a Bulgarian inquiry in the summer of 1912, Romanian prime minister Titu Maiorescu refused to commit himself to a specific program. After the extent of the Bulgarian victories became clear, however, the Romanians began to press for concessions. In particular they wanted the Bulgarian portion of Dobrudzha (Rom: Dobrodgea), the fertile area between the Danube and the Black Sea. This region was predominately Bulgarian in population. The surrender of Bulgarian-inhabited territory was totally unacceptable to the Sofia government. The Bulgarians hoped that their Russian patrons would prevent this Romanian extortion.

By far the most serious dispute afflicting Bulgaria was the one with Serbia. Some leading military and political figures in Serbia had never been happy with the March 1912 treaty. They thought that their government had conceded too much of Macedonia to Bulgaria. Among these was the Serbian prime minister, Nikola Pašić. Regarding the March 1912 treaty he wrote, "In my opinion we conceded too much."[8] The strategic situation at the time of the armistice increased Bulgarian concerns. The bulk of their army was in Thrace along the Chataldzha lines and besieging Adrianople. Meanwhile, throughout both the disputed and undisputed zones of Macedonia, Serbian officials were beginning to establish a Serbian administration. Bulgarian concerns escalated on 13 January 1913, when the Serbs formally requested a revision of the March 1912 treaty.[9] The Serbian failure to obtain an Adriatic port and territory in northern Albania because of Austro-Hungarian resistance was one reason for this request. The Serbs hoped to retain most of Macedonia in compensation for their thwarted expectations in Albania, and because they had always considered Macedonia to be "South Serbia" anyway. The Bulgarians did not respond to the Serbian request for revision of the treaty. They considered this to be a provocation. They recognized that the Serbian presence in Macedonia was a growing threat to their national aspirations. They could not respond to this threat, however, until the resolution of the war with the Ottoman Empire and the transfer of the bulk of their army from Thrace to the western frontier of Bulgaria.

The resumption of fighting on 3 February 1913 was mainly at the three besieged cities of Adrianople, Janina, and Scutari. Hostilities had never stopped at Janina because the Greeks had not signed the armistice. After a brief Greek attack, the Ottoman commander surrendered on 6 March. The fall of Janina enabled the Greek command to shift forces that had participated in the siege eastward to Macedonia to bolster the Greek claims there in the growing dispute with Bulgaria. Later on the 26th of the same month, Adrianople fell to the Bulgarian Second Army. Serbian troops from the Serbian Second Army assisted in the assault. This did not resolve the strategic situation, however. Significant Ottoman forces remained at Chataldzha and on the Gallipoli Peninsula.

The Ottoman forces at Scutari continued to hold out against the Montenegrins. Serbian reinforcements arrived in February 1913. While the Serbs bolstered the Montenegrins, they also antagonized the Austrians, who wanted Scutari for the new Albanian state. On the urging of the Vienna government, the Great Powers pressured both Montenegro and Serbia to end the siege. When this had no effect, a fleet of Great Power warships, Russia excluded, imposed a naval blockade on Montenegro. In a sense the Adriatic/Scutari operation marked the end of the Great Power system. This was the last occasion in which the Great Powers cooperated to force their will on a Balkan issue. On 10 April, the Serbs withdrew from Scutari. The Montenegrins continued the siege alone. Finally, on 22 April, the exhausted defenders of Scutari surrendered. The Montenegrin triumph was short-lived. Under threat of direct military intervention from Austria-Hungary, the Montenegrins withdrew from their prize on 5 May. The Scutari crisis marked the second time in six months that the Austro-Hungarians had threatened force to prevent the Serbs to become established on the Adriatic Sea. Soon afterward talks between the Balkan states and the Ottomans resumed in London.

Meanwhile, during the spring of 1913, the disputes between Bulgaria and its neighbors continued to escalate. The problem with Greece over southern Macedonia and Salonika was the most immediate. On several occasions, actual fighting broke out between Bulgarian and Greek forces north of Salonika at Nigrita and Angista. Attempts at negotiation foundered on the issue of Salonika. Both sides regarded the city as vital to their plans for development.

Another difficulty for Bulgaria loomed to the north. Romanian demands for compensation against Bulgarian annexation of Ottoman territory led the Great Powers to call an ancillary ambassadors' conference at St. Petersburg. This conference began at the end of March 1913. On 9 May, the St. Petersburg ambassadors' conference announced its decisions to award the Bulgarian Danubian port of Silistra to Romania. This was less than the Romanians expected. They had wanted all of Bulgarian (southern) Dobrudzha. Silistra, however, was more than the Bulgarians wanted to surrender. The dissatisfaction of both sides in the matter gave promise of future difficulty. For the Sofia government, the St. Petersburg conference was an alarming indication that the Russians would not support Bulgarian interests to the maximum extent.

At the same time the conflict between Bulgaria and Serbia grew. By April 1913 Serbian prime minister Nikola Pašić indicated that Serbia would go to war against Bulgaria if the Great Powers did not limit Bulgarian Macedonia to the right (east) bank of the Vardar River.[10] This was a significant deviation from the March 1912 agreement. The problem with Serbia was the most serious of the disputes Bulgaria faced. Serbia occupied most of the Macedonian territory Bulgaria had gone to war with the Ottoman Empire to obtain. A member of the St. Petersburg government later wrote in regard to the looming Bulgarian-Serbian conflict, "All the sympathies of [Russian Foreign Minister Sergei] Sazonov and myself were with the Serbians, for it appeared from their objectionable actions that the Bulgarians had forgotten that we had saved them in the most acute period of the struggle with Turkey."[11] This attitude threatened to undermine Russian support for the March 1912 Bulgarian-Serbian treaty. Russian arbitration became problematic. Resolution of the dispute with Serbia was critical for Bulgaria. If the Sofia government could obtain a settlement with Belgrade, it could turn its attentions to the south. Bulgaria had a larger army then did Greece. Furthermore, Greece lacked a Great Power patron. Yet the resolution of the dispute with Serbia meant further concession territory in Macedonia beyond the March 1912 treaty. This was impossible for Sofia. Macedonia had been the goal of Bulgarian foreign policy since the abrogation of the San Stefano treaty in 1878. Under these circumstances the Bulgarian government decided to request formal Russian arbitration under the terms of the treaty.

Not surprisingly, the Greeks and Serbs quickly recognized mutual interest in combining against Bulgarian claims to Macedonia. If the disputes should result in war, Bulgaria was stronger than either of them separately, but together they stood a reasonable chance of success. The Greeks and Serbs had been in contact for some time. On 5 May 1913 the Greeks and Serbs signed a treaty, followed by a military alliance on 14 May and on 1 June a formal alliance, the Treaty of Salonika. These agreements divided Macedonia between them.

Having allied against Bulgaria, both Greece and Serbia approached Romania. Romania, the biggest state in southeastern Europe, had the largest army among the Balkan states. The Romanians remained dissatisfied with the results of the St. Petersburg ambassadors' conference and hoped to obtain Bulgarian Dobrudzha. The Romanians made no formal commitments. Nevertheless their anti-Bulgarian interests were clear.

On 26 May 1913 the Serbs again demanded a formal revision of the March 1912 accord.[12] The Bulgarians were no more inclined to consider this request than they had been in January. Soon after this the negotiations between the warring sides finally reached an agreement in the British capital. Some prodding from the Great Powers was necessary. The Greeks and Serbs, in particular, were in no hurry to bring the Balkan War to a conclusion. They wanted to delay the signing in order to array their forces for the pending war against Bulgaria. The Bulgarians, for their part, were anxious to conclude the treaty so that they could transfer the bulk of their army still in Thrace to Macedonia to confront their erstwhile allies.

The Treaty of London, signed on 30 May, ended the Balkan War and limited the Ottoman Empire in Europe to the territory of Thrace east of a straight line between the Aegean port of Enos (Tk: Enez) to the Black Sea port of Midia (Tk: Midye). This line ensured that the Ottomans could only defend their capital on the west from the antiquated Chataldzha lines. These fortifications had been just sufficient enough to stop the exhausted Bulgarians in November 1912. They might not do so again, especially if the Bulgarians had Great Power support. The Ottomans also surrendered claims to Crete and the Aegean Islands. The Treaty of London further allowed the Great Powers the right to settle the question of Albanian frontiers.[13] The Albanian stipulations were a success for Austria-Hungary and Italy and a setback for Montenegro, Russia, and Serbia. By now the Serbs were determined to retain Macedonia irregardless of the resolution of the Albanian issue.

A meeting in the Serbian city Niš on 1 June between Ivan E. Geshov, the Bulgarian Prime Minister, and the Serbian Prime Minister Nikola Pašić failed to resolve the crisis. Upon his return to Sofia, Geshov resigned. The position of the Russians now became crucial. They had been reluctant to act on their responsibility for arbitration under the terms of the March 1912 treaty. Whatever decision the Russian tsar made would alienate one of the Balkan states. Yet the Russians apparently made little effort to determine their own best interests in the dispute.

As the situation in the Balkans escalated, the St. Petersburg government dithered. By the end of June Stoyan Danev, the new Bulgarian prime minister, and Prime Minister Pašić agreed to travel to St. Petersburg to attempt to resolve the crisis. Before either leader departed, however, the situation in Macedonia exploded. Tension between Bulgarian and Serbian troops along the lines in Macedonia rose as both sides engaged in raiding and sniping. On the night of 29–30 June, General Mihail Savov, commander of the Bulgarian forces, ordered attacks against the Serbs and Greeks. His instructions read, "So that we do not ignore the Serbian attacks, which would reflect poorly on our morale, and to press the enemy further, I am ordering you to attack the enemy energetically along the entire line without disclosing your strength and without becoming involved in a prolonged battle."[14] The Bulgarian attacks ended any chance that Russian influence could resolve the Bulgarian-Serbian dispute. Danev's government made desperate attempts to stop the fighting. These were to no avail. They only confused the Bulgarian military command as to the intentions of the government. Despite Bulgarian hopes, no help was forthcoming from Russia. The St. Petersburg government stood aside in this Second Balkan War or Inter allied War while the Greeks and Serbs used the ill-considered Bulgarian probes as a pretext to implement their agreement of the previous month.

The allies surged forward against the Bulgarians. In eastern Macedonia the Serbs inflicted heavy casualties on the Bulgarians. By 8 July the Serbs had pushed them across the Bregalnitsa River. In Salonika the Greeks quickly overwhelmed the small and isolated Bulgarian battalion stationed there to embody Bulgarian claims to the city. The entire Bulgarian garrison was killed or captured. Meanwhile elsewhere in southern Macedonia the Greeks attacked the Bulgarian Second Army on two flanks and inflicted a major defeat in the vicinity of the city of Kikis north of Salonika during the first four days of July.[15] The Bulgarians retreated north toward pre-war Bulgaria.

The Bulgarian defeats compelled retreats from eastern and southern Macedonia. By the middle of July, the Bulgarian army had moved back to approximately the pre 1912 Bulgarian frontiers. Despite heavy losses, all the Bulgarian forces remained intact. Motivated by the threat of enemy invasion of the homeland and benefiting from shortened lines of communication and supply, the Bulgarian army began to stabilize its positions against the Greeks and Serbs. At this point, however, two new dangers arose to confront Bulgaria in the north and the southeast. In the north the Romanian army mobilized on 5 July to enforce Romanian claims to southern Dobrudzha. On 10 July the Romanians declared war on Bulgaria. That same day Romanian forces crossed the Bulgarian border and occupied Dobrudzha to a line from Tutrakhan on the Danube to Balchik on the Black Sea. Then on the night of 14–15 July, a large Romanian force crossed the Danube at Oryahovo, Gigen and Nikopol. The Bulgarians offered no resistance. Their forces were totally engaged in southeastern Macedonia. Dim Bulgarian hopes for Russian intervention never materialized.

Meanwhile the Ottomans took advantage of the deepening Bulgarian catastrophe to reclaim some of the territories they had lost in the First Balkan War, especially Adrianople. Ottoman forces crossed the Enos-Midiya line on 12 July and headed for Adrianople. Most Bulgarian troops were in eastern Macedonia. The few remaining soldiers had no chance against the Ottomans. After spending so much time, effort, and lives to take Adrianople, the Bulgarians abandoned it without firing a shot. Some Ottoman soldiers continued on past the pre war frontier. While the Romanian invasion induced despair in Bulgaria, the Ottoman caused apprehension. Ottoman rule had ended only 33 years before. Given the ongoing catastrophe, many Bulgarians feared it might return.

Amidst all these disasters, the Bulgarian army managed several small victories. In northwestern Bulgaria a determined defensive effort at Kalimantsi on 18 July stopped the Serbian advance into Bulgaria. In the south,

Bulgarian forces bottled the oncoming Greeks in the narrow Kresna Gorge of the Struma River at the end of July. King Constantine, then with his soldiers, faced capture. In the far northwest a small Bulgarian garrison held the city of Vidin against a Serbian and Romanian siege. These successes helped the Bulgarians to retain some shreds of military dignity. They also helped persuade the Greeks and Serbs to end the war. Nevertheless they were not enough to prevent the inevitable defeat.

By the end of July a new government had assumed office in Sofia. The failure of St. Petersburg to intervene on behalf of Bulgaria caused the pro-Russian government of Stoyan Danev to resign on 13 July. A pro-Austrian government led by Vasil Radoslavov took over in Sofia four days later. It immediately began to seek a way out of the war. With this pursuit came a new orientation in Bulgarian policy. Tsar Ferdinand, himself of Austro-German origin, and his new prime minister, Radoslavov, increasingly aligned the country toward the Triple Alliance and away from Russia.

Nevertheless the Russians and the other Great Powers applied some pressure in Belgrade and Bucharest to end the war. After a desultory meeting at Niš, representatives of the warring states convened in the Romanian capital on 30 July. There the delegates settled down to negotiation. The Great Powers maintained a presence at the Bucharest talks through their ambassadors to Romania. The Second Balkan War came to an end with the signing of the Treaty of Bucharest on 10 August 1913. The Bulgarians conceded most of Macedonia to Greece and Serbia and southern Dobrudzha to Romania.

The next month the Bulgarians reached a settlement with the Ottomans in the Treaty of Constantinople, signing this treaty on 30 September 1913. It deprived Bulgaria of most of the gains made in eastern Thrace. The ground taken at the cost of many Bulgarian lives at Lozengrad, at Lyule Burgas–Buni Hisar, and in front of Chataldzha reverted to Ottoman rule.

The Treaty of Bucharest greatly altered the political situation in southeastern Europe. The Serbs replaced the Bulgarians as the dominant Slavic power in southeastern Europe. Serbia controlled all of Kosovo, most of Macedonia, and much of the Sandjak of Nov Pazar. Because of the alienation of Bulgaria, Serbia also became Russia's sole connection in southeastern Europe. This situation augmented Serbian power. Serbia was hardly a match for Bulgaria in terms of Russian strategy. Bulgaria was located close

AUSTRIA-HUNGARY

BOSNIA

ROMANIA

Belgrade

SERBIA

Bucharest

DOBRUDZHA

BULGARIA

MONTENEGRO

Sofia

Scutari

Kumanovo

Constantinople

ALBANIA

Midia

Adrianople    Chataldzha

Salonika

Enos

OTTOMAN EMPIRE

GREECE

Janina

1912 Borders
1913 Borders

**Balkan Peninsula — 1913**

to the traditional Russian objective of Constantinople. Indeed, the Bulgarians had almost taken it in November 1912. After the Second Balkan War, however, the Russians had to support Serbia or risk losing their influence in southeastern Europe all together.

Greece had also increased in size and power as a result of the Balkan War settlement. Most of the Aegean Islands now came under Greek rule. Crete, although controlled by Greece since the crisis of 1898, became a formal part of the Greek kingdom. Also the Greeks made significant gains in Epirus and Macedonia. Most import of these was the city of Salonika, with its cosmopolitan population and its mercantile economy. Greece had also improved its international position by the Serbian alliance.

For Bulgaria, the treaties of Bucharest and Constantinople were disastrous. For the second time in less than forty years Macedonia had eluded unification with Bulgaria. Although exhausted by almost a year of fighting against the Ottoman Empire and the Balkan Allies, the Bulgarians remained determined to obtain their nationalist goals in Macedonia. Russia's inability to save Bulgaria altered the situation. The Radoslavov government increasingly oriented itself to Vienna and the Triple Alliance in an effort to gain redress. The Russian loss was the Austrian gain. Before 1912 the Austrians had no strong position in southeastern Europe, but afterward they had Bulgaria. Regarding the Treaty of Bucharest, Dimitŭr Tonchev, leader of the Bulgarian delegation at Bucharest, observed, "Either the Powers will change it, or we ourselves will destroy it."[16] From the moment of the signing of the Treaty of Bucharest, the Bulgarians were determined upon its revision.

The Balkan Wars caused considerable human and material losses. In both wars military casualties were high. The Bulgarians lost 32,000 dead, the Greeks 5,169, the Montenegrins 3,076, and the Serbs 36,550.[17] In addition, cholera and dysentery epidemics, which probably began during the initial retreat of the Ottoman Army in Thrace and spread in the advances and retreats of all the combatants, swept through the civilian populations of southeastern Europe. The fighting devastated the areas where it took place. Civilians in Kosovo, Macedonia, and Thrace also became victims of atrocities perpetrated by all the combatants. The costs of the war greatly exceeded the resources of these small and underdeveloped countries.

Nevertheless, the Treaty of Bucharest did not represent a significant stabilization of southeastern Europe. The Bulgarians were determined upon a revisionist policy directed at Greece and especially Serbia. This led them to sponsor partisan bands operating in Serbian-ruled Macedonia. Despite efforts to achieve normalization of relations by both parties, the Ottomans continued to challenge Bulgarian rule in newly acquired western Thrace.

The Greeks also pursued aggressive policies in southeastern Europe after the Treaty of Bucharest. They supported a pro-Athens uprising in southern Albania. They claimed territory there under the name Northern Epirus. They also became involved in a serious dispute with the Ottomans over the disposition of several Aegean Islands, including Samos, Chios, Mytiline, and Limnos.[18] Only the mutual exhaustion of both parties prevented war from breaking out over this issue.

Probably the most serious post-Bucharest conflict concerned Serbian aspirations in the new Albanian state. Success in the Balkan Wars encouraged the Serbs to pursue their goals in northern Albania. Despite Austro-Hungarian and Italian prohibitions, they continued to seek access to the Adriatic Sea. To this end the Serbian government continued to stage a series of provocations in northern Albania. Although the Great Powers ambassadors' conference in London had decreed recognition of an independent Albanian state, no set borders and no viable government had yet defined the new state. Serbian forces never entirely evacuated northern Albania after the autumn of 1912. Some Serbian military formations were still there a year later. Their presence resulted in an Austro-Hungarian ultimatum on 18 October 1913, demanding the withdrawal of all Serbian forces from northern Albania.[19] For the third time in one year the Austrians had threatened war over a Balkan issue. The Serbs indicated a formal acquiescence to the Austro-Hungarian demands. Nevertheless, Serbian regular and irregular forces remained on hand in northern Albania. At the same time the Serbs faced armed unrest in the newly occupied areas of Kosovo and Macedonia. With their army depleted and exhausted from its efforts during the Balkan War, the Serbs sought assistance from Russia. Despite some promises of help, nothing was forthcoming during the first half of 1914. The Russians appeared to be ready to lose their final position in southeastern Europe.

The Serbian provocations were not limited to activities in northern Albania. Serbian intelligence circles operating on the periphery of the Belgrade government encouraged more specific actions. On 28 June Gavrilo Princip, a young Bosnian Serb with connections to Serbian intelligence, assassinated Franz Ferdinand, the heir to the throne of Austria-Hungary, and his wife in Sarajevo. Although the assassin clearly had a link to the Serbian military, the exact role of the Serbian government in the affair remains murky. After dithering almost a month, the Austrian government delivered an ultimatum to the Belgrade government on 23 July. The Serbs received no firm commitments from the Russians. Greek Prime Minster Venizelos thought that the threat of a Bulgarian attack was too great for Greece to honor the June 1913 alliance with Serbia.[20] As a result the Serbs accepted most, but not all, of the Austro-Hungarian terms. Their refusal to permit Austro-Hungarian investigators to work within Serbia led to a declaration of war on Serbia on 28 July 1914. Bulgaria immediately declared a policy of strict neutrality.[21] The country still needed some time to recover from the Balkan Wars.

The Serbs had around 400,000 men at arms in eleven divisions, and their Montenegrin allies around 45,000.[22] The Serbian army, like the country it defended, was overwhelmingly composed of peasants. All the Serbian units were deficient in uniforms and equipment. They had not been able to make up its losses in men and equipment from the Balkan Wars. The Serbian Second and Third Armies faced the Austro-Hungarian frontier. Other units screened the southeastern frontier against a possible Bulgarian attack. The army was under the command of Crown Prince Alexander, with Vojvoda (Field Marshall) Radomir Putnik, who had led the Serbs to victory in the two previous wars as his deputy and actual military leader. Service in the wars against the Ottomans and the Bulgarians had seasoned these soldiers. Their material well-being, however, had eroded due to the previous wars. Also as a consequence of the Balkan Wars, cholera and typhus had appeared in Serbia.

Austro-Hungarian Balkan forces, after initial confusion regarding the hostility of Russia, included the nineteen divisions.[23] The overall quality of this force was dubious. The Austro-Hungarian military had faced declining financing for some time. Nor did its commander, General Oskar Potiorek, inspire confidence. He had bungled security arrangements in Sarajevo in June. The Austro-Hungarians undertook three invasions of Serbia during the autumn of 1914. The first began on 12 August, when the Fifth Army crossed the Drina River into Serbia. It soon encountered stiff resistance and logistical difficulties. At the Cer Mountain in northeastern Serbia a large battle developed, which soon turned to the advantage of the Serbian defenders. Defeat at the Battle of Cer Mountain forced the Austro-Hungarians back into Habsburg territory by 20 August. The Fifth Army tried again on 7 September. An invasion from northeastern Bosnia resulted in high Austro-Hungarian casualties but occupied little territory. This effort ended on 26 September. The Serbs counterattacked into Bosnia and Slavonia but made little headway.

The third Austro-Hungarian effort occurred in November and December 1914. On 17 November General Potiorek once again attacked into northwestern Serbia from Bosnia. On 2 December his forces entered Belgrade. The Serbian government had already moved south to Niš on 25 July, upon the mobilization of the Serbian army. Vojvoda Putnik counterattacked on 3 December. By 9 December, the Habsburg forces once again had to retreat. They evacuated Belgrade six days later, on the 15th. The Austro-Hungarian army lost 273,000 soldiers in the autumn campaigns against Serbia, while the Serbs lost 132,000.[24] The incompetent General Potiorek belatedly lost his command.

The fighting in the fall of 1914 exhausted both sides. Austro-Hungarian loses in Serbia were significant. At the same time, the Habsburg disaster in Galicia, where casualties were even greater than in Serbia and where Russian forces were advancing, precluded further action against Serbia for the time being.

The cycle of fighting in southeastern Europe began in October 1912 and continued with little interruption through the outbreak of general European fighting in 1914. Attempts by the Great Powers to stop or control this conflict at the ambassadors' conference and the Treaty of London met little success. Only threats of direct intervention, as the Austro-Hungarians made against Serbia in December 1912, against Montenegro in April 1913, and again against Serbia in October 1913, had any immediate success. The Austro-Hungarian ultimatum in July 1914 was a continuation of this process. Its direct military intervention in southeastern Europe did not produce any immediate result. Austro-Hungarian military failure in the autumn of 1914 led to the involvement of all the Great Powers in southeastern European conflict the next year.

*All photographs in this section courtesy of Bibliotelescope*

**FIGURE 1.**
*Storm trooper posing with dead enemy soldiers*

FIGURE 2.
*Bulgarian Army supply unit*

FIGURE 3.
*Bulgarian artillery firing*

Тодоровъ

Генералъ-Лейтенантъ *(signature)*

**FIGURE 4. ABOVE**

*Crown Prince Boris III, General Zhekov,*
*and General Batzarov near Struga 1918*

**FIGURE 5. LEFT**

*General Nikola Zhekov*

**FIGURE 6. ABOVE**

*Bulgarian officers and soldiers at the
Macedonian Front in 1915*

**FIGURE 7. BELOW**

*English prisoners*

FIGURE 8.
*Anglo-French prisoners, Macedonian Front*

FIGURE 9.
*Captured French pilot*

# THE
# ESTABLISHMENT
## OF THE
# MACEDONIAN
# FRONT

# 3

The defense of Serbia in 1914 was a rare early success for the Entente. Despite having deflected three Austro-Hungarian invasions, Serbia remained vulnerable to additional attacks from the Central Powers. Manpower and resources, depleted in the fighting in 1912–13, had scarcely recovered from the combats against Austria-Hungary. Meanwhile typhus and cholera, which originally had developed during the fighting in 1912 and had spread through military movement and refugees, proliferated throughout the country. Serbia's Entente allies paid little initial attention to the situation in southeastern Europe. The entry of the Ottoman Empire into the war on the side of the Central Alliance on 14 November 1914 and the military woes of Russia on the Eastern Front were far more significant. In an effort to deal with both of these issues, the Entente, at the instigation of British First Lord of the Admiralty Winston Churchill, undertook a campaign to open a warm-water route to Russia and to force the Ottomans out of the war. After an initial attempt to force the Dardanelles, the water connection between the Mediterranean and the Black Seas, failed, the Entente landed British, French, and ANZAC (Australia and New Zealand) forces on the Gallipoli Peninsula on 25 April 1915 in an effort to clear the Ottoman defenses. Because of Russian misgivings, the Entente declined Prime Minister Venizelos's offer of three Greek divisions for the operation. The Russians did not want to share control of Constantinople with the Greeks or with the British and French. The near seizure of the old imperial city by the Bulgarians in November 1912 had made the Russians skittish. In any event, neither the Germanophile Greek King Constantine nor the Greek army had little interest in participating in this venture.[1] Consequently, as a result of the failure of his pro-Entente policy, Venizelos stepped down as prime minister on 6 March 1915. The Gallipoli venture caused both warring sides to increase their attentions on southeastern Europe.

For the Central Powers, logistical support for the Ottomans became critical. Serbia, astride the land route between Berlin and Constantinople, was a major obstacle for the passage of soldiers and supplies. Also its presence on the southern flank of Austria-Hungary threatened the Habsburg Empire, which was already weakened not only by losses in the Serbian campaigns but also by enormous casualties in the fighting against the Russian army in Galicia. German chief of staff Erich von Falkenhayn stated in May 1915, "It is most important that we gain Bulgaria quickly and at any price, because the key to the entire situation (in Eastern Europe) lies in Sofia."[2] In July 1915, with the Western Front stabilized and with the immediate danger to Austria-Hungary thwarted, the Germans decided to eliminate the Serbian problem. An important consideration for the success of this operation was the attitude of Bulgaria. This caused the Austro-Hungarians and Germans to renew their efforts to attract Bulgaria to the Central Alliance.

After the renewal of fighting in southeastern Europe in 1914, the Bulgarians entertained offers from both sides. Although the personal inclinations of the Austro-German Tsar Ferdinand of Saxe-Coburg-Gotha and German-educated Prime Minister Vasil Radoslavov lay with the Central Powers, both recognized that the renewal of fighting in southeastern Europe afforded Bulgaria the opportunity to gain redress for the losses of the Balkan Wars. At the same time they paid close attention to the course of the war, especially in Eastern Europe.

The advantage of Bulgaria for the Entente was clear. A Bulgarian assault on the Chataldzha lines, perhaps abetted by Russian action in the Black Sea, could result in the fall of the Ottoman capital and in the ultimate success of the Gallipoli operation. The long-sought communications and logistical channels between Russia and its Western allies would be opened. In the spring of 1915, during the Russian advances in Galicia and the British and French landings in Gallipoli, the Bulgarian government adopted a positive stance toward the Entente and considered intervention on the side of the Entente. The Entente, however, could not meet Bulgaria's price of Macedonia. Most of Macedonia had been in Serbian hands since the Treaty of Bucharest of August 1913. Because Serbia controlled Macedonia, the Entente's options for its disposal were limited. The Serbs were not eager to surrender their Balkan War prize, especially after their victories in the autumn of 1914. Serbia's Prime Minister Pašić indicated clearly the Serbia would not part with its territory to lure Bulgaria into the war.[3] A Bulgarian response was to increase support for an anti-Serb partisan campaign in Macedonia.

After the Entente became bogged down at Gallipoli and suffered a major defeat at Gorlice-Tarnow in Galicia on the Eastern Front, the Entente offer lost considerable appeal in Sofia. The Bulgarian government decided in the summer of 1915 to join the Central Powers in an assault on Serbia in order to obtain Macedonia. The Sofia government had already concluded a 500 million franc loan with Germany the year before.[4] This undoubtedly was a factor in the predisposition of Ferdinand and Radoslavov for the Central Powers.

The Bulgarians proposed a military convention; according to this agreement they would obtain all Macedonia, defined in the terms of the 1912 Bulgarian Serbian agreement as both the contested and the uncontested zones.[5] Furthermore Bulgaria would receive that part of Serbia east of the Morava River. This included the large city Niš. In addition, if Greece joined the Entente Bulgaria was to obtain the territory Bulgaria lost to Greece at the Treaty of Bucharest. This meant southeastern Macedonia, including Drama, Seres, and the Aegean port of Kavala. If Romania joined

the Entente, Bulgaria would regain southern Dobrudzha and a consideration of territory in northern Dobrudzha. Also according to paragraph 7 of
the alliance, the Germans promised to give Bulgaria military material "of
every type as long as possible in conjunction with German needs."[6] The
Austro-Hungarians and Germans essentially agreed to the Bulgarian conditions and responded with a formal alliance. This offered Bulgaria a five-
year alliance with a secret annex guaranteeing the immediate possession
of all Macedonia. Bulgaria then signed a military alliance with Germany
on 6 September.[7] In this convention, the Germans undertook, among other
things, to send to Bulgaria the soldiers, war material, and money necessary
to wage war. Tsar Ferdinand was most likely the major motivator for this
military convention. Neither the Ministerial Council nor the army staff
was informed of the proceedings.[8] This served to emphasize Ferdinand's
control over military affairs even though this time, unlike during the Balkan Wars, he did not exercise his constitutional prerogative to act as commander in chief of the Bulgarian armed forces.

As a part of the overall understanding, the Austro-Hungarians and
Germans arranged an agreement between the Bulgarians and the Ottomans to rectify the Bulgarian-Ottoman frontier in Thrace. The Bulgarians had contemplated such an arrangement since the Treaty of Constantinople of September 1913 but could not quite work out the details. Their
inherent distrust of their former enemies undoubtedly contributed to this
problem. The relationship of the Bulgarian military with the German army
was problematic from the outbreak of the First World War. Many Bulgarians supported Russia. Russia had fought the Ottoman Empire 1877–78
to liberate Bulgaria. Many soldiers had received their military educations
in Russia, and some even volunteered to serve with the Russian army. Most
notable among these was the Balkan war hero and Bulgarian minister to
St. Petersburg, General Radko Dimitriev. Upon the outbreak of the war in
August 1914, he resigned his diplomatic position and accepted a command
in the Russian army.[9] Many of those officers who remained in Bulgaria retained their Russophile perspectives.

Overlooking some obvious candidates, including the deputy com-
mander in chief of the Bulgarian army during the Balkan Wars, General
Mihail Savov, Ferdinand selected a relatively junior colonel named Nikola
Todorov Zhekov.[10] Although Savov had led the Bulgarian army to tre-

mendous victories over Ottoman forces at Lozengrad, Lyule Burgas–Buni Hisar, and Adrianople, he had ordered the attack on Serbian positions on the night of 29–30 June 1913, which had precipitated the disastrous Second Balkan War. Ferdinand's own role in these events remained obscure. He had little interest in revisiting the disaster of 1913 by returning Savov to command. Real or perceived Russophile sympathies tainted a number of other senior officers.

Zhekov was only a colonel in the summer of 1915. He was born in Sliven in 1864 or 1865. He had received his military education in Bulgaria and, like many officers in the Bulgarian army, at the Italian General Staff Academy in Turin. He served in the Bulgaro-Serbian War of 1885 and in the Balkan Wars, where he participated in the siege of Adrianople as the chief of staff of the Bulgarian Second Army. Zhekov apparently caught the eye of Tsar Ferdinand while serving as the school for reserve officers, and sought the attention of the monarch for career purposes.[11] In anticipation of Bulgaria's joining the Central Alliance and with the support of the tsar, Zhekov received the rank of major general on 2 August 1915.

Another relatively junior officer, Lieutenant Colonel Petŭr Ganchev, signed the convention for Bulgaria. He was a former adjutant of the tsar and former military attaché in Berlin. Ganchev served as the chief Bulgarian negotiator in the arrangements with the Central Powers. Afterward he remained at German Army headquarters in Pless, Silesia, as the representative of the Bulgarian army. From there he often communicated directly to Ferdinand. Zhekov and Ganchev embodied the interests of the Bulgarian tsar. During the Balkan Wars, Tsar Ferdinand had fulfilled his constitutional role as commander in chief of the Bulgarian army. He chose not to assume this position in the First World War, probably because he wished to avoid the risk of direct association with another military defeat. Nevertheless, through Zhekov and Ganchev, Ferdinand sought to exercise a strong influence over the military conduct of the war. By September 1915, most of the leadership of the Bulgarian army recognized that a German alliance offered the best opportunity to attack the Serbs and to unify Bulgaria with Macedonia.

The Bulgarians were no more prepared to undertake a major military effort so soon after the Balkan Wars than the Serbs. Like its Serbian counterpart, the Bulgarian army did include many motivated battle-hardened veterans in its officer corps and in the enlisted ranks. Even though the territories Bulgaria had obtained as a result of the Balkan Wars were not heavily populated, they provided a new source of recruits for the Bulgarian army. The willingness of the Bulgarian population to support another war so soon after the previous one, however, remained problematic. Many of the infantry weapons and artillery pieces it did possess were obsolete, or were of French and Russian manufacture.[12] This meant that ammunition and replacement parts for these weapons would be very difficult to obtain after Bulgaria joined the Central Powers. A report by General Mihail Savov, the Balkan War deputy commander of the Bulgarian army, stated on 15 February 1915 that "The material condition of the army is an unsatisfactory condition, with the possible exception of clothing."[13] The Bulgarian army was especially deficient in clothing. On the eve of the war, the army lacked 35 percent of the greatcoats, 32 percent of the tunics, 39 percent of the trousers, and 43 percent of the boots it needed.[14] After he learned of the signing of the convention with the Central Powers, Bulgarian chief of staff Kliment Boyadzhiev went to General Zhekov and warned that the Bulgarian army lacked the resources to undertake another conflict.[15] Zhekov ignored the caution. He depended upon massive infusions of supplies from Germany to enable the war effort.

Because of their alliance with Austria-Hungary and Germany, the Bulgarians anticipated little difficulty in overrunning Serbia. Tsar Ferdinand announced upon declaration of war with Serbia on 14 October 1915, "The victorious Central Powers are already in Serbia and are advancing rapidly."[16] With the help of their Austrian and German allies, the Bulgarians anticipated an easy and rapid victory. The mobilization, drawing on the experience of the Balkan Wars, was rapid and organized. At the time of mobilization the Bulgarian infantry division was supposed to consist of 45,280 men, including 860 officers and 44,420 NCOs and enlisted men. At the time of mobilization the Bulgarian army had 8,900 officers, 600 medical doctors, and 522,395 NCOs and enlisted men.[17] Although its material base was weak, this was a formidable force. The Bulgarian First and Second Armies prepared to invade Serbia, while the Third Army, consisting of the 4th Preslav Division and the 5th Danube Division under General Stefan Toshev, guarded the Romanian frontier.

The Bulgarian government was anxious to avoid complications with Greece. In response to a German request, Tsar Ferdinand and Radoslavov agreed to turn over Doiran and Gevgeli, two districts on the border between Greek and Serbian Macedonia, to Greece at the end of the war as a goodwill gesture.[18] The Bulgarians also promised the Greek government that their army would not enter these two districts. When the Bulgarians announced general mobilization on 24 Septemer, they stationed two divisions, the 2nd Thracian and the 10th Black Sea, on the Greek frontier.[19] This force was clearly intended to cover the border with Greece. The Greeks responded by mobilizing their army and navy.[20] The Greek government, having failed to do so the previous year, finally appeared to prepare to honor its arrangement with Serbia.

The Serbs had asked for 150,000 Entente soldiers upon Bulgarian mobilization on 22 September 1915.[21] This was the same number the Greeks had agreed to provide in the 1913 treaty. As the orientation of Bulgaria toward the Central Powers became clear in the early autumn of 1915, so did the peril of Serbia. This caused the Entente to consider aid for Serbia. The idea of an Entente intervention in southeastern Europe on behalf of Serbia apparently originated in France during the autumn of 1914. By February 1915, it evidently had become a French effort with the purpose of a landing at the neutral port of Salonika and an advance into the soft underbelly of Austria-Hungary.[22] The successful Serbian defense in the autumn of 1914 appeared to lend some credence to the idea. An effort to supply the Serbs from Salonika up the railroad to Skopie and to Niš was already in place. The French Ministry of War considered that this route could serve to send reinforcements to the Serbs.[23] The Gallipoli operation, however, soon obscured the idea of Entente intervention in southeastern Europe.

Having returned to office on 24 August as a result of victory in parliamentary elections, Prime Minister Venizelos renewed his attempts to pursue a pro-Entente policy. On 3 October, he agreed to the landing of British and French forces at Salonika, providing that Greek sovereignty remained intact and that the Entente forces not occupy Macedonia only to turn it over to Bulgaria.[24] The Entente understood that the Greeks would not march with them at this time. Although the British were concerned that without Greek support, there would be insufficient Entente troops to help the Serbs, the French were blithely nonchalant. The French proposed to send a force of 150,000 men up the Vardar River valley to assist the beleaguered Serbs. The British, however, hoped that the mere presence of their forces in Salonika would persuade the Greeks to join the Entente. Although the arrival of these troops in Salonika clearly represented a real threat to Bulgarian plans, the Entente did not really consider Bulgarian issues in formulating their plans to aid Serbia. The first British and French soldiers disembarked on 5 October. The commander of the force, General Maurice Sarrail, arrived in Salonika on 13 October. The previous July, Sarrail had received orders to proceed to Gallipoli to take command of the two French divisions there. He was to replace General Henri Gourand, who had been severely wounded and lost an arm at the end of June. Before he could assume this command, he learned on 28 September that he would go to Salonika.[25] The initial British troops were from the 10th Division, also withdrawn from Gallipoli. The commander of this force was General Sir Byron Mahon. Their initial objective was to establish contact with the beleaguered Serbs. This meant an advance up the Vardar River valley and control of the railroad line extending along that valley linking Salonika and the main city of northern Macedonia, Skopie, and extending on to Niš in central Serbia. A narrow gauge branch line of this vital rail line extended north from Skopie to Mitrovitsa in Kosovo. By utilizing these rail lines the Entente forces could supply the retreating Serbs. The French imagined a grander plan, however. Having contained the Bulgarians in Macedonia, they envisioned an offensive toward Sofia, with another thrust supported by the Greeks moving up the Struma valley.[26] This was the same route the Greek army had taken in the Second Balkan War, and they had very nearly been trapped by the Bulgarians at the Kresna Gorge. In any event, this proposal was far ahead of the capabilities of the initial Entente force that arrived at Salonika.

Events changed rapidly in Greece. On 5 October, the same day the first British and French soldiers landed in Salonika, Venizelos resigned as Greek prime minister. The king's supporters in parliament compared the appearance of the Entente in Salonika to the German invasion of Belgium.[27] They also pointed out that the Greek-Serbian Treaty of June 1913 could not be implemented, and that under Venizelos's policy Greece would again be involved in the misery of war. This was the second time that year that Venizelos had lost the support of the Greek king and had to resign.

The Bulgarians initially took little notice of the disembarkation of French and British troops in Salonika. They were in the midst of preparing for their attack on Serbia. Soon after the Bulgarian declaration of war on Serbia on 14 October, the Greek government decided upon a policy of armed neutrality benevolent toward the Entente.[28] On 28 October 1915, Greek Prime Minister Stefanos Skouloudis, however, assured Bulgarian minister Pasarov of positive feelings of the Greek government toward Bulgaria. Bulgaria's Prime Minister Radoslavov responded with a decision to maintain strict neutrality toward Greece.[29] Furthermore Bulgarian finance minister Dimitŭr Tonchev, while on a mission in Berlin, reported that the Germans sought friendly relations with Greece.[30] This report reinforced the decision for neutrality toward Greece. With the attack on Serbia underway and thus far successful, the Bulgarians were still not overly concerned about their southern frontier.

Meanwhile the Central Powers gathered their forces to end the Serbian problem and to establish a direct line of communication to Constantinople. Under the overall command of General August von Mackensen, the Austro-Hungarian Third Army and the German Eleventh Army led by General Max von Gallwitz began the fourth invasion of Serbia in a little over a year, on 6 October. Facing them was a depleted and exhausted Serbian army under the command of the seasoned Vojvoda Putnik. The Serbs had spread their armies thinly to cover their northwestern, northern, and eastern frontiers. This prevented them from concentrating against the enemy attacks. The Austro-Hungarians crossed the Sava River west of Belgrade, while the Germans crossed the Danube east of the former Serbian capital. Then on 14 October, the Bulgarian First and Second Armies moved into Serbian territory. The Bulgarians had planned a powerful thrust into Serbia to cut off Macedonia since the beginning of the year.[31] The Bulgarian First Army, consisting of the 1st Sofia, 6th Vidin, 8th Tundzha, and 9th Pleven Divisions under the command of General Kliment Boyadzhiev, the former chief of staff, advanced into the Timok region of northeastern Serbia. There it made contact with General Gallwitz's Eleventh German Army on 6 November in the vicinity of Niš. It then turned to the southwest toward Kosovo in pursuit of the retreating Serbs. On 11 November, the Bulgarian First Army entered Niš. Soon afterward it reached the Morava River, the central axis of Serbia. The Bulgarian First Army pursued the retreating Serbs into Kosovo, but halted at the Albanian frontier. During this campaign, Zhekov strove to maintain Bulgarian operational autonomy. When the German High Command asked the Bulgarian High

Command to move the First Army's 5th Danube Division to link with the Austro-German movement south of Danube, the Bulgarians refused. Other problems were more important, and this issue was "only of local tactical interest."[32] Zhekov wished to retain as much operational independence as possible.

Meanwhile, the Bulgarian Second Army, consisting of the 3rd Balkan and 7th Rila Divisions and the Cavalry Division, swept into Macedonia, the object of Bulgarian policy since the failed San Stefano Treaty of 1878. General Georgi Todorov commanded the Second Army's thrust into Macedonia. Beginning on 14 October, the Bulgarians employed both old and new means to reassert their authority in Macedonia. The Bulgarians returned to the town of Shtip on 19 October through the traditional Balkan band of irregulars, a *cheta* led by Ivan Bŭrlov. The same day a Bulgarian airplane landed in the town.[33] On 23 October, units of the Second Army entered Skopie and Veles on the Vardar River. In doing so the Bulgarians both blocked the retreat of the Serbs to the south along the Vardar valley and cut them off from the oncoming French forces.

The French initially regarded their Bulgarian foes with some condescension. They reckoned that the spirit of the army was "poor" because of the inherent Bulgarian Russophilia. With German leadership, however, the Bulgarian army became, in the opinion of the French staff, "a formidable instrument."[34] The French army in Salonika soon received confirmation of this opinion.

On 14 October, the day of the Bulgarian attacks, Vojvoda Putnik telegraphed Sarrail, to ask for help. "The military situation requires that French troops advance to Niš as soon as possible."[35] The next day three French infantry battalions crossed the Greek frontier and proceeded on into Serbia. The British lagged behind. Only on 22 October did they receive permission from the British secretary of state for war, Field Marshall Earl H. H. Kitchener, to proceed across the Greek frontier into Serbia.[36] This force moved toward to the village of Doiran, where the Vardar River passed in a narrow area between mountains and Lake Doiran.

The Bulgarian attacks threatened to crush the Serbian forces against the oncoming Austro-Hungarian and German armies. General Putnik attempted to hold off the onslaught to gain time for the British and French to arrive up the Vardar valley from Salonika. The advance of the British and

French up the Vardar was a risky operation. If they moved too fast, the Bulgarians could pinch off the advance units. If they moved too slowly, they would afford little help to the Serbs. Also the position of their Greek hosts was not clear. Greek refusal to allow the Entente use of the railway lines leading north to Bitola and to Skopie and Niš complicated their movement to the north.[37] The new Greek government clearly was cool to the Entente presence in Salonika, and King Constantine and his entourage inclined toward the Central Powers. If the Greeks chose to join the Central Alliance, the Entente expedition would be in serious difficulty.

The pressure of the Austro-Hungarians, the Germans, and the Bulgarian First Army in the north and the Bulgarian Second Army advancing from the east forced the Serbs to retreat in a southwesterly direction into Kosovo. There, in the region that resonated through five hundred years of Serbian history, Vojvoda Putnik attempted to make a stand against the invaders near Pristina. The Bulgarian First Army moving on the Serbian left defeated the Serbs on 24 November. The Bulgarians undoubtedly appreciated the symbolism of defeating the Serbs at Kosovo Pole. The Serbs then retreated across the Albanian mountains in three columns, one across southern Montenegro, one through central Kosovo across northern Albania, and the southernmost from Prizern to the port of Dürres. All converged on Lake Scutari, and from there reached the Adriatic. Albanian irregulars also harassed the Serbs along all of their difficult routes of retreat. The Central Powers chose not to chase the defeated Serbian army across Albania. The Germans preferred to husband their resources. The Bulgarian First Army pursued the Serbs to the Albanian frontier. The Bulgarian Second Army turned to deal with the advance of the British and French up the Vardar.

War with the Entente soon came to Bulgaria itself. On 21 October, Entente warships subjected the Bulgarian Aegean coast to bombardment. Installations at the small ports of Badoma and Porto Lagos, and Dedeagach, the main Bulgarian Aegean port, suffered some damage from the bombardment.[38] Lacking an Aegean navy, the Bulgarians could do little but record the extent of the damage and worry that the Entente might take advantage of the Bulgarian weakness by staging a landing somewhere along their coast.

Meanwhile the Bulgarian advance continued. On 16 November in Parachin, Serbia, the Bulgarian General Staff met with the German General Staff together with the commander of German forces in Serbia, Field Marshall von Mackensen, to deal with the changing situation in the south. By this time, the Bulgarians were alert to the danger poised by the arrival of Entente forces in southeastern Europe. After expelling the Entente forces from Serbian Macedonia, the Bulgarians wanted to pursue them into Greek territory. At Parachin, the Germans agreed to assign four divisions and some artillery to support the Bulgarian turn to the south.[39] General Zhekov seems to have understood this support as implicit sanction for undertaking an attack against the Entente forces around Salonika.[40] The Germans, however, did not consider this agreement to be binding in case the Entente forces then landing in Salonika grew too large to attack. The Balkan effort was subordinate to their obligations elsewhere for the Germans. As von Falkenhayn, later wrote, "The Entente could send a division to Macedonia more easily than the Germans could a battalion."[41] This was an implicit acknowledgement of the manpower limitations the Germans faced. It also indicated the transportation difficulties in southeastern Europe and the Entente command of the sea. Von Falkenhayn cited logistical difficulties and the strength of Entente defenses around Salonika, as well as the danger of driving Greece into the arms of the Entente as reasons to forgo a drive on Salonika. He also feared that the elimination of the Entente treat in Salonika would free the Bulgarians from their obligations to the Central Alliance.[42] In any event, von Falkenhayn "requested" that the Bulgarian Second Army not cross the Greek frontier in pursuit of the retreating Entente forces.[43] At no time in the war was the Bulgarian army able to undertake an initiative without German support. It lacked the material basis to do so. It did not do so this time.

Neither the Austrian nor the Bulgarian military command shared its German ally's perspective on the fighting in Macedonia. The Austrians evidently agreed with the Bulgarians that the Central Alliance needed to pursue the Entente forces across the Greek frontier.[44] Austro-Hungarian chief of staff Franz Conrad von Hötzendorf himself wanted to pursue the Entente forces across the Greek frontier all the way to Salonika.[45] The Central Alliance, however, did not function as a partnership of equals.

Now deeply concerned about the developments to the south, the Bulgarians began to monitor closely the growing numbers of Entente soldiers arriving in Salonika. A Bulgarian report from 14 November indicated that there were 124,800 Entente soldiers in Salonika, of whom 62,000 were at the front in Serbia.[46] The Bulgarian figures were fairly accurate. French figures state that by 15 November the Entente had a total of 150,000 men in three French and five British infantry divisions.[47] The precision of the Bulgarian figures is probably due to the fact that Bulgarian agents could circulate freely in Salonika at that time because Bulgaria and Greece were not at war. That same day Radoslavov, the usually complacent Bulgarian prime minister, wrote in his diary of the need to expel the Entente forces from Macedonia.[48] Bulgarian political leaders began to recognize the peril the Salonika front represented. Tsar Ferdinand himself admitted, "I understood much too late the terrible danger that threatens our army from the French and British."[49] Additional intelligence from Salonika increased anxieties in Sofia. At the end of November, the Bulgarian consul in Salonika, T. Nedkov, reported that the British had not yet decided to undertake "serious" action in the Balkans, and that they still hoped that Greece could would join the Entente.[50] Because Bulgaria and Greece were not at war, Consul Nedkov could freely observe and report on the potential danger growing in Salonika.

In consideration of the threat of the Entente presence at Salonika, the Germans agreed that the Bulgarians could occupy Doiran and Gevgeli.[51] This meant that the Bulgarians could enter the areas near the Greek frontier. Gevgeli itself was only 79 kilometers up the railroad line from Salonika. By this time in fact the Bulgarians were already in Doiran and were approaching Gevgeli. Nevertheless the Germans, with the concurrence of the Bulgarian government, continued to insist that the Bulgarian army refrain from violating the Greek frontier.

The movement of Entente soldiers into Serbian Macedonia forced the oncoming Bulgarians to adjust their advance. French units advanced on the left side of the Vardar River into Serbian Macedonia, while a mixed French and British force moved up along the right bank. This force consisted of three French divisions and one British division totaling around 60,000 men, including forty-three artillery batteries, eleven cavalry squadrons, and 276 machine guns. Units on the left wing of the Bulgarian Second

Army turned toward the south to meet the new threat. The Bulgarian Second Army had 160,000 men, with eight cavalry squadrons and sixty-five batteries totaling 260 guns.[52] Given the disparity of forces, the Entente advance up the Vardar valley was foolhardy. Only the expectation that the retreating Serbian army would link with the Entente forces moving up into Macedonia can explain this advance from Salonika.

The Bulgarian Second Army met both of these columns beginning on 3 December and defeated them separately. The Bulgarians had no reservations about fighting the armies of the Great Powers. Like the Serbian Army, the Bulgarian army had gained considerable experience confidence in the Balkan Wars. The Bulgarian attack stopped the left bank column east of Krivolak and forced it to retreat. Even so, the French soldiers made a good initial impression on the Bulgarians. A Bulgarian report of 4 December 1915 stated, "It must be admitted that the French executed a retrograde maneuver in an exemplary manner, given their success in escaping from our trap."[53] Near Gevgeli on 10 December, the Bulgarians again attacked the French and forced them back over the Greek frontier.

At the same time other units from the Bulgarian Second Army moved on to the British force north of Lake Doiran. On 7 December, the Bulgarian army attacked British positions in Serbia at Kosturino. Within five days the Bulgarians pushed the outnumbered British back into Greek territory. There the British established defensive positions southwest of Lake Doiran. The Bulgarians perceived stronger resistance from the French than from the British, to some extent because the mountainous terrain prevented the Bulgarians from bringing their heavy artillery to bear on the French.[54] In any case the success against the British and French armies was a source of great satisfaction for the Bulgarians. The Germans continued to stymie the Bulgarian success. Zhekov telegraphed to German headquarters at Pless, "We need to cross the Greek frontier or we will have to break off our attacks, which would be very undesirable."[55] By early December 1915 the Bulgarians clearly understood the need to pursue the defeated Entente forces back to Salonika.

Meanwhile, elements of the Bulgarian Second Army advanced in a southwesterly direction, taking Bitola on 4 December. Three days later the Bulgarian army entered Ohrid. This western Macedonian town had symbolic importance for the Bulgarians because until 1767 it had been the location of the Bulgarian patriarchate, an Orthodox church administrative center that represented one aspect of Bulgarian claims to Macedonia. Now all of Serbian Macedonia was under Bulgarian control. The Bulgarians had realized their chief war aim.

After their retreat into Greek territory, these Entente forces remained on the defensive until the summer of 1916. The Entente forces suffered relatively high casualties in this Serbian adventure. One out of every ten Entente soldiers was killed, wounded, or missing.[56] The Bulgarian General Staff's daily bulletin for 29 November (11 December n.s.) boasted that Macedonia up to the Greek and Albanian frontiers was cleansed of Serbian and Entente forces.[57] This victory over the Serbs and the Entente imparted to the Bulgarian Second Army a certain measure of vindication after its near collapse in the Second Balkan War in the summer of 1913. The Bulgarian command realized, however, that a serious threat remained largely intact across the Greek border.

The Bulgarian army reached the Greek frontier on 11 December. Because of the German refusal to permit movement into Greece, however, it stopped there. To avoid incidents they stayed two kilometers from the actual frontier, a "gunshot" from the Greek frontier.[58] For the time being, the Greek Army interposed itself between the Greek frontier and the Entente forces, which had withdrawn further south toward Salonika. The success of Bulgarian arms against the Entente advance certainly increased the confidence of General Zhekov that a Bulgarian pursuit of the retreating Entente forces could push them back into the sea. Prime Minster Radoslavov, however, worried that a Bulgarian advance into Greek territory would force the wavering King Constantine to side with the Entente.[59] This concern superseded his previous musings on the need to intervene in Greece. Nevertheless, the problem in the south continued to be a source of anxiety for both the Bulgarian government and the military.

That same month the Bulgarian minister in Berlin, Dimitŭr Rizov, wrote to Sofia, "Ever since our army stopped at the Greek frontier, Salonika has become a nightmare for me, because I am convinced, that if the British and French are not expelled from Salonika soon, a terrible catastrophe will befall us."[60] Rizov's concerns were prescient. The Sofia government was beginning to understand that the relatively easy victory in the war against Serbia would not stand as long as Entente forces threatened Bulgaria along its southwestern frontier.

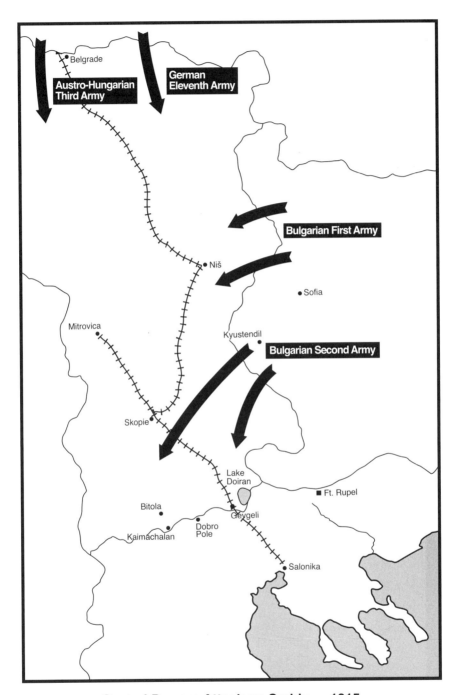

**Central Powers Attack on Serbia — 1915**

Zhekov remained convinced of the need to pursue the defeated Entente forces into Greece. He insisted to von Falkenhayn that the Central Powers must drive Entente troops in Salonika back into the sea. Bulgarian troops should remain on Greek soil. Any Greek troops should evacuate positions near Bulgaria. "*We* have committed our entire existence to this war, *we* have engaged in a bloody war and have sustained enormous losses. These circumstances entitle me to ask Your Excellency (von Falkenhayn) to keep them in mind in decisions regarding territorial and economic questions between Bulgaria and Greece."[61] For Zhekov and the Bulgarian army, the occupation of Greek Macedonia was vital to the preservation of Bulgaria's success thus far in the war.

After their defeat in Serbian Macedonia, the Entente armies began to entrench themselves in Salonika. General Sarrail reported to the War Council in Paris, "Undoubtedly our retreat has decreased our prestige in the east, but if we shift our actions to another location, we will undermine the hope that we persevere on the Western Front where we have struggled in vain so far, and have to look again for that area where we can obtain the desired result."[62] Despite some British misgivings, the Entente conference at Chantilly 6–8 December confirmed Sarrail's sensibilities. The presence of the Entente force in Salonika required the Central Powers to maintain forces in the Balkans that might be used elsewhere.[63] A Bulgarian officer who spent nine days in Salonika reported on 20 December 1915 to the new army chief of staff, Major General Konstantin Zhostov, that the British and French armies were not showing any signs of leaving the city after their defeat in Serbia.[64] They were preparing fortified positions and building hospitals. He noted that morale among the Entente forces after their defeat was low and that the British troops demonstrated little attention to their responsibilities. He also noted that the Greeks were not enthusiastic about their British and French guests. The appearance of a Bulgarian officer among enemy soldiers in a neutral city demonstrated the anomalous situation on the Macedonian Front at its formation. This was one of the final Bulgarian reports from Salonika. On 30 December 1915 the commander of the French forces in Salonika, General Maurice Sarrail, ordered the arrest and detention of the diplomatic representatives of the four Central Powers.[65] This effectively closed the eyes of the Central Powers there. Central Powers diplomats remained in Athens, however. This was another indication of the growing distance between authorities in Athens and Salonika.

Much of the Greek army viewed the British and French as "intruders."[66] During this time there were a number of incidents between Greek authorities and their Entente guests. In December the Greeks sent sixty railcars of grain across the frontier. The next month the Greek cavalry with sabers drawn intimidated a British unit.

Nevertheless the establishment of barracks and other signs of permanence indicated that the Bulgarians would have an enemy presence close to their southern frontier. This report indicated that the Entente presence in Salonika was rapidly becoming permanent. If the Central Powers were to expel the Entente they would have to act precipitously. Not all Bulgarians favored an attack on Salonika. General Zhostov, the Bulgarian chief of staff, lacked enthusiasm for a march on Salonika. He considered that with the conquest of Macedonia, Bulgaria's war goals were attained. On his own initiative, he informed the Germans that no more troops were needed in Macedonia because of the difficulties of maintaining provisions.[67] General Zhostov was not a strong advocate of the Central Alliance or a continuation of the war. Later, after a tour of the Western and Italian fronts he suggested to Radoslavov that Bulgaria could now switch sides and join the Entente. Obviously the military efforts of Bulgaria's allies did not impress General Zhostov. Zhostov's views made him unpopular with the tsar's court and the government. He wrote that to them he was a "black cat."[68] His sudden death in August of the next year removed a major critic of the war from the Bulgarian army.

With Central Powers forces on his northern frontier contemplating invasion and Entente forces in occupation of his second largest city, King Constantine of Greece found himself in a difficult situation. Not surprisingly in these circumstances, he sent mixed messages to Sofia. Back in November, as the Bulgarians approached the Greek frontier, he warned that if the Bulgarian army chasing the Serbs crossed the Greek frontier, the Greeks would have difficulty maintaining neutrality.[69] Radoslavov still thought that Bulgaria should act to preserve Greek neutrality. On the other hand, personal assurances from Greek King Constantine to Tsar Ferdinand that "the Bulgarian army need not fear anything, that they will have full freedom of action" if they entered Greek territory provided additional incentive to cross the Greek frontier and expel the Entente forces from Salonika.[70] King Constantine also told the Bulgarian military attaché in Athens, Major Kableshkov, "I have nothing against the entry of the Bulgarian army into Greece. . . . The expulsion of the Anglo-French from Salonika is imperative and must be accomplished as soon as possible."[71] Clearly King Constantine was in a difficult position. His statements belied the German insistence that an attack on Salonika would undermine Constantine's position on the throne. They only encouraged some in the Bulgarian military to press for action.

On 27 December 1915, the first German units arrived to take positions in the Vardar valley.[72] Other German forces joined them, and soon after the turn of the year these units constituted the German Eleventh Army. This formation held positions between the Vardar River and Lake Doiran. It guarded against a possible Entente advance up the Vardar. Also it stabilized the Macedonian Front and ensured against any Bulgarian adventurism in that region.

For the Bulgarians, the satisfaction over the expulsion of the Entente from Macedonia was tempered by the realization that the Entente forces would remain in Salonika unimpeded by the Central Powers. General Zhekov later ruefully admitted,

> In the military convention, concluded for the circumstance of war against only Serbia, . . . military activity against Entente soldiers in Macedonia was not anticipated. This unforeseen eventuality created special concerns for our high command and forced it to take extra measures against a new and unexpected enemy that had become an accomplished fact with the disembarkation of the Entente forces at Salonika.[73]

Zhekov wrote with the advantage of hindsight, knowing that in September 1918 this Entente force finally launched an offensive that caused the collapse of Bulgaria.

As the smallest and weakest of the Central Powers, the Bulgarians had little choice but to accept the Germans' decision to forgo an offensive against Salonika. Von Falkenhayn conceded, "It is true that the expulsion of the Entente would have had the very desirable result for the Bulgarians that they would have been free from any direct danger, but that was only of very doubtful advantage for the general conduct of the war."[74] Nevertheless, for the Germans, Salonika represented a large internment camp. If Bulgarian-German offensive eliminated it, the Entente soldiers could disperse to other fronts. The Bulgarian victories against the Entente in southern Macedonia restored Bulgarian military confidence lost during the defeats of the Second Balkan War of 1913.[75] In the fall of 1915, the Bulgarians enjoyed a clear numerical advantage over the British and French. The demoralized British and French troops retreated in some disorganization to the safety of the Greek frontier. Had the Bulgarians pursued them across the border immediately, they had a reasonable chance for success. The Bulgarians, however, could not undertake such an effort on their own. They lacked the ability to project their power beyond the Greek frontier. They needed German logistical support at the very least. This was not forthcoming.

The equivocal position of the Greek government complicated any Bulgarian response to the Entente appearance in Macedonia. While the Bulgarians had little reason to trust the Athens government, the Germans supported King Constantine. Von Falkenhayn cautioned General Zhekov, "I do not believe that the Greeks allowed the landing in Salonika in order to injure us. It is simply happened because of their fear."[76] A preemptive Bulgarian thrust across the Greek frontier might tip King Constantine and his army over to the Entente. On the other hand, a restrained policy toward Athens could ensure Greek hostility toward the intruding Entente forces and lead to their expulsion from Greece without any Bulgarian investment of blood and material.

Nor were the Germans entirely consistent in their attitude toward the Salonika landings. They sent troops to support the Bulgarians along the Greek frontier. Also they participated in a diplomatic demarche in Athens threatening an invasion of Greece. Finally, in the spirit of the alliance, they appeared to consider Bulgarian demands to march on Salonika. Yet they maintained a firm grip on policy throughout the fall of 1915 and winter of 1916. They recognized that in the end the elimination of the Entente forces around Salonika did not suit their strategic interests.

Although the French had sent supplies up the Vardar valley to Serbia and had contemplated a direct military intervention in aid of Serbia since 1914, they made few concrete preparations to implement the operation. Nor did they secure much enthusiasm from their British allies or their neutral Greek hosts. The disembarkation of the large Entente force in Salonika in October 1915 was in itself a significant success. The force could not, however, accomplish its objective of extending aid to the Serbs. The Bulgarian thrust across Macedonia cut the British and French off from their Serbian allies. After the withdrawal of the Serbs into northern Albania, the Bulgarians turned their attention to the British and French in southern Macedonia.

Bulgarian regrets over the failure to pursue the defeated Entente forces to Salonika, however, were to a certain degree retrospective. At the time of the establishment of the Entente positions around Salonika, the Bulgarian government under Radoslavov remained committed to the German position. Not even every Bulgarian general advocated an advance into Greece. General Zhostov, the Bulgarian chief of staff, lacked enthusiasm not only for a march on Salonika but also for the Central Alliance. In addition, any such action would require additional heavy artillery not readily available because of the demands of other fronts and because of the difficult topography of southeastern Europe. By the springtime the Entente forces had established defensive positions in northern Greece. The Bulgarian army did cross the Greek border the next summer, but by then the Entente forces were firmly ensconced in the hills north of Salonika. Two years later, these forces launched a large offensive that knocked the exhausted Bulgarians out of the war and began the disintegration of the Central Alliance.

The Macedonian Front arose from a complicated set of circumstances. On the Entente side these included desire to aide the Serbs and the recognition that the Gallipoli operation had failed. Access to Serbia for the Entente depended upon Greece, since the presence of the Austro-Hungarian navy in the Adriatic and the lack of a viable port in Albania precluded a major operation there. The diplomatic conditions for operation changed as Entente ships entered the port of Salonika. The Entente forces arrived in Greece as intruders rather than guests. The Entente forces could not help the Serbs against a combined Austro-Hungarian–Bulgarian–German attack. The Central Powers quickly overran Serbia. On the other hand, despite Bulgarian urging, the Central Powers did not act to eliminate the Entente presence in Greece. The Germans in particular did not want to commit the resources to such an operation. The multinational makeup of both forces hampered the implementation of unified policy. In this regard the Germans were able to control their Austro-Hungarian and Bulgarian allies more effectively than the British and French were able to cooperate.

The consequence of this situation was stalemate along the northern Greek frontier. In this respect the Macedonian Front followed the precedent set on the Western, Eastern, and Italian Fronts.

After thirty-seven years of reticence, the Great Powers had intervened in southeastern Europe militarily. This intervention was the consequence of the collapse of their congress in 1914. They intervened in a struggle that once again involved Bulgaria against Serbia. Both sides justified their presence in southeastern Europe by claiming that by maintaining forces in Macedonia they forced the other side to do so. This kept these forces from being utilized elsewhere. For the time being Greece and Romania remained on the sidelines.

# DEVELOPMENT
## OF THE
# MACEDONIAN
# FRONT

# 4

The formation of the Macedonian Front, like that of the Western and Eastern Fronts, during the First World War, was accidental. Neither the Central Powers nor the Entente had anticipated establishing a line of conflict along the Greek frontier with Bulgaria and Serbian Macedonia. Both maintained forces along this front as a means of preventing the other side from employing those troops and military resources elsewhere. The Greeks interposed some military units along their frontier in between the two hostile forces to maintain the illusion of their sovereignty.

At a Central Alliance military conference on 5 January 1916 in Niš, Bulgarian military and government leaders met with von Falkenhayn and the superfluous Kaiser Wilhelm. General Zhekov insisted upon an attack on Salonika to expel the Entente troops. Neither Tsar Ferdinand nor Prime Minister Radoslavov supported him.[1] No important decisions ensued from these talks. Afterward Zhekov persisted in raising the issue during the sub-

sequent visit of the German kaiser to Bulgaria, but to no avail. Von Falkenhayn insisted that the upcoming offensive at Verdun precluded an effort in
Macedonia. Zhekov later dismissed this as an "excuse" to cover the "family
politics" of the Germans toward the Greek king.[2] Even so, the Central Powers managed to reach some agreement on the Greek issue. On 6 January
1916, the representatives of Austria-Hungary, Bulgaria, and Germany in
Athens informed the Greek government that their armies intended to cross
the Greek frontier.[3] Although initially the Greeks agreed to this demarche,
the evacuation of Gallipoli provided the Entente with reinforcements for
Salonika, and distractions at Verdun prevented the immediate implementation of this threat. It was not implemented. The Germans did attack Salonika from the air. On the night of 31 January, a German zeppelin bombed
the port area of the city, killing one British, one French, and one Greek soldier and eleven civilians, and destroying a bank.[4] Within a month, Entente
flyers were bombing Bulgarian installations on the other side of the Greek
frontier. By April they were even flying over Sofia, dropping leaflets and a
few bombs.

Across the Greek border the Entente forces continued to dig in. As
early as 21 November 1915 they had begun to plan to establish defenses in
the area around Salonika, and even to broach the possibility of an evacuation. The Entente forces did not anticipate an immediate Bulgarian attack
into Greek territory.[5] The safe haven of Greece allowed them to recover
from their defeat in the late autumn of 1915. It also permitted them the opportunity to established fortified positions in northern Greece without im-
pediment from the Central Powers. The Entente leadership did not trust
the Greeks. They had good reason not to do so. At the beginning of February Colonel Ionnis Metaxas, chief of staff of the Greek army and later the
authoritarian ruler of Greece, stated, "If Venizelos himself was in power today and could order the Greek army to fight on the side of the Entente, the
army would refuse."[6] Nevertheless, at the end of December 1915, the local
Greek commander in Salonika signed an agreement promising not to in-
terfere with Entente military operations in Greek territory.[7] This provided
a certain measure of security for the Entente efforts there.

Bulgarian concerns about the increasing Entente presence in Salonika
finally had some effect on their German allies. On 9 February 1916, during a visit of Tsar Ferdinand to German General Staff Headquarters in

Pless, General Zhekov and General von Falkenhayn agreed to fortify their positions along the southern border of Bulgaria.[8] Further, they decided to resolve the question of an offensive against Salonika by 15 March 1916. General von Mackensen had previously informed German General Headquarters in mid-January 1916 that because of logistical difficulties no offensive could ensue against Salonika before the middle of April.[9] While this agreement offered the Bulgarians stronger defensive positions along their southern frontier, it postponed the decision to undertake an offensive against the Entente in Salonika. Afterward von Falkenhayn continued to resist the idea of an attack on Salonika. He pointed out that because of the limitations of the railroad line south of Niš and the roads in the region, the accruing of materials for an offensive could not be complete until April. Further, he warned, "It would be very questionable to undertake an attack, when no one knows, what will happen elsewhere through the middle of April, in such a case it may be appropriate to consider, if we should not meanwhile undertake an operation in another direction."[10] General Zhekov himself later admitted that the onset of winter in the difficult terrain of southern Macedonia and the logistical situation made life difficult for Bulgarian soldiers.[11] These issues made the continuation of the offensive problematic. As von Falkenhayn was aware, the offensive against Verdun would be well underway by time agreed upon for the decision against Salonika. At this point von Falkenhayn would not even accept a Bulgarian proposal to occupy strategic points inside Greek territory that could be used to construct defensive positions against Entente attacks.[12] Soon afterward, however, he did agree that the Bulgarians could enter the Greek port of Kavala "in case of need."[13] For all practical purposes, the Pless agreement of 9 February confirmed that the Macedonian Front had become permanent.

Despite their assurances to their Bulgarian allies, the Germans had no intention of undertaking any action against Salonika. One reason undoubtedly was because of the German involvement at Verdun. Also the evacuation of Gallipoli made an attack against Salonika less attractive for the Germans. Von Falkenhayn latter claimed that the Bulgarians had lost some of their enthusiasm for the attack by the winter of 1916.[14] His concerns, however, that had once the Bulgarians clearly attained their goal of Macedonia, they would be less likely to support the other war aims of the

Central Powers and might have been vulnerable to an Entente offer of a separate peace or even adopt a pro-Entente policy had some substance.[15] With Macedonia safely under control, the Bulgarians would have had little incentive to remain active in a war in which they had attained their goal. That might have been advantageous also for the Germans, however. They would not have had to deploy soldiers and deliver supplies to an inactive ally. Zhekov remained adamant on the issue of an offensive into Greece. Nevertheless, with the conquest of Serbian Macedonia the Bulgarians had realized their main war aim. Further effort on their part would not necessarily mean further gains. With the German government maintaining pro-Greek and pro-Romanian policies, the Bulgarians had nothing further to obtain. They remained in the war essentially to protect their conquests.

One response of the Bulgarian command to the somewhat anomalous situation on the Macedonian Front was the traditional Balkan expedient of encouraging partisan activity. They had already employed partisans to attack the Serbs in Macedonia in the aftermath of the Second Balkan War. By March 1916 the Bulgarians were supporting partisan bands all along the Greek frontier.[16] These irregular units functioned at first mainly as information gatherers. Also they fought against Greek bands that operated in the areas along the frontier. The partisans allowed the Bulgarian command greater freedom of action along the supposedly inviolable Greek frontier. The Bulgarians also obtained intelligence from Slavic-speaking Macedonians who had deserted from the Greek army.[17] The Bulgarians also drew upon the Macedonian population for soldiers. They eventually mobilized 133,837 men from the occupied Macedonian regions.[18] Most of these came from the area granted the Serbs by the Treaty of Bucharest, Vardar Macedonia. The Bulgarians regarded the population there as Bulgarians.

The Bulgarian command remained concerned about growth of Entente power around Salonika. If this force undertook another offensive it could invade Bulgaria and even threaten the link between the Central Powers and the Ottomans. The Central Powers forces arrayed the Bulgarian First Army and the German Eleventh Army in Army Group Mackensen, headquartered in Skopie under the command of the group's namesake. The German Eleventh Army initially consisted of the German 101th Division and the Bulgarian 9th Pleven and 5th Danube Divisions, together with a German staff. The Bulgarian First Army consisted of the 3rd Balkan and 8th Tundzha Divisions. It occupied positions from the Debar and Struga on the Albanian frontier to the bend of the Cherna River to Belasitsa Mountain. The German Eleventh Army extended from Kozhuh Hill to the Vardar River. The Bulgarian Second Army, consisted of the 11th Macedonian, 2nd Thracian, 6th Vidin, and 7th Rila Divisions, had an independent command in Levunovo. It held the line from the Strumitsa River valley to the Struma River. The composition of these armies changed over time. The main Bulgarian positions were located in the high ground between Lake Doiran west to the Vardar River. The headquarters of the Bulgarian command remained in Kyustendil, in southwestern Bulgaria. On order from General von Falkenhayn on 12 March 1916, the Bulgarians began to fortify their positions along the Macedonian Front.[19] There would be no effort to cross the Greek frontier for the time being.

After their retreat from Serbian Macedonia, the Entente forces quickly established themselves in an extended defensive perimeter around Salonika. Beginning in April 1916, they expanded north toward the Greek frontier. Initially the British held the line from the Gulf of Ofano on the Aegean Sea to the Vardar River with the 22nd, 26th, 28th, 10th, and 27th Divisions. General George Milne, who replaced General Mahon, led the British forces. The French, under the command of their Eastern Army, the largest Entente force in Greece, had four infantry divisions, the 57th, 122nd, 156th, and 17th Colonial, including some Senegalese battalions. They had also three artillery divisions. They initially held in general the territory between the Struma valley and the Vardar.

The Entente command drew on several additional sources of soldiers for their operations in Macedonia. One was source Italy. As General Joseph Joffre, the commander of the French army, pointed out, "Among the allied powers, Italy has the greatest interest in preventing Serbia and Montenegro from concluding a separate peace that would install the Germans and Bulgarians on the Adriatic. For that reason, Italy has the greatest interest to assure the prompt reorganization of the Serbian army."[20] This was true in that the Italians placed great importance on the control of the Adriatic Sea. Nevertheless, the Italians were not eager aid the Serbian army. They perceived in the Serbs rivals for the domination of Albania. Already in October 1914, the Italians had occupied the island of Saseno in the Bay of Valona, and occupied the city of Valona itself on 25 December 1914.[21] Valona was the main port of southern Albania. Albania, established as an independent state only in December 1912 at the London ambassadors' conference, had lapsed into disorder after the outbreak of the First World War. The new monarch appointed by the Great Powers, Prince William of Wied, had abandoned his throne on 3 September 1914 and returned to his home in Germany. The presence of the retreating Serbian army in northern Albania made the Italians uncomfortable. An additional 80,000 Italian troops landed in Albania in the autumn of 1915.[22] Their commitment in Albania stretched Italian resources. Nevertheless, under some pressure from the British and French, the Italian government decided to establish a presence on the Macedonian Front in 1916. Around 23,000 men of the 35th Infantry Division, under the command of General Pettit di Roreto, arrived at Salonika on 11 August. While the Italians were represented on the Macedonian Front, their main interest in Southeastern Europe remained in Albania. This placed them in combat with their Austro-Hungarian enemies, but also in conflict with their Serbian allies regarding northern Albania and neutral Greece in southern Albania.

Russia also agreed to send soldiers to Macedonia. The Russian troops who arrived at Salonika were part of a larger force first dispatched to France. Two infantry brigades remained in France for service on the Western Front, and two eventually went to Salonika, where they formed the Russian Expeditionary Force in Macedonia. The Second Infantry Brigade consisting of 224 officers and 9,388 men arrived from Archangel in August.[23] These soldiers represented Tsar Nicholas's desire to maintain Russian interest in the Balkans.[24] Their presence on the Macedonian Front placed them in direct conflict with the fellow Slavs and fellow Orthodox Christians whom the Russians had freed from Ottoman rule only thirty-four years earlier. The liberators of Bulgaria were then poised to invade Bulgaria.

The most important source of additional soldiers for the Macedonian Front was the Serbian army. In yet another imposition on the neutrality of Greece, the survivors of the trek across northern Albania had found refuge on the Greek island of Corfu. To facilitate the reorganization of the Serbian Army, the French occupied the island of Corfu in January 1916. The idea of moving these soldiers to Salonika originated in a Serbian staff study presented at Chantilly during an Entente command conference there from 5–7 December 1915. This study, by Colonel Dušan Stefanović, suggested that the addition of the Serbian and Montenegrin armies to the Entente forces already in Salonika could enable the Entente to succeed with another offensive into Macedonia.[25] The 30,000 men of the Montenegrin army were soon lost when the Austro-Hungarians overran their country in January 1916. Nevertheless by 1 June 115,488 Serbian soldiers, after a period of recovery on the Greek island of Corfu from the ordeal of their retreat across the Albanian mountains the previous fall, joined the Entente forces in Salonika.[26] They were organized into six infantry divisions and one cavalry division. These in turn made up the First Army, under the command of Vojvoda Živojin Mišić; the Second Army, commanded by Vojvoda Stepa Stepanović; and the Third Army, commanded by General Pavle Jurišić-Šturm. The Third Army was reorganized in 1917 and its divisions divided between the First and Second Armies. All the Serbian forces were under the command of Serbian Crown Prince Alexander. The Entente command anticipated that these soldiers would be highly motivated to fight against the Bulgarians in order to return to their homeland. Serb forces extended from Nonte to Paralovo, with the First Army including the Morava and Vardar Divisions, Second Army, the Šumadija and Timok Divisions, and the Third Army, the Drina and Danube Divisions.

This mixture of nationalities and units in Macedonia reflected the complexity of the Entente. General Sarrail had a difficult time managing all of this diversity. The force thus assembled totaled in the summer of 1916 to 313,000 men, including 82,000 French, including colonial soldiers from Madagascar, Senegal, and Indochina, 87,000 British, 97,000 Serbian, 30,000 Italian, and 17,000 Russian soldiers.[27] Of the European Entente powers fighting in the summer of 1916, only the Belgians and the Portuguese lacked a military presence in Salonika. In August 1916, a contingent of unarmed and unequipped Albanians arrived there, sent by the pro-Entente Albanian leader Essad Pasha.[28] Each army present had its own agenda and its own chain of command reaching back to the home country. The British and Italians had little interest in an active policy in Macedonia. The Russians maintained the traditional interests of their monarch and government in southeastern Europe. The French and especially the Serbs advocated offensive actions in Macedonia. All the Entente could manage at first were occasional air raids. Throughout the summer the Entente air forces bombed Bulgarian targets, at Fort Rupel, Prilep, Bitola, and distant Sofia.

As soon as the Entente forces moved up to the Greek frontier, the Bulgarians began to fortify the positions they had established just north of the border.[29] This border had been established only at the end of the Balkan wars and was still poorly delineated. The Bulgarian command, led by General Zhekov, continued to press the Germans for an offensive to drive on Salonika and eliminate the Entente presence there.[30] The Bulgarians were especially eager to extend their right flank to the southern end of the Rupel gorge, where the Struma River flowed on down to the Aegean. They also perceived an opportunity in the outrage many Greeks felt about the Entente presence in their country. One Greek officer told the German military attaché in Athens that if the Bulgarians crossed the border into Greece, "we will greet the Bulgarians as liberators."[31] German objections to a move into Greece ceased. On 26 May, soldiers from the Bulgarian 7th Rilski Division crossed the border and approached Fort Rupel, which commanded the approaches of the Struma River into Greece. This was an important point of access into Greece from the north. On instructions from the Athens government, the garrison surrendered. The bloodless Bulgarian occupation of Fort Rupel clearly demonstrated the frustration of King Constantine with the Entente occupation of the northern portion of his country. Essentially, for the Bulgarians the seizure of Fort Rupel was a defensive action. By controlling Fort Rupel, they ensured that no Entente force could follow the invasion route into Bulgaria the Greek Army had utilized during the summer of 1913 in the Second Balkan War. At the same time, the Bulgarians also improved their lines west of the Struma River with the occupation of Belasitsa Mountain inside Greek territory. This too was with the concurrence of the Greek army. Later, on 3 June, the Bulgarians also advanced into Greek territory on the western bank of the Vardar and established defensive positions.

After this success, Zhekov continued to press for further action on the Macedonian Front. In July 1916 the Bulgarian army received reports that French and Serbian troops were burning the villages of "good Bulgarians" on the Greek side of the frontier.[32] This ethnic cleansing offended Bulgarian nationalist sensibilities. It also deprived the Bulgarians of sources of local information on the Entente-controlled side of the Greek frontier.

Nevertheless, the Germans continued to resist Bulgarian entreaties to undertake an offensive on the Macedonian Front in the summer of 1916. Von Falkenhayn assured Zhekov that the Entente had no intention of mounting an offensive there.[33] He also cautioned against further intrusion into Greece. On 9 July 1916 von Falkenhayn telegraphed Zhekov, in response to Zhekov's repeated requests to attack into Greece: "At the present moment, when difficult battles are taking place on the French and the Russian Fronts, perhaps decisive for the war, and with not only every soldier, but also every cartridge and every grenade counted upon, it is highly undesirable, that we establish a new front." This time von Falkenhayn did not expressly forbid a Bulgarian attack into Greece. He warned Zhekov, however, "I ask Your Excellency therefore, in view of the situation that you examine your desire, to advance into Greece, in regards to the question of what Bulgarian strength will be free for the Romanian Front."[34] In the case of an Entente attack on the Macedonian Front, he did he not preclude a Bulgarian counteroffensive.[35] In any event, Zhekov remained committed to an offensive on the Macedonian Front. He explained to the German naval attaché in Sofia, "If the Bulgarian Front must be weakened to free up units to use against Romania, it is necessary to improve the security of Bulgarian positions there against enemy initiative."[36] Zhekov clearly understood that if Romania entered the war, the Entente forces on the Macedonian Front would try to seize the initiative. His use of the term "Bulgarian Front" is instructive. This indicated that Zhekov realized not only that with the conquest of Macedonia, Bulgaria had realized its war aims, but also that the Bulgarians remained the major factor in the Central Alliance position in southeastern Europe.

Von Falkenhayn remained concerned about the Greek situation. He feared the Bulgarians would undertake some act of aggression that would propel the Greeks into the arms of the Entente. General Zhekov sarcastically responded to his concerns:

> I have already given the strictest orders from the beginning of the operations in Greek territory to avoid conflict with Greek troops, and I

can assure Your Excellency, that Bulgarian soldiers, in spite of the rumors from various sources, are well disciplined. On the other hand
if the Greeks open fire on us, it would be a crime to remain inactive. We are not shaky barbarians or headhunters, as some would de-
scribe us.[37]

General Zhekov's sense of exasperation because of Bulgaria's status as a
junior ally in the Central Alliance was evident in this response. The Bulgarian army had a more recent experience of war than the German army.
Furthermore, Bulgarian efforts during the Balkan Wars were not entirely
without success.

The catalyst for the renewal of serious military activity on the Macedonian Front for the first time since the previous fall was the anticipation
of Romania's joining the Entente in the summer of 1916. Both sides understood that the entry of Romania into the war would alter circumstances on
the Macedonian Front. General Zhekov feared the massing Entente armies
in the south and a hostile Romania in the north would place Bulgaria in
the same perilous position as during the Second Balkan War in the summer of 1913.[38] He explained the Bulgarian strategic situation to the Austro-
Hungarian chief of staff, Conrad:

> The greater part of the Bulgarian army is arrayed on the Macedonian
> Front, where our enemy undoubtedly will undertake an offensive im-
> mediately upon the entry of Romania into the war against us, we need
> to hold sufficient power for the defense of the Black Sea and Aegean
> coasts against a possible attack, we need to put sizable force on the
> Dobrudzha frontier not only to guard our flank but to gain the nec-
> essary space to act across the Danube.[39]

The Bulgarians had not abandoned their intention of advancing against Salonika. Probably at least in part to forestall the Bulgarian offensive there,
the Germans proposed a mutual withdrawal in northern Greece through
diplomatic channels in Athens in August 1916.[40] The Central Powers would
withdraw to a line from the Devoi River in southern Albania to Lake Kas-
toira to Lake Doiran to the mouth of the Struma River. In return, they expected the Entente pull back to Lake Langaca to Topcin to Katerini. Under
this proposal, Central Powers and Entente troops would be separated by

20–30 kilometers and the Entente would retain Salonika. This extraordinary de facto armistice would have left the Central Powers free to undertake a possible offensive against Romania. Undoubtedly the proposal was also intended to bolster the Greek government in Athens. The Entente had no interest in accepting the German proposal. They wanted neither to support King Constantine, nor to yield the strategic positions they had already occupied in northern Greece.

The Bulgarians had prepared for an offensive in Macedonia for some time. They had urged an offensive on the Macedonian Front since the beginning of the year. The Bulgarian General Staff, convinced that the Germans would not support an attack on Salonika, urged instead in 1916 an offensive on the Macedonian Front in Greece to shorten their lines.[41] They developed a specific operational plan in June 1916.[42] Only in August, with the pending entry of Romania onto the side of the Entente, did the Germans finally sanction a Bulgarian action. Beginning on 17 August, the Bulgarian First Army, commanded by Lieutenant General Kliment Boyadzhiev, crossed the Greek frontier and advanced against the Serbian Third Army south of Lake Prespa and to a line from Lerin (Gk: Florina) to Lake Ostrovo (Arnisa) to Kaimakchalan mountain. The Greek frontier guards who had previously formed a fragile line along the border withdrew. Elements of the Bulgarian First Army entered Florina on the evening of 17 August. The Greek garrison there was interned and sent to Germany. The conquest of Florina represented the greatest extent of Bulgarian advance into north central Greece.

The Bulgarian offensive soon ran into difficulties. Because its front was over 130 kilometers wide, the First Army had trouble concentrating its power on its objectives.[43] The advancing Bulgarians could utilize only light artillery against their adversaries; the difficult terrain limited the deployment of heavy artillery and caused logistical problems. This impeded further progress on the western flank. Nevertheless the Bulgarians inflicted heavy casualties on the opposing Serbian Third Army. Serbian losses during the Bulgarian offensive included 657 dead, 2,555 wounded, and 706 missing.[44] This was the first major combat for the reorganized Serbian army since its arrival in Salonika. The Bulgarians sustained even heavier casualties in the fighting. In the Florina operation, they lost 32 officers and 1,047 soldiers dead and 66 officers and 4,333 soldiers wounded.[45]

In the second part of the flank attack, launched simultaneously with the western attack, the Bulgarian Second Army moved into eastern Macedonia beginning on the night of 17 August. Although initially hesitant, von Falkenhayn finally agreed to the Bulgarian seizure of the three most important towns in eastern Macedonia: Kavala, Seres, and Drama.[46] The entire effort was under Bulgarian command. On their left flank, the Bulgarians had for some time feared an Entente descent upon Kavala, the main Aegean port in eastern Macedonia. Through the spring and much of the summer the Entente fleet had harassed the Bulgarian Aegean littoral.[47] The possibility of an Entente attack on or even landings at Kavala clearly concerned the Bulgarians as they contemplated the occupation of eastern Macedonia.[48] The Bulgarians had only a tiny navy confined to the Black Sea. An Entente presence there potentially could have turned the eastern flank of the Central Powers on the Macedonian Front. The Bulgarian effort here achieved immediate success. The Bulgarian Second Army entered Greek territory in eastern Macedonia and took Drama and Seres. It occupied Kavala on 12 September. Elements of the Greek army's 4th Corps stationed there offered no resistance. These soldiers were disarmed and interned in Germany. Apparently at Kavala, however, some members of the Greek garrison refused internment and escaped to Salonika.[49] The unity of the Greek military was fraying. Some officers, disgusted with the capitulations to the Bulgarians, turned to the Entente for redress. With this operation the Bulgarians shortened their land lines and extended their Aegean coast. This offensive also gave them control of the railroad between Drama and Gevgeli on the east bank of the Vardar River. The Bulgarians had occupied all of this territory during the Balkan Wars and regarded it as a part of their Macedonian legacy.

The Bulgarians had advanced on both wings of the front. In the east, at least, they had sustained very light losses. The British official history termed it a "brilliant stroke."[50] Even the usually Bulgaropobic Erich Ludendorff later admitted that the advance on the flanks had merit.[51] Nevertheless, the Entente troops were still active, and Salonika remained far away.

Just as the Bulgarians opened their offensive in Macedonia, German command changed at the highest level. Because of the failure of the Verdun battle to produce a decisive result, the heroes of the Eastern Front, General Paul von Hindenburg and his deputy Erich Ludendorff, replaced von

Falkenhayn on 29 August. This change of command was not advantageous to Zhekov. He had gotten along well with von Falkenhayn. The deposed German commander himself asserted that there was never "the slightest friction" between the German and Bulgarian General Staffs.[52] This assessment is overly sanguine. Nevertheless, when German High Command changed, relations started to go bad because Ludendorff in particular demonstrated "egoism and brutality" in his relations with his Bulgarian allies.[53] Zhekov found Ludendorff, in particular, to be arrogant and condescending. Neither von Hindenburg nor Ludendorff thought highly of the commander in chief of the Bulgarian army. Von Hindenburg described Zhekov as "a man of remarkable powers of observation, not by any means blind to great conception, but essentially restricted in his outlook to the sphere of the Balkans."[54] This is a reasonably fair assessment. As the military commander of the most junior partner in the Central Alliance, and not entirely comfortable with the Ottoman connection, Zhekov naturally focused his attentions on the Balkans. Moreover, von Hindenburg, like his predecessor von Falkenhayn, had little interest in any Bulgarian effort on the Macedonian Front. He later wrote, "If we had compelled the Entente forces to withdraw from Macedonia we should have had them on our necks again on the Western Front."[55] This dismissive attitude toward the Macedonian Front demonstrated that the fundamental difference between the Bulgarian and German commands continued with the advent of von Hindenburg and Ludendorff. Bulgarian national interests were secondary for the Germans. Ludendorff dismissed Zhekov as "a loyal supporter of the Alliance, but [who] did not possess those outstanding qualities which are required of a leader in a modern war. Besides, he lacked the necessary training."[56] Just as Zhekov could comprehend the Central Alliance only in Bulgarian terms, so Ludendorff had similar limitations in German terms.

Meanwhile, events north of the Danube were moving toward conflict. On 27 August 1916 Romania declared war on Austria-Hungary. That same day Romanian troops advanced into Transylvania. Bulgaria joined the war against Romania three days later. A joint Bulgarian-German-Ottoman force consisting mainly of the Bulgarian Third Army, but commanded by Field Marshal von Mackensen, invaded Romania from northeastern Bulgaria on 1 September. General von Mackensen had left the German Eleventh Army to command the Central Powers offensive against Romania.

This army moved into Dobrudzha, a fertile region between the northward crook of the Danube River and the Black Sea known to the Bulgarians as "Golden Dobrudzha" because of the valuable wheat crop produced there. The Romanian Third Army, with the support of two Russian infantry divisions, defended the Dobrudzha. The ephemeral Treaty of San Stefano of 1878 had assigned most of the region to Bulgaria. Until the Treaty of Bucharest of 1913, the southern part of the Dobrudzha had belonged to Bulgaria. The Bulgarian government aspired to acquire all of Dobrudzha. With the Central Powers' invasion of Dobrudzha, the First World War became a two-front war for the Bulgarians. From this point on many Bulgarians referred to the fighting in Macedonia as the "Southern Front."

One consequence of the spread of the fighting was that Bulgarian soldiers confronted their Russian liberators on both the Macedonian and Dobrudzha Fronts. Another problem from the past arose with the transfer of an Ottoman force across Bulgaria to Dobrudzha. The only available reinforcements for Dobrudzha came from the Ottoman army. The presence of the Ottomans was disconcerting for the Bulgarians. In mid-September a hastily arranged Austro-Hungarian and German counteroffensive under the command of former German chief of staff von Falkenhayn drove the Romanians out of Transylvania.

At the same time the Bulgarians advanced in eastern Macedonia, the Entente armies on the Macedonian Front again became active. As General Zhekov had anticipated, the Entente undertook an offensive to prevent the Central Powers forces in Macedonia from intervening against Romania. The arrival of the Serbian army in Salonika in the summer had given the Entente a numerical advantage over the Central Powers forces in Macedonia. The Entente offensive was to start within ten days of signing the treaty of alliance with Romania in Bucharest on 17 August 1916.[57] It began that same day. General Sarrail had originally planned an offensive for March, but received little cooperation from his British allies. The British had never been convinced of the utility of the Macedonian operation. They continually contemplated removing their troops for use elsewhere.[58] In June, Sarrail received instructions from Paris to prepare an offensive using only French and Serbian forces.[59] Initially General Milne indicated that if Romania did not attack Bulgaria, British troops would not participate in an offensive on the Macedonian Front.[60] The French government intended this to be an inducement to the Romanians to enter the war on the side of the Entente. An Entente offensive from Salonika could hold the Bulgarian army in Macedonia in place, and enable the Romanians to make their major effort in Transylvania without fear that the Bulgarians could shift significant forces from the Macedonian Front to invade Romania from the south. The Entente effort was really a simultaneous offensive launched at the same time as the Bulgarian effort rather than a counter-offensive. Its ultimate goals were vague. Sarrail intended the Entente forces to advance in the direction of Sofia. Because of the difficult topography of the region, this was not a realistic objective. Sofia lies behind the Rila mountain complex and is not directly accessible from the south through a river valley system.

The Entente was able to mass a force of over 300,000 men, including British, French, Italian, Russian, and Serbian soldiers and 1,000 artillery pieces.[61] On the eve of the Entente offensive, General Joffre telegrammed General Sarrail, "Now that Romania has entered the war, the mission of the Eastern Army is to undertake the necessary effort to limit the freedom of action of the Bulgarian army to allow the Romanians to operate with their maximum force against the Austrian army."[62] Joffre had hoped that Bulgaria might be induced to seek a separate peace. Now he abandoned the concept of breaking though to Sofia. Interestingly enough, the idea of a Bulgarian separate peace at this time also occurred to some Germans. When Romania entered the war in 1916, the Germans suspected an Entente effort to achieve a separate peace with Bulgaria.[63] Radoslavov's "offhand" denial of this rumor did not appear to have reassured the German secretary of state.

After three days of heavy artillery fire, a joint British and French offensive effort near Lake Doiran ensued. In this First Battle of Doiran the Bulgarian defenses held. Attacks continued until 23 August, but failed to dislodge the Bulgarians from most of the defensive positions they had established there. Bulgarian counterattacks relied on the Balkan War tactic of the bayonet charge and restored the Bulgarian situation to some degree.

On the Entente right wing, mainly British units attacked the newly established Bulgarian positions along the Struma River beginning on 21 August. Although they did destroy several bridges over the Struma to prevent further Bulgarian advance, their efforts to push the Bulgarians back from the Struma met only local success. British troops did manage to cross the Struma River between Lake Butkova and Lake Tahinos. The tenacity of the Bulgarian defense limited British presence east of the Struma there and in two other locations to three small bridgeheads. Fighting continued through the autumn, with little change in position.

The Entente forces achieved more success, however, further the west. After 23 August, the Bulgarian First Army made little progress against strengthening Entente resistance. Bulgarian casualties mounted. By the end of August, the First Army's advance into Greece had ceased. The difficult terrain hampered communication and logistics. Adequate heavy artillery could not accompany the Bulgarian advance.

After Bulgarian activity halted, the Entente acted. Between Lake Prespa and Lake Ostrovo, four French and six Serbian divisions from the Serbian First and Third Armies moved against the center and left flank of the Bulgarian First Army. Included under French overall command was the Russian brigade. The Entente offensive began on 12 September with two days of artillery fire. Ground attacks began two days later. The situation rapidly deteriorated for the overextended Bulgarians. Because of their commitment in the north against Romania, they had little manpower and few material resources left to commit to the Macedonian Front. Units of the Bulgarian First Army had to retreat from their forward positions immediately, sometimes abandoning their artillery in the process.[64] As a consequence of this setback, General Boyadzhiev, who had opposed the initial Bulgarian offensive because of the relative weakness of his force, was replaced by Lieutenant General Dimitŭr Geshov. Also the Bulgarian First Army itself came under the command of the German Eleventh Army, led by Lieutenant General Arnold von Winckler.[65] The Germans imposed the same command strictures in stiffening the Austro-Hungarian army against the Brusilov offensive earlier that summer.

The Bulgarian First Army's western flank, between Bitola and Lake Ohrid, managed to contain the Entente offensive. On 23 September, however, French troops entered Florina after heavy fighting. The Germans later complained that the Bulgarian infantry did not stay in their positions to await an enemy attack, but launched their own attacks even before artillery preparation.[66] Probably the Bulgarian infantry were conducting their traditional bayonet assaults, which terrified their opponents but which often resulted in high Bulgarian casualties. The Entente attacks pushed the Bulgarians back toward the old Greek-Serbian frontier. This eliminated the gains of the Bulgarian effort the previous month. The center of the First Army encountered extremely hard fighting southeast of Bitola. The overextended Bulgarians soon found themselves in jeopardy.

In this difficult situation the Bulgarians sought assistance from their allies. With the Battles of Verdun and Somme still raging on the Western Front and the Brusilov offensive on the Eastern Front only beginning to wane, the Germans had very limited sources of reinforcement. One source of support was Bulgaria's erstwhile Ottoman enemies. In June 1916, Enver Pasha, the Ottoman commander in chief, had proposed to send a Turkish division to fight against Romania in case Romania did join the Entente.[67] Then in response to a German request of 12 September 1916, Enver agreed to send the 11,979 men of the 50th Infantry Division to the Macedonian Front.[68] It took up a position on the eastern flank of the Macedonian Front, from the mouth of the Struma River along the Aegean coast. In November the 12,609-man strong 46th Infantry Division took up positions along Lake Tahinos. Together the divisions formed the XX Corps. Ottoman soldiers remained in Macedonia until May 1917, when the demands of fighting in Palestine and Mesopotamia, and the relative quiet of the Macedonian Front, caused first the withdrawal of the 46th Division and then the 50th Division. The Bulgarians were never entirely comfortable that military units of their old antagonists were back in Macedonia. The officers and men of the Ottoman 50th Division, though needing training, made a good impression on the Bulgarians. Nevertheless, as General Zhekov pointed out to Lieutenant Colonel Ganchev with regard to the Ottoman presence in Dobrudzha, "such help is given to Germany, not Bulgaria."[69] Even so, Bulgarian manpower resources were limited. General Zhekov undoubtedly understood that the Germans were responding to Bulgarian requests for reinforcements by bringing in Ottoman troops. With the arrival of the Ottomans, all members of the Central Alliance were represented on the Macedonian Front.

Von Hindenburg sought to reassure his Bulgarian allies. Neatly undercutting the Bulgarian commander in chief, he telegraphed to Tsar Ferdinand through Colonel Ganchev that "the situation of the Bulgarian First Army is not as desperate as General Zhekov indicated under his first impression."[70] After some dithering, von Hindenburg confirmed General Zhekov's order that the Bulgarian First Army withdraw from Florina to positions south of Bitola.[71] The situation at Florina finally attracted the attention of the Germans, who of course were focused on the Western and Eastern Fronts.

Meanwhile on 12 September a large battle developed at Kaimakchalan (Serb: Kajmakčalan) massive, a high stony ridge with two summits both about 35,000 meters long and 24,600 meters high. Troops from the Serbian First Army's Drina Division (detached from the Third Army) attacked the Bulgarian First Army's 11th Macedonian Division's fixed positions on the ridge. After over two weeks of heavy fighting and with high losses on both sides, Serbian troops, with French support, succeeded in overrunning Bulgarian positions on the twin summits of Kaimakchalan on 30 September. The heavy losses reflected the intensity of the fighting. The Serbs lost 4,643 killed, wounded, and missing, about three quarters of them from the Drina Division.[72] The Serbs claimed 68,000 Bulgarian casualties and 7,700 prisoners. This was the first Serbian military victory since the exit from Serbia the previous year.[73] The fighting at Kaimakchalan presaged the fighting two years later at Dobro Pole, which was a part of the same ridge system further to the northeast. Both battles involved infantry attacks up steep inclines against fixed defenses. In 1916 the Bulgarians had not had the time to develop strong defensive positions.

A major problem for the Bulgarians was that their army was overextended. The Bulgarian First Army was increasingly hard pressed in south central Macedonia. The Bulgarian Second Army was containing the Entente offensive on the eastern part of part of the Macedonian Front. The Bulgarian Third Army was invading Dobrudzha. Then on 1 October, the 10th Romanian Division crossed the Danube and invaded Bulgaria at the village of Ryahovo, between Ruse and Tutrakhan, in the rear of the Bulgarian Third Army. This Romanian action cchoed their invasion of Bulgaria during the Second Balkan War. General Zhekov had to divert elements of the Third Army as well as reserve units to contain the Romanian invaders.[74] The Bulgarians soon stopped the Romanian invasion and pushed it back.

Its successful containment and elimination must have been a source of some satisfaction to the Bulgarian commander. The relatively easy victories in Macedonia the previous year seemed a long time ago.

Another problem was the precipitous retreat of the First Army. It was so involved in the fighting at Kaimakchalan that it failed to consider the necessity of establishing secondary defensive positions behind this fortified ridge. When the Serbs gained the advantage at Kaimakchalan, the Bulgarian General Staff failed to give the order to retreat in a timely manner.[75] As a result, after receiving the order to pull back, the First Army had no fall-back positions. As a result additional guns, equipment, and men were lost.

The fall of Kaimakchalan persuaded the Germans that the center of the Macedonian Front was in difficulty.[76] Entente attacks continued after the Kaimakchalan victory. The German Eleventh Army began its withdrawal to the north. Colonel Ganchev stated in Pless that the position of the entire Eleventh Army on the Macedonian Front was critical and requested that a German division be sent there. In November, the Bulgarians requested four German and six Austro-Hungarian divisions.[77] The Bulgarians had exhausted all of their reserves. When asked by his French captors what was behind the front, a Bulgarian prisoner answered, "Our Lord God and His Majesty the Tsar."[78] Finally the arrival of additional German soldiers on the Macedonian Front in October seemed to reassure the Bulgarians.[79] Their presence was proof that their allies had not abandoned them.

Heavy fighting continued southeast of Bitola. Entente forces, including the First, Second, and Third Serbian armies, and Franco and Russian units, crossed the Cherna River where it bends to the north to join the Vardar. Then they launched heavy attacks on Bulgarian positions northwest of the bend beginning on 3 October. East of the bend the Serbian Drina Division attacked the continuation of the Kaimakchalan ridge at Dobro Pole. The Entente forces had 103 battalions and around 80 batteries to the Central Powers' 65 battalions and 57 batteries in the area.[80] The onset of the rainy, muddy, Balkan autumn complicated the situation for both sides. The Bulgarian 3rd Balkan Division, bolstered by some small German units, held out southeast of Bitola until 11 November, when the Second Serbian Army broke through its defensive positions.

By the beginning of November, General Otto von Below had decided to abandon Bitola. General Zhekov opposed this retreat because of the effect it would have on Bulgarian morale. Crown Prince Boris despaired when he wrote to his father that the Bulgarians would have to abandon Bitola. "Alas, everything has been in vain. The situation worsens."[81] His depression was warranted. Despite a visit to von Below in threatened Bitola on 12 November, Zhekov could not prevent the evacuation of the city one week later. The Bitola situation was a good demonstration of the power relationship between the Bulgarian and German commands. Although Zhekov was the commander of the Bulgarian army, he could not override the orders of the German commander of the Macedonian Front. This was the cause of great frustration for the Bulgarians. Bitola was much more important to Bulgaria than to Germany. Units from the Serbian First Army and some French and Russian troops entered Bitola on 19 November. This was four years to the day after the Serbs had taken Bitola from the Ottomans in the First Balkan War.[82] The conquest of Bitola on the anniversary of its initial conquest was a source of tremendous satisfaction to the Serbs.

Fighting continued in front of the new positions north of Bitola until 27 November. By this time the Entente forces were worn out. They had reached the end of their logistical abilities. General Sarrail admitted in his memoirs, "Serbs, Russians and French were exhausted."[83] The onset of winter and rugged terrain of southeastern Europe also imposed limits on the ability of the Entente to advance further. Also German reinforcements had revived Bulgarian confidence. In the fighting north of Bitola, French and Serbian troops suffered a serious reverse. Elsewhere the front stabilized across the Cherna River southeast of Bitola.

The Bulgarians likewise were exhausted. They had missed their opportunity to eliminate the Macedonian Front. They would not get another one. The fighting along the central section of the Macedonian Front cost the Central Powers 299 officers and 4,706 men dead, and another 832 officers and 32,079 men wounded.[84] The Macedonian Front settled into a dormant period for the winter. The withdrawal of the Bulgarians to positions north of Bitola was not without benefit. Their lines were shortened and their logistical situation improved. After the autumn of 1916, French and Serbian soldiers experienced the same difficult mountain situation the Bulgarians had already experienced.

The battle of the Cherna Bend provided both sides with reasons for satisfaction. For the Entente it represented the first success on the Macedonian Front. Serbian troops had the satisfaction of returning to their country one year after their expulsion. For the Central Powers, the defense along the Macedonian Front was critical for the success of the operations against Romania.[85] During the heavy fighting in Macedonia, Bucharest fell to the Central Powers on 4 November, and the Bulgarian advance into Dobrudzha continued. On their western flank in Macedonia, the Bulgarians conducted a successful fighting retreat. Their lines did not collapse and permit a large-scale breakthrough by the French and Serbs. At the same time, neither side achieved an overwhelming victory. The stalemate on the Macedonian Front persisted.

In particular the Bulgarians were satisfied with their resistance to the superior numbers in the Entente attack. General Zhekov later singled out the fighting at the bend of the Cherna River as "legendary" in terms of the tenacity of Bulgarian resistance. He later wrote that "our defense was conducted without regard of casualties."[86] A German official history also somewhat overstated, "If the huge bare Macedonian mountains could talk, they would undoubtedly speak of heroic deeds and heroic suffering."[87] Another cause of satisfaction was the successful Bulgarian defense of their positions east of the Cherna. The Bulgarians' 3rd Balkan Division held against the Serbian attacks along the ridge line from the heights of Sokol to Dobro Pole to Veternik. After the fighting tapered off, a Bulgarian prisoner explained his motivation to captors this way: "An attack on Salonika is German business, an attack on us is Bulgarian business."[88] This statement belied the efforts of Bulgarian generals and statesmen to drive out the Entente forces in Salonika. Nevertheless, it explains the basic motivation of the Bulgarian soldier after the conquest of Macedonia in 1915. Undoubtedly the ferocity of the fighting was predicated to some degree on the recent antagonisms between the Bulgarians and the Serbs. This was the first time Bulgarian soldiers had retreated during the First World War.

The fighting in Macedonia during the fall of 1916 was a precursor for the Battle of Dobro Pole, which occurred slightly to the northeast two years later. In both battles determined French and Serbian assaults broke into Bulgarian positions and forced the Bulgarians to retreat. At the Cherna Bend, the Bulgarian defensive positions were not as well developed at they

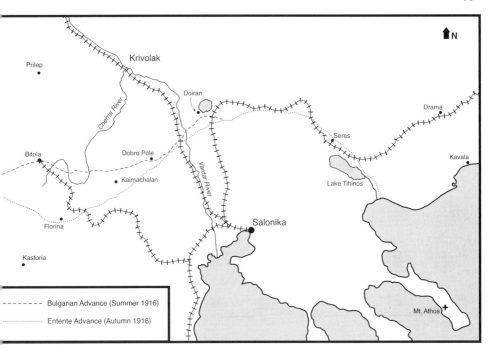

**1916 Battles**

were two years later at Dobro Pole. Unlike at Dobro Pole, the Bulgarian army retained its cohesion and morale. It conducted a fighting retreat at Cherna Bend in the autumn of 1916. Also the Germans successfully bolstered the Bulgarians with sufficient forces to enable them to establish new defensive positions behind Bitola. In this the Germans acted in the same manner that they had earlier that summer when the Austro-Hungarian army collapsed in the face of the Brusilov offensive. No Bulgarian unit collapsed, however, in the autumn of 1916. The morale and material condition of the Bulgarian forces had not yet eroded to the fatal extent it reached two years later.

The efforts by both belligerents to establish the Macedonian Front led to the intrusion of all the Great Powers into southeastern Europe. The restraint the Germans imposed on the Bulgarians prevented a Central Powers offensive from eliminating the Entente presence in Salonika. Had they acted by the spring of 1916, they would have had a reasonable expectation of success. By the summer of 1916 Entente forces in around Salonika had grown much larger, especially by the addition of the refurbished Serbian army. This greatly lessened the chance of a Central Powers attack.

By the autumn of 1916 all of the southeastern European countries were also involved in the conflict, with the partial exception of Greece. Since neither side developed a clear strategy for the Macedonian Front, both lapsed into the default of the offensive. Simultaneous offensives ensued in August 1916. For the Central Powers the main impetus for the offensive came from the Bulgarians, who perceived in the proximity of the Entente forces to their homeland and to their recent gains a serious danger. On the Entente side, the French and the newly rehabilitated Serbian commands urged offensive measures on the Macedonian Front. The consequences were offenses launched almost simultaneously. Just as in August 1914 on the Western Front, when similar circumstances prevailed, the consequence was stalemate. Both sides made some gains. The Bulgarians advanced into eastern Macedonia and occupied Drama, Seres, and the Aegean port of Kavala. This was the last successful Bulgarian advance on the Macedonian Front. Their attempt to envelop the Macedonian Front on the western wing, however, failed. Thereafter the Bulgarians lost the initiative on the Macedonian Front. For the rest of the war they would be on the defensive there. Together with the attack on Romanian Dobrudzha, the Macedonian offensive of August 1916 represents the maximum extent of Bulgarian military efforts during the First World War. Even though the west wing of the Macedonian offensive was not successful, the eastern wing of the Macedonian attack and the Dobrudzha offensive did gain victory. That a small country like Bulgaria could undertake simultaneous First World War offensives and obtain victory in two out of three of them is a significant achievement.

The simultaneous Entente offensive parried the Bulgarian thrust in the west and carried French and Serbian units into Serbian Macedonia. It then stalled at Bitola. This was the first significant Entente success since the arrival at Salonika the year before. After the fighting reached Bitola, both sides became exhausted. As a result, neither side was able to achieve a decisive result in the autumn of 1916.

# THE LULL

# 5

For the Bulgarians, the results of the 1916 campaign in Macedonia were decidedly mixed. They had advanced in eastern Macedonia, and they had, despite considerable losses in territory and manpower, managed to hold on against a strong Entente offensive in central Macedonia. Their position north of Bitola was less than ideal. The Entente forces were well established across the Cherna Bend. The Bulgarians had noted, however, rumors that the British wanted to withdraw from Salonika.[1] The prospect of a British withdrawal and the ending of the Salonika operation was more than merely rumor. The British were pressing their French allies to abandon the Bitola salient, and even to end the Salonika operation.[2] Yet the Central Powers had no plans to take advantage of the Entente discord. Because manpower and material resources were limited, they adopted a defensive stance along the Macedonian Front in 1917.

Adding to the Bulgarian material burden were significant numbers of prisoners of war. By the summer of 1917 the Bulgarians had at least 12,000 Serbs and 2,000–3,000 pro-Venizelos Greeks.[3] There were also British, French, Romanians, and Russians among these prisoners. The Bulgarians employed many of them in agricultural and mining activities throughout Bulgaria. Their exact number remains obscure. Another distraction during in February and March was an uprising in the Morava region of Serbia, occupied by Bulgarian soldiers. This Serbian revolt forced the Bulgarians to transfer temporarily some units from the Macedonian and Romanian Fronts.[4] By the end of March, the Bulgarians, together with some Austro-Hungarian and German troops, had suppressed the Morava revolt.

In the early months of 1917, a political problem arose between the Bulgarian government and the Bulgarian high command over contacts between General Zhekov and the Bulgarian opposition. The Radoslavov government, together with Colonel Ganchev, the Bulgarian representative to the German High Command in Pless, schemed to replace Zhekov with General Mihail Savov. The presence of Colonel Ganchev indicated that Tsar Ferdinand had some role in this effort. One German report noted that "Savov is more able than Zhekov, but entirely unreliable."[5] The Germans wisely remained aloof from this effort. Some sense of their preference can be inferred from their references in dispatches to Radoslavov as "our friend."[6] The less pliant Zhekov enjoyed no such confidence from the Germans. Ultimately Zhekov retained his position, but this squabble undermined both the government and the army command.

Bulgarian relations with their German allies were beginning to fray. This process had begun with relatively petty issues the previous year. Bulgarian disputes with the allies were becoming more frequent by the summer of 1916. The request by the Bulgarian governor of Macedonia on 11 June 1916 for use of a house named *Tsar Kyril* in Skopie, then utilized by the Germans as a stable, received a curt *"nein"* from the German authorities.[7] The Bulgarians responded in kind to German requests. Later that year Ludendorff complained that the German Eleventh Army did not receive the assistance that it "had a right to expect" from the Bulgarians.[8] The Bulgarians greatly resented what they perceived to be German arrogance.

Causes for Bulgarian resentment against the Germans accumulated. After the heavy fighting of the previous autumn, the Bulgarian command approved three weeks' leave for some soldiers from the Bulgarian Second Army's 11th Macedonia Division's 25th Infantry Regiment in February 1917. General von Hindenburg, in an unwarranted act of interference in Bulgarian affairs, wrote to Zhekov to strongly disapprove of this leave. He lectured the Bulgarian commander: "The distribution of strength on our common front is not such that we can allow our troops such relief."[9] This kind of imperious admonition contributed little to a sense of comradeship between the Bulgarian and German commands.

The peril of their position on the Macedonian Front and the apparent German lack of concern agitated the Bulgarian command. One issue between the Bulgarians and Germans was the Central Powers' command structure on the Macedonian Front. On 22 April 1917, the Bulgarian First Army and the German Eleventh Army, which consisted of four Bulgarian divisions plus one German division and one German brigade with a German staff, came together in a formation known as "Army Group Scholtz" under the command of Lieutenant General Friedrich von Scholtz, a hero of the 1914 Tannenberg battle. The Bulgarian Second Army remained under separate command. The previous German commander in Macedonia, General Otto von Below, moved to the Western Front, and then from there to the Italian Front later the same year, where he participated in the successful Austro-German effort at Caporetto. Although 90 percent of the soldiers were Bulgarian, the staff of Army Group Scholtz and the staffs of the 61st and 62nd Corps were German.[10] This imbalance between numbers and command was a cause of considerable Bulgarian resentment. Zhekov complained that the staff of Eleventh Army did not take into account Bulgarian problems, such as the difference in fighting in level and mountainous conditions.[11] Crown Prince Boris echoed Zhekov's concerns. In the aftermath of the Bulgarian retreat from the Bitola in 1916, he had telegraphed his father, Tsar Ferdinand:

I must also say with sadness and bitterness that while I was here, I began to have the clear conviction that the German commanders in Macedonia understand almost nothing about mountain warfare and always keep the reserves back too long and they always send them too late. They are not able to understand that climbing in the mountains is not like maneuvering in the plains.[12]

The Eleventh Army's German staff failed to take into account the difficult Macedonian terrain in their tactical perspective.

Zhekov particularly resented that in November 1916, Ludendorff sent an "imperative" telegram to Tsar Ferdinand, expressing his dissatisfaction with the "weak behavior" of Bulgarian soldiers during the Cherna Bend battle and demanding that the Bulgarian commander be strictly punished because of this "weak behavior." Ferdinand refused to accept the telegram.[13] Zhekov perceived in this incident a German effort to assume control of the Bulgarian military.[14] Nevertheless, on into 1917 the German military attaché in Sofia, Colonel Edward von Masow, insisted that Zhekov was the "true friend" of Germany.[15] This Ludendorff episode marked the intensification of worsening relations between the Bulgarian and German military commands. It reverberated through the next year. In an unproductive meeting at German headquarters in Pless on 4 January 1917, Zhekov told Ludendorff, "I only ask for one thing, that you do not try our patience any further, because we are already at our limits and I fear that soon every injustice against Bulgaria will effect not only Bulgaria disastrously, but also effect the fate of the entire Central Alliance."[16] This warning proved prescient the next year.

After the stabilization of the Bulgarian lines north of Bitola at the end of November 1916, military activity waned due to the onset of winter and the exhaustion of both sides. What the Bulgarians called the "Little War" continued. Small numbers of soldiers, sometimes in mixed Bulgarian and German units, fought the Little War in patrols in front of the fixed defensive positions and raids into enemy territory. In attacking the enemy the Bulgarians sought to collect intelligence, prisoners, enemy weapons, and munitions, and to disrupt potential Entente attacks on Bulgarian positions.[17] Another reason for this activity was to maintain the soldiers' discipline and morale. This Little War continued in front of the Bulgarian lines until the end of the Big War.

The Germans offered little help for the depleted Bulgarian forces in Macedonia. The best that General von Below would do was to promise to "envision" the transfer of a German division to the Macedonian Front if an offensive against the Entente became necessary.[18] The Bulgarians continued to feel vulnerable in the south. The Entente forces were better equipped and more numerous than those of the Central Powers. The material and morale situation in the Bulgarian army deteriorated due to the duration of the war. General Zhekov worried that his allies had abandoned Bulgaria.

Meanwhile the campaign in Dobrudzha had achieved success for the Central Powers. By the beginning of 1917, the Bulgarian Third Army and its Central Powers partners had occupied almost all Romanian territory west of the Pruth River. Only Moldavia remained under the control of the Romanian government, now relocated from Bucharest to Iaşi. Although hostilities continued, Romania was effectively out of the war. The Russian revolution further isolated Romania. This situation enabled the Bulgarians to transfer four divisions from the Third Army to the Macedonian Front. The 1st Sofia and 6th Vidin Divisions took up positions north of Bitola, while the 4th Preslav Division took a part of the Cherna Bend line to the southeast. A "mixed division" was divided between the area around Ohrid and eastern Albania. The addition of these troops strengthened Bulgarian defenses. Even so, General Zhekov admitted that the Central Powers forces remained at a disadvantage. He later wrote: "While the addition (of the Third Army elements) was not insignificant, it did not come close to changing the balance of power in our favor."[19] They also were at a disadvantage in terms of artillery. As long as they remained on the defensive, however, this was not necessarily a fatal situation.

Although they lacked the manpower and material resources to attempt another offensive toward Salonika, the Bulgarians enjoyed some defensive victories on the Macedonian Front in 1917. After meeting with Entente leaders in Rome in January 1917, General Sarrail urged that the success on the Macedonian Front of the previous autumn continue with a spring 1917 offensive. While the conference yielded no definite decision, it solidified Sarrail's position in Salonika.[20] Upon his return to Greece, he developed plans for a renewed attempt to break through the Bulgarian and German positions and reach Prilep in central Macedonia. The new offensive began on 11 March north of Bitola, where the fighting had ended the previous fall. French and Serbian attacks and Bulgarian counterattacks along this front emulated the fighting on the Western Front.

Tsar Ferdinand panicked at initial reports of heavy fighting. He telegraphed Crown Prince Boris that the Bulgarians were "gravely defeated," and blamed General von Below for sending German troops back to Germany and "sacrificing ours."[21] Ferdinand tended to be excitable. His telegram also indicated the distrust of German motives that permeated the Bulgarian military and the recognition that Bulgarian issues were subordinate to those of the Germans.

In any event, the tsar's concerns about the fighting near Bitola were unfounded. The Bulgarian defenses held. A French report noted that in the fighting, "The enemy there frequently used gas and incendiary shells and flame throwers."[22] The consequences for the attackers were the same as on the Western Front: high casualties and limited territorial changes. The weather was particularly bad during the fighting. General Sarrail finally ended the offensive on 19 March. The Bulgarians lost 975 dead and 2,507 wounded in the March fighting, and the Bulgarians and Germans together lost as many as 2,000 prisoners.[23] Neither the Bulgarians nor the Germans had the resources to sustain such losses indefinitely. The Entente, however, failed to develop sustained attacks necessary to break the lines.

The second Entente attempt of 1917 to break through the Macedonian Front began on 22 April. This action was intended as a means to take the pressure off the Romanians and the Russians, both of which were teetering on the edge of defeat. All the Entente forces in Macedonia participated in this effort. The first to act were the British. After two days of intense artillery fire, infantry attacks by the 122nd British Division and two Greek regiments began on the night of 24 April. The offensive consisted of several attempts to push through the Bulgarian positions west of Lake Doiran. For a time the British attack pressed the Bulgarian defenders. The commander of the Bulgarian 9th Pleven Division, General Vladimir Vasov, testified to the intensity of the fighting in his diary: "I had a bad time last night. For a while it became almost impossible to maintain the forward Doiran positions. I considered whether or not to evacuate the positions. I decided to counterattack the enemy with fresh troops from the main position. Thank God the counterattack succeeded."[24] In this ensuing second battle of Doiran, the second of three at this location, the Bulgarian First Army prevented the British from making any significant gains. Bulgarian artillery fire was especially effective, so much so that the British thought that the Bulgarians had the advantage in artillery. This does not seem to have been the case, however.[25] A renewed attempt to advance on 8 and 9 May also failed. The Bulgarian defenders lost 315 killed, 948 wounded, and 75 missing.[26] General von Scholtz's praise for the successful defense gave some indication of the difficult conditions on the Macedonian Front: "In consideration of the hot weather, the difficult terrain, and the fatigue during the winter because of the lack of cover, the difficulty in provisioning man and beast, the steadfastness and combativeness of the troops was praiseworthy apparent."[27] British experience indicated that at least in the Doiran sector, the Bulgarian First Army had sufficient munitions during the spring of 1917.

The second battle of Bitola, also known as the second battle of the Cherna Bend, began on 5 May 1917, with a combined French and Serbian attempt to renew the advance of the previous autumn. The 9th Serbian division opened the attack. The Serbs had lost some of their enthusiasm of the previous autumn. The arrest and trial of several senior Serbian commanders, including Colonel Dragutin "Apis" Dimitrijević, at Salonika undermined Serbian morale.[28] This trial concerned the personal and political rivalries among some important Serbian military leaders.[29] It included false accusations of an assassination attempt against Crown Prince Alexander. The trial was conducted hastily and peremptorily. On 26 June a Serbian firing squad executed Dimitrijević and two associates. The revolutionary turmoil in Russia also undoubtedly disconcerted the Serbs. The weakness of the Russian provisional government meant the loss of the Serbs' main patron among the Entente allies. Undoubtedly the Serbs, in a position of size and dependence on the Entente similar to that of the Bulgarians on the Germans, undoubtedly resented their situation. This situation undermined the Entente offensive.

During this battle, the Bulgarian First Army, using the tactic of strong counterattacks, repelled all French, Italian, Serbian, and Russian attempts to advance. The French and Serbs gained some ground in front of Bulgarian positions at Dobro Pole, and further east the British took some territory along the banks of the Struma River. All Entente forces suffered heavy casualties. In all the spring fighting, the Entente lost 13,000–14,000 men.[30] General Sarrail reported:

> The enemy positions were taken. But the solidity of the shelters under rocks, which facilitated machine gun fire and shielded the enemy in-

fantry from our artillery, the extremely heavy and prolonged enemy artillery fire, laborious counter fire because of the numerous enemy batteries, notorious reinforcements and problems with our airplanes, our troops, in spite of their courage, were not able to maintain their gains.[31]

General Sarrail finally canceled the offensive on 23 May. The Entente undertook no further major attacks that year.

Crown Prince Boris noted that the morale of the Bulgarian army improved with the successful defensive fighting in the Cherna Bend.[32] Even if the Bulgarians could not advance, they could still fight effectively in the defense. Nevertheless, the spring 1917 offensives further eroded the Central Powers' manpower and material on the Macedonian Front. As a consequence the Central Powers took no offensive action there in 1917. This was in contrast to the Western Front, the Italian Front, and the Eastern Front, all of which saw Central Powers offensives that year. Except for artillery exchanges and some raids and counterraids in the Little War, there were no offensive efforts by either side for the remainder of the year. Air raids by both sides continued throughout the year.

In their spring 1917 offensives the Entente forces sustained high losses and made insignificant gains. They exhausted for the time being their offensive capabilities. Fighting in the spring offensives was particularly heavy at the Bulgarian defensive positions at Dobro Pole, a fortified ridge east of the Cherna Bend. The Bulgarians recognized the importance of holding the positions at the Dobro Pole section of the front in this area. After the fighting in the Cherna Bend died down, General Nikola Ribarov of the 3rd Balkan Division of the First Army wrote:

> Once the defenses of Dobro Pole are compromised, all the intermediate positions will have the potential for immediate offensive, not just for support, and because of the bad roads and the extraordinarily difficult terrain over which we must retreat, we cannot take the better part of our heavy artillery with us-after a few dates it is doomed to be in the hands of the enemy.[33]

General Ribarov understood that the heavy artillery that was vital to the Bulgarian defensive positions at Dobro Pole was immobile because of the difficult terrain. He predicted exactly what happened the next year at Dobro Pole.

For most of the remainder of 1917, intra-alliance squabbles distracted the Entente command in Salonika. Both the Italians and the Serbs resisted Sarrail's attempts to persuade them to extend their fronts. At the same time, the morale of the Russians deteriorated rapidly because of the revolutionary events at home. Another important distraction was the political situation in the host country. Even before the spring offensives, events in Greece were moving in the direction of the Entente. By 1 October 1916, the pro-Entente Greek corps at Salonika consisted of around 12,000 soldiers, two thirds of whom were veteran soldiers.[34] These troops augmented the already established advantage in manpower of the Entente forces on the Macedonian Front. On 9 September 1916, Venizelos arrived in Salonika with the intention of forming a pro-Entente Greek government. For the next nine months, two Greek governments existed, the royal government in Athens, ostensibly neutral in the war but leaning toward the Central Powers, and the Venizelos provisional government in Salonika, which tilted toward the Entente and cooperated with General Sarrail. This is the period of the national schism. In December 1916 the British and French landed troops at Piraeus in an attempt to pressure the Royalist government in Athens. Strong Royalist resistance thwarted this move. After sustaining some casualties, the Entente forces withdrew.[35] Usually Sarrail supported the Venizelists, but not always. In December 1916 he recognized a local Albanian authority in Koritza instead of supporting Greek claims.[36] He thought this would ensure a more stable situation on his left flank. This also preserved Italian interests in Albania from Greek encroachment. On his right flank, he supported the accession of Mount Athos to the Venizelos regime on 26 March 1917. About the same time, the Entente removed the pro-Royalist governor of Corfu and replaced him with an individual more favorable to their cause. At the end of May, Sarrail sent mainly French troops and a small British contingent from the Macedonian Front south into Thessaly. Up until then, the Royal government in Athens had controlled Thessaly. The region had functioned as a neutral zone between the pro-Entente and pro-Royalist forces. British and French landings also took place on the Isthmus of Corinth and at Piraeus to impart maximum pressure on King Constantine. Sarrail was concerned that the Bulgarians and

Germans might take advantage of the situation to launch attacks around Bitola or at Gevgeli.[37] The Central Powers, however, lacked the strength to undertake any attack on the Macedonian Front. By the end of July, British and French units returned from the south to resume their positions in Macedonia.

On 11 June, King Constantine finally bowed to Entente pressure, abdicated his throne, and departed for Switzerland. His son Alexander succeeded him as king and acquiesced in the pro-Entente policies of the Venizelos government. The schism in Greek politics was over. Royalist forces, after refitting, would join the Entente on the Macedonian Front. This made the Macedonian Front even more of a Balkan War.[38] On 2 July the newly reunified Greek government declared war on the Central Powers. While the Greek declaration of war preoccupied Tsar Ferdinand, it did not make a big impression in Kyustendil at Bulgarian army headquarters.[39] Zhekov anticipated that after the declaration attacks might ensue at Kavala and in the west between Lakes Ohrid and Prespa. These never materialized. The Bulgarians did utilize the Greek entry into the war on the side of the Entente to press the Germans to agree to a Macedonian offensive.[40] The Bulgarians did not have the resources to undertake an offensive on the Macedonian Front by themselves. With the developing situation in Russia and the British offensive in Flanders, the Germans had no resources to spare.

Even though General Zhekov had insisted on the imposition of a Bulgarian military administration of the occupied Greek territories the previous year, the Germans agreed only after the Greek declaration of war on the Central Powers.[41] Before then the Germans had disparaged Bulgarian presence on Greek territory. A German report of 12 April 1917 had strongly criticized the Bulgarian failure to provide sustenance for the civilian population of Drama and Kavala.[42] Even after the Greek declaration of war, Field Marshal Paul von Hindenburg, the chief of the German General Staff, urged Zhekov to ensure the Greek population had sufficient food, and warned him, "I see in the harsh treatment of the Greek population only serious military disadvantages."[43] The implication that the Bulgarian authorities were abusing Greek civilians, while not without some basis, was unwelcome in Kyustendil. The German field marshal's condescending admonition toward his Bulgarian allies reflected in part a continuing pro-Greek bias in the German military. This was especially irritating to the Bulgarians. They perceived this as German intrusion into their internal affairs.

A separate peace with Russia might have provided a means to resolve this issue. Nevertheless, this option never received much serious consideration by the pro-German Radoslavov government. The Russian collapse in 1917 ended any chance of a separate peace. Furthermore, after the Russian breakdown, a Central Powers victory appeared likely to many Bulgarians. Disputes with Austria-Hungary and Germany as well as with the Ottoman Empire converged in the problem of Dobrudzha. A supplementary note to a secret agreement between Bulgaria and Germany promised that in case of war between the Central Powers and Romania, Bulgaria could incorporate southern Dobrudzha plus that portion of Dobrudzha assigned to Romania by the Treaty of Berlin.[44] This note appeared to indicate that Bulgaria would obtain the entire region. After the defeat and occupation of most of Romania by the Central Powers in 1917, the Bulgarian government expected to annex most of, if not all, Dobrudzha. To general dismay, on 7 April 1917 the usually pro-German Colonel Ganchev reported that the Germans intended to control Dobrudzha.[45] At the same time, the Germans were seizing the available food resources there. The inability of the Bulgarian Third Army, then occupying Dobrudzha, to obtain even its own provisions from the German-controlled military government there further aggravated the Bulgarians. A report signed by the chief of the Directorate of Economic Planning and Social Welfare, Major General Aleksandŭr Protogerov, insisted, "We consider that it is the right of the fighting Third Army, which has made, makes and will make sacrifices, to obtain provisions from the area it has fought for. Furthermore, it has the right to rely on food from Romania, as compensation for its defeat."[46] This situation was a source of great frustration for the Bulgarians. Dobrudzha offered a new and potentially rich source of sustenance to alleviate the food shortages in Bulgaria. Furthermore, Bulgarians had considered that at the region was rightfully theirs. Most of the Central Powers forces that overran this region were from the Bulgarian Third Army. After they had conquered Dobrudzha, the Bulgarians had to share the spoils with their allies.

The Bulgarian military command came to resent General von Mackensen himself. The problem arose in part from von Mackensen's command over the Bulgarian Third Army in Dobrudzha. This emphasized that the Germans had no confidence in the Bulgarian Army command. Another aspect of the problem came from von Mackensen's establishment of a military directorate in Constanța, the main Romanian port on the Black Sea. This seemed to indicate to the Bulgarians that the Germans intended to make their exploitation of Dobrudzha permanent. A meeting between the German kaiser and the Bulgarian tsar in Cherna Voda, Romania, in September 1917 failed to resolve this issue.[47] The Constanța problem naturally exacerbated the entire Dobrudzha issue.

The dispute over Dobrudzha did provide the Bulgarian government with one advantage. In the spring of 1917, when German unrestricted submarine warfare led to the outbreak of war with the United States, Radoslavov cited this disagreement as a reason why Bulgaria would not break relations with the Americans.[48] After the American entry into the war, the Germans pressed their allies to break off relations with Washington.[49] Radoslavov did fear that the arrival of American troops on the Western Front might free Entente soldiers for use in Macedonia.[50] The Bulgarians, however, having no quarrels with the United States, had no wish to end their relationship. Despite German disapproval, Bulgaria retained diplomatic relations with the United States throughout the war. The connection, however, brought the Bulgarians little real benefit either during the war or during the subsequent peace process.

The Dobrudzha issue especially inflamed already strained relations between the Bulgarians and the Ottomans. They had always been tenuous allies. As recently as 1913 in the Balkan Wars they had been adversaries. The Ottoman cession of the lower Maritsa valley in 1915 had been instrumental in bringing Bulgaria over to the side of the Central Powers. This territory gave Bulgaria complete control of the railroad to Bulgaria's only Aegean port, at Dedeagach, as well as the Adrianople railroad station and the southern suburbs of that city.[51] Bulgarian presence loomed close to the important Ottoman city of Adrianople. They had briefly occupied the city during the Balkan Wars. The Ottomans never accepted this loss of Thracian territory as permanent.[52] While the Ottomans raised no specific territorial claims to Dobrudzha, they did attempt to use their participation in the Romanian campaign and subsequent military losses there as a bargaining point. Three Ottoman divisions had participated in the conquest of Dobrudzha, and afterward Ottoman forces continued to garrison that region.[53] The Constantinople government wanted to regain not only the Maritsa valley, but also all of Western Thrace up to the Mesta River, an area Bulgaria had conquered during the First Balkan War. The Ottomans first raised the issue of compensation in December 1916 through German state secretary Arthur Zimmerman.[54] This issue infuriated the Bulgarians. Dimitŭr Rizov, Bulgarian ambassador in Berlin, warned German foreign secretary Zimmermann, "There is no more effective means to revive moderate Russophile sentiment in Bulgaria than for Turkey to receive territorial compensation from us."[55] Already by the beginning of 1917, some Germans feared that the Bulgarians were so disaffected by the conduct of the war that they might seek a separate peace with the Entente.[56] The Russian ambassador in Stockholm, Anatoli Neklyudov, came to the same conclusion after a secret meeting with ambassador Rizov in February 1917. He reported, "It seems to me that it is not out of the question that the Bulgarian ambassador and Tsar Ferdinand himself are capable of breaking the alliance with Germany and seeking a separate peace."[57] Neklyudov's speculation was overly optimistic. Nevertheless, having served as Russian minister in Sofia from 1911 until 1915, he had some experience with Bulgarian sensibilities, and with Ferdinand's personality.

By the autumn of 1917 relations with Bulgaria's Ottoman ally were disintegrating. Zhekov complained about the presence of Ottoman troops in Dobrudzha fighting alongside the Bulgarian Third Army. "We never wanted the cooperation of Turkish soldiers and if we accept them it must be under the condition that they be replaced by German soldiers."[58] Von Hindenburg on the other hand considered the Ottoman demands to take part in the management of the Dobrudzha to be "justified" because of their participation in the Dobrudzha campaign.[59] Although von Hindenburg attempted to be evenhanded in his treatment of his allies, his pronouncement did little to allay Bulgarian concerns about the Ottoman presence in Dobrudzha and in Thrace.

The food crisis in Bulgaria was becoming more pronounced throughout 1917. A German report of 15 April 1917 estimated that the Bulgarians had on hand enough bread for twelve days, meat for seven days, vegetables for twenty-five days, oil for fifteen days, fodder for eight days, and hay for four days.[60] It blamed shortages on poor transportation between Dobrudzha, where there was food, and Bulgaria. The situation did not improve over the summer. In October 1917, Major General Protogerov, asked Radoslavov to demand immediately from the Germans 100 million kilograms of grain from the crop yield in Romania.[61] At the end of November, Lieutenant General Dimitŭr Geshov of the First Army reported that while the offensive spirit of the soldiers was unfavorable, their defensive sensibility and their ability to defend their positions were good.[62] His report attributed the lack of offensive spirit in part to the feeling among the soldiers that Bulgaria had attained its national goals and that their only remaining obligation was to defend the frontiers. It also ordered the bread ration restored to one kilogram per frontline soldier and 750 grams for rear-echelon troops. The situation deteriorated through the year. By December there was only 600 grams of bread for rear-echelon soldiers, and 800 grams for officers and soldiers at the front.[63] Civilians could expect only 400 grams of bread or grain or 300 grams of flour per day.

At the same time, the clothing of the Bulgarian army was wearing out. An Army Group Scholtz staff officer reported that in the Bulgarian First Army, "The clothing situation leaves much to be desired. Tunics and pants are often in tatters."[64] Because of the miserable clothing situation, dissatisfaction increased in the ranks. The Bulgarians also complained that the Germans failed to provide them with sufficient military equipment. A report of 25 April 1917 grumbled that "since the beginning of the war we have received only 680 of the 1150 machine guns the Germans promised us."[65] The Bulgarians thought that the Germans were failing to fulfill their alliance obligations. The Germans blamed many of the economic woes in Bulgaria on the poor railroad system. A report of 7 November 1916 stated that Bulgarians had no reserves of railroad personnel or material and had to rely on the Germans for support.[66] The Bulgarian railroad system did not function with the same efficiency that characterized German railroads.

The Bulgarians needed German military material and manpower to continue their war effort. Nevertheless, they increasingly resented the German presence in Macedonia. German confiscation of food resources there especially aggravated the Bulgarians. The Bulgarian army's Directorate for Economic Concerns complained that the Germans treated Macedonia as a "conquered land."[67] The Bulgarians considered that Macedonian food resources belonged to Bulgaria, not Germany.

Despite the German alliance, the old connection with Russia remained strong for many Bulgarians. The Bolshevik seizure of power in Russia held peril and promise for the Macedonian Front. The Bulgarian military understood this and closely followed events in revolutionary Russia from its very beginning.[68] Tsar Ferdinand feared that the Russian Revolution might excite the Russophile sensibilities of the Bulgarian population.[69] A report of 21 April 1917 noted that "here and there soldiers complain about the brutality, cruelty and illegitimate actions of some officers."[70] This was not unusual in First World War armies. The possible end of the war in the east, however, seemed to indicate that the Bulgarian alliance with Germany was justified. As Bulgaria prepared to participate in the peace negotiations with Russia, Zhekov urged the Bulgarian government:

> We must emphasize clearly and nobly, that Bulgaria did not participate in the present war for revenge, but from duty and obligation. The uncertainty was great, the risks were innumerable, nevertheless the Bulgarian nation joined with those nations who recognized our historical rights and decided to satisfy the need of their spirit, as they rectify the injustices of Berlin in 1878 and Bucharest in 1913. Bulgaria did not embark on a war of conquest in 1912. If it had, it would not have found the moral strength to participate in the present struggle. Bulgaria fights for a great and noble goal, freedom and unity.[71]

Zhekov's justification for the Bulgarian war effort to some degree separated Bulgaria from the other Central Powers. The other three all had annexationist goals based on non-nationalist criteria. They all sought to expand their European empires. There was even a whiff of Wilsonian idealism in Zhekov's explanation of Bulgaria's war aims. Perhaps this was deliberate, as Bulgaria maintained diplomatic relations with the United States throughout the war. Other than the opportunity to obtain some of the material largess from Russia and Ukraine, Bulgaria had no real national interests in the Brest-Litovsk negotiations.

A declaration of support for Bulgaria's territorial aspirations by the Austro-Hungarian and German governments at the end of 1917 failed to produce the intended effect. General Zhekov considered it to be merely "poetic" because it lacked a firm guarantee that Bulgaria could retain the territories conquered from Macedonia, the Morava region, and Dobrudzha.[72] The negotiations beginning at Brest-Litovsk in December 1917 raised the possibility of a negotiated general peace. The Bulgarians feared that their hard-won acquisitions in Macedonia and Dobrudzha would be negotiated away for the sake of a broad peace settlement. Radoslavov had always insisted that Bulgaria fought the war for its unification.[73] The present war was a continuation of the Balkan Wars as a struggle of the liberation and unification of all Bulgarians. A failure to reach this goal would mean eventually another war.

In aftermath of signing armistice in Russia on 26 Dec 1917 at Brest-Litovsk, Zhekov asked von Hindenburg not to withdraw German troops from Macedonia. The Germans had already transferred men and artillery to the west in preparation for the spring offensives. Zhekov emphasized that "for we Bulgarians the security of the position of the southern front is of vital importance and in any case we cannot risk the, even though timely, piecemeal withdrawal of any participants, since such a weakness in our present position would paralyze the tenacity and morale of the army," and pointed out that "Our forces on the southern front are scarcely level with those of the enemy."[74] Zhekov recognized that the material circumstances of his forces were eroding, and that this was beginning to have an effect on the morale of the Bulgarian soldiers.

He did consider withdrawing the remainder of the Bulgarian Third Army from Dobrudzha after the conclusion of peace with Russia.[75] The Germans had exerted considerable pressure on him to return the Bulgarian Third Army to the Macedonian Front to allow the German forces there to be utilized on the Western Front. Ludendorff told Zhekov that such an exchange was "absolutely necessary."[76] This had placed the Bulgarians in a quandary. They understood that the Macedonian Front needed more soldiers. Despite their growing disenchantment with their German allies, however, they wanted the Germans to remain in Macedonia as a representation of German commitment to Bulgarian claims and Bulgarian victory. Also, the dispute with the other Central Powers over the disposition of Dobrudzha made the complete withdrawal of Bulgarian forces impossible. A part of the Third Army remained in Dobrudzha for political, not military, purposes. There it enforced Bulgarian claims to the region. The Dobrudzha issue was an unfortunate distraction for the Bulgarians. This was an overreach for Bulgaria, just as Salonika had been during the Balkan Wars.

On the Entente side of the Macedonian Front inter-allied relations were also difficult. Sarrail also had to cope with demands by the Italians to move their 35th Division from the Cherna Bend to Albania. This was to enforce Italian interests in Albania. Similarly the Serbs wanted to move their troops to the region of Pogradec to be closer to Serbia proper. Another distraction for the Entente occurred on 18 August 1917, when a huge fire burned down much of the city of Salonika. The southwestern section, including the old section of the city and the waterfront, was devastated.

At the end of December 1917, General Sarrail was recalled to France. The failure of the 1917 offensive and his own prickly personality contributed to his recall. General Louis Guillaumat, a veteran of the fighting around Verdun, succeeded him. The onerous task of coordinating the various national contingents around Salonika prevented General Guillaumat from any immediate offensive activity after assuming command. He made progress the next year in reorganizing the Entente armies and in integrating the new Greek army into the existing forces.

At the end of the year, the Central Powers obtained another success on the Macedonian Front, through no effort on their part. The Russian division, which had augmented Entente forces in 1916, and which had taken part in the spring 1917 offensives, ceased to function as an effective military unit. Concerning the morale situation among the Russian soldiers, the commander of the Russian 2nd Brigade wrote to General Sarrail on 18 May 1917, "I have found that nervous fatigue has spread through them to an extreme degree."[77] He asked that a date be fixed to take the Russians out of the line. This did not occur. The Russians remained for the time being in the line. Despite efforts of the provisional government in Petrograd to maintain military order among the units on the Macedonian Front, the Russian soldiers became increasingly restive. After the October Revolution, the government ceased to be effective. Elements of the brigade fraternized with Bulgarian and German soldiers.[78] By the beginning of 1918, all Russian units had left the front lines in Macedonia. Entente efforts to induce Russian soldiers to volunteer to remain in Macedonia failed. A few assisted the Entente as laborers, but most languished in camps until their repatriation to Russia in 1919 and 1920. The collapse of discipline in the Russian forces undoubtedly made an impression on the Bulgarians.

The Bulgarians acted at the end of 1917 to strengthen their position along the Aegean. Always concerned about the possibility of a British naval landing on the Thracian shore, the Bulgarians established the Fourth Army on 25 November 1917 for coastal defense. The Bulgarian Fourth Army consisted of the 10th Black Sea Division and the 2nd Cavalry Division. General Sava Savov initially commanded this minimal force. Most Bulgarian soldiers were on the Macedonian Front. Nevertheless, the Bulgarians had some experience from the Balkan Wars at repelling naval landings. On 7–11 February 1913, they had defeated an Ottoman attempt to land troops at the port of Sharkoi on the Sea of Marmara. This victory preserved the Bulgarian positions at Chataldzha outside of Constantinople.

During 1917 the fighting on the Macedonian Front was limited. When the Entente undertook several offensive actions, mainly during the spring, Bulgarian defenses generally held. No significant Entente gains ensued. Nevertheless, the Bulgarians were weaker at the end of the year than they had been at the beginning. They were in no position to undertake offensive action against the Entente forces. Their material basis for conducted the war had eroded. Their food and clothing situation was especially problematic. Their relations with the Central Powers allies had become fraught with difficulties over the conduct of the war and the disposition of the spoils. One consequence was a crisis in morale among the Bulgarian soldiers, reaching from the ranks all the way to the high levels of command.

Meanwhile the situation of the Entente forces on the Macedonian Front had stabilized. By the end of 1917, the Russians were no longer available for military action due to the disruption of the revolutions at home. The addition of Greek forces united by a Venizelist government installed in Athens, however, more than compensated for their absence. A new commander, more energetic and less fractious than his predecessor, had assumed command. Both British and French forces were well equipped, the other Entente forces less so. At the end of 1917 the Entente force in Macedonia had grown to 185,000 French and French colonial troops, 174,000 British, 90,000 Serbian, 57,000 Italian, 19,000 Russian, and 49,000 Greek troops, for a total of 574,000 men.[79] It had assumed a defensive posture on the territory taken in the 1916 offensive between the Struma River and Lakes Prespa and Doiran.[80] When the new French commander, General Guillaumat, arrived in Salonika, the Entente was in good position to undertake an offensive in 1918.

The Bulgarians did not undertake any major military initiatives on the Macedonian Front during 1917. Had the Germans supported a Caporetto-type offensive, the Macedonian Front might have been eliminated. The Germans' interests were elsewhere, and by 1917 the Bulgarians clearly lacked the ability to carry out a major effort on their own. The most they could do was to fight a "Little War" all along the front. Meanwhile, Bulgarian material and morale were beginning to wear down.

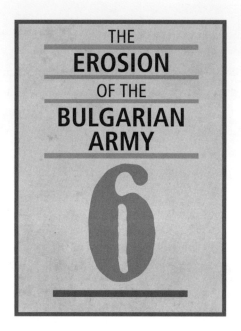

# THE EROSION OF THE BULGARIAN ARMY

## 6

At the beginning of the war Bulgarian morale was largely positive. While the Bulgarians were not enthusiastic to be at war again so soon after the Balkan Wars, they were grimly determined to rectify the injustices they perceived to be the consequence of the 1913 Treaty of Bucharest. Nevertheless, after a year of military success the mood in Bulgaria remained fairly good. A German report from June 1916 noted:

> Undoubtedly public opinion in Bulgaria, which at the beginning of the war was for the most part pro-Russian, has changed. It has become clear to countless observers, who over the past two years here from informal conversations with all strata of people, from soldiers' letters, from political literature indicate that the majority of the people are convinced of the correctness of the policies of the Central Powers.[1]

Even so there was dissension in the Bulgarian ranks from the start. At the beginning of the war several instances of antiwar activity had occurred within the army, and a military court sentenced at least seventeen soldiers to death.[2] From the beginning of 1916 to 1 July 1917 the Entente command in Salonika counted 11,370 deserters from all the Central Powers forces on the Macedonian Front, including Austro-Hungarians, Bulgarians, Germans, and Turks.[3] Bulgarians undoubtedly were the majority of these soldiers. Probably many of these Bulgarians were from the mixed ethnic areas overrun the during the autumn 1915 campaign. This meant they were from Macedonia, but had been drafted into the Bulgarian Army after 1915. For many of these soldiers national identity had little to do with their efforts to escape the fighting.

1918 opened on a positive note with the signing of the protocol for peace at Brest-Litovsk. An "optimistic" Radoslavov told the German ambassador in Sofia, Alfred von Oberndorff, that the news caused war weariness among Bulgarian officers to vanish. The ambassador expressed some concern, however, that peace with Russia could lead to a rapprochement between Bulgaria and Russia.[4] In that case, the German position of primacy in Bulgarian affairs would greatly diminish. The earlier conclusion of the armistice with Romania on 6 December 1917 had already allowed the Bulgarians to transfer some of the units of the Third Army, then in Dobrudzha, to Macedonia.

The Macedonian Front remained quiet through the spring of 1918. Meanwhile the morale of the Bulgarian soldiers there continued to erode. In the early summer of 1918 Zhekov visited the front to ascertain the situation. Upon his return to headquarters in Kyustendil, Zhekov reported to Tsar Ferdinand on 12 June 1918, "Today it is impossible to have any illusions, that the spirit of the soldiers is the same as at the beginning of the war, or even of last year."[5] The general recognized that the Bulgarian army faced a serious morale problem in the summer of 1918. Up until then, the Bulgarians had achieved some success in the World War. They had participated in the campaign against Serbia in 1915, overrunning and occupying the major Bulgarian war objective, Macedonia, and pushing British and French expeditionary forces back to the Greek frontier. Since the 1915 defeat of the Serbs, the Bulgarian army had held its own against the larger and better-equipped Entente forces established in southern Macedonia. In 1916 and 1917, Bulgarian forces had participated in the Central Powers' conquest of Romania. By the summer of 1918, however, these victories were no longer sufficient to sustain the army physically or emotionally. Concerns about the situation at home, severe food and material shortages, as well as growing suspicions about Central Powers allies, seriously undermined the morale of the Bulgarian army.

This situation was especially worrisome to the Bulgarian command because five years earlier during the Balkan Wars, the Bulgarian army had undergone a similar crisis of morale. The morale problem in the spring and summer of 1913 had been an important factor in precipitating the catastrophic Second Balkan War. Then disorders in the ranks arose from a variety of resentments, mainly war weariness.[6] The military command ordered disastrous attacks on Serbian positions to focus the energies of the army and to prevent the Bulgarian morale from further deterioration. These attacks provoked strong Greek and Serbian counterattacks. Soon afterward, Ottoman and Romanian forces invaded Bulgaria. The Bulgarian army was overwhelmed, and Macedonia was lost. While the Bulgarian soldiers in the summer of 1913 had been at arms for only nine months, those in the summer of 1918, many of them veterans of the Balkan Wars, had been in service for over two and a half years. If the army high command could not find a way to alleviate the soldiers' discontent during the summer of 1918, Bulgaria risked another disaster possibly worse than that of 1913, especially with a large Entente force in southern Macedonia dug in as close as twenty miles to the pre–World War I Bulgarian frontier.

A major cause of the morale problem was the soldiers' realization that the situation at home was as bad as what they experienced at the front. The soldiers understood that the black market, war profiteering, and governmental inefficiency were major causes of the lack of food and material throughout Bulgaria. Laws designed to counter these problems had little effect.[7] Zhekov's report to the tsar noted that some mutinous frontline soldiers had declared, "Here we defend the security of the state with our blood, and at home they sell it for money."[8] A June 1918 report on the morale of the army noted, "The soldiers' hearts are tormented by the hunger of the children."[9] Fears at the front about the war profiteers, governmental corruption, and inefficiency had become so pervasive that many soldiers had come to believe, as one report noted, "the enemy is behind us."[10] The challenges the Bulgarian soldiers and their families faced seemed more serious behind the Bulgarian lines than in front of them. The soldiers appeared to be helpless to assist their families.

One particularly worrisome aspect of the domestic economic situation for Bulgarian high command was the opening of a fissure in Bulgarian society and among the Bulgarian soldiers themselves. Most Bulgarian soldiers were peasants. The high prices for agricultural goods benefited the peasant majority, but caused greater hardship among the urban minority. The high command became apprehensive that the urban soldiers might become susceptible to revolutionary propaganda. The Bulgarian military command was well aware that the Russian Revolution had urban origins.[11] At the same time, somewhat contradictorily, a July morale report noted that "the town dweller, who is more intelligent and for that reason is the bearer of the national idea, is lost in worry about his family, and his energies are paralyzed."[12] The high command considered that urban soldiers were more patriotic than peasants and worried that the nationalist ideology that sustained the war effort was becoming diluted by hunger.

Closely linked to concerns about the situation at home was the declining quantity and quality of rations at the front. The problem with food had begun in 1916. Bulgaria could not produce enough foodstuffs to feed its population. Much food was exported out of the country to Germany and Austria-Hungary. This only increased the cost of food in Bulgaria and inflated the Bulgarian economy. On 17 July 1916, General Zhekov reported to the Bulgarian Ministry of Finance that "from the old harvest there is no grain left, and from the new harvest as of today nothing has been received, there is nothing in the stores of the kingdom, with the exception of several railcars of corn meal, but they are reserved for the army and the amount they contain is so small that it will only last for 8–10 days."[13] This was the situation when the Bulgarian army was about to participate in the offensive against Romania and at the same time absorb a strong attack from the Entente forces in northern Greece.

The problem of sustenance continued on into 1917. In March 1917, General von Below of the German Eleventh Army asserted that Bulgarian supply difficulties were "critical" due to the inefficient Bulgarian railroad system.[14] By then the military began to confiscate food in the countryside.[15] The conquest of most of Romania by Bulgaria and the other Central Powers did little to improve the situation. By 5 November 1917, a decree from the Bulgarian government forced General Zhekov to order a reduction in rations for his soldiers.[16] Zhekov's order shrank the bread ration from one thousand to eight hundred grams of bread per man. The entire country, including the military forces in the field, faced famine.

Not surprisingly, by the summer of 1918, massive discontent emerged in the Bulgarian army. Poor harvests in 1917 and the spring of 1918 had made the food situation even more desperate. At that time General Zhekov, in an effort to assuage the soldiers' spirits and to fill their stomachs, ordered an increase to nine hundred grams of bread per day for frontline soldiers.[17] The Bulgarian supplies of grain, however, were insufficient to meet this demand. Only low-quality bread, made mainly from cornmeal, was available. In his report to the Bulgarian Tsar Ferdinand, General Zhekov noted, after a tour of the front, that "The lack of food, mainly bread and meat, causes alarming unease and makes morale plummet."[18] Few vegetables, and no meat, were available to supplement the small bread ration. The Germans typically downplayed the seriousness of the food shortages in the Bulgarian army. A German report of 12 June stated, "The (Bulgarian) army's food supply, although it remains scanty and limited, is secure until 1 August, since von Scholtz's headquarters helps constantly."[19] By the end of June, the food situation had worsened still further. The quantity of the bread ration had declined to around six hundred grams per day, and the quality of the bread had deteriorated to a concoction consisting almost totally of cornmeal, including ground-up cobs.[20] July brought no relief. By the end of that month, some units were down to only five hundred grams of bread per day. Nor had the quality improved. In the Bulgarian Second Army, deployed in southeastern Macedonia, the bread ration consisted of "barley bread with straw."[21] Also occasionally available was a rancid soup.[22] These rations made many soldiers sick. Obviously the dwindling quantity and quality of the rations affected not only the Bulgarian soldiers' physical strength but also their psychological vigor.

Another tangible problem affecting the morale of the Bulgarian army during the summer of 1918 was the poor condition of its clothing. This problem had its origins in the large number of uniforms worn out during the Balkan Wars. Also Bulgarian units did sometimes squander limited material resources. At the beginning of the war, the 1st Sofia, 8th Tundzha, and 9th Pleven Infantry Divisions used up the uniforms allotted for the entire army.[23] The material situation in the Bulgarian army quickly deteriorated in the difficult campaigns of the autumns of 1915 and 1916, as well as the Romanian campaign. After his June 1918 tour, General Zhekov noted that the state of the clothing in the army was even worse than that of the rations. Some units had reported one quarter of their men with bare feet.[24] Soldiers' greatcoats were often so tattered and worn that they were insufficient for use in the mountains even during the relatively clement summer weather. Upon assuming command of the 2nd Thracian Division, which held the positions at Dobro Pole, in July 1918, General Ivan Rusev reported, "The mass of soldiers have nothing on their feet, sentries are barefoot, outer clothing is rags, underwear, either rags or completely absent."[25] Zhekov realized that soldiers could not exhibit a great deal of élan when they were ordered into battle barefoot. In July only two regiments were allowed to draw upon "very limited amounts" of footgear and uniforms.[26] By the summer of 1918, the Bulgarian army was becoming a hungry and naked mass.

The medical services of the Bulgarian army by the summer of 1918 were in bad condition. They lacked most important medicines. Many sections of the front were in remote or rugged locations that made access to medical services difficult. Some units of the 2nd Thracian Division were more than three hours from medical aid.[27] The influenza epidemic at the end of the summer of 1918 only made things worse for the Bulgarian soldiers at the front.

Under these circumstances discipline deteriorated in the Bulgarian army. The soldiers increasingly resented the authority of their officers. One young captain wrote upon assuming a new post at the front, "Upon my arrival at my battalion, I formed the impression that there was no discipline, nor did the officers have any authority over their men."[28] There was little trust between the officers and men. At least one fragging incidence directed against a junior officer occurred in the same unit.

Other important debilitating issues concerned Bulgaria's relations with the Central Alliance. Many Bulgarians had begun to doubt the loyalty of their Ottoman, German, and Austro-Hungarian allies. Few had great confidence in the Ottoman Empire. Ottoman sultans had ruled Bulgaria for five hundred years. Persistent Ottoman pretensions to western Thrace, most of which was acquired by the Bulgarians during the Balkan Wars, caused great disquiet in Bulgaria. The Bulgarians recognized that to a certain degree they had to compete with the Ottomans for German favor. In the spring of 1918, the perceptive Crown Prince Boris warned Lieutenant

Colonel von Masow, the German military attaché in Bulgaria, "The revival of Turkish aspirations in Europe is intolerable for us. Germany on this issue has two choices. She has to decide whether to defend a state whose domestic situation is in disarray and whose role in Europe has dwindled, or to be with a vigorous young state. A mistaken policy would compromise the future of German-Bulgarian relations."[29] During their desperate Western Front offensives in the spring of 1918, the Germans had little inclination to become involved in squabbles among their allies. Consequently Bulgarian anxieties continued to increase. A diplomatic report from Constantinople dated 18 May 1918 emphasized, "The Turks have aggressive intentions toward Bulgaria."[30] A formal Ottoman request for the return of western Thrace arrived in Sofia in July.[31] The Ottomans appeared to be on the verge of stabbing their Bulgarian allies in the back. Zhekov told the German naval attaché in Sofia that the Bulgarian army would revolt if the Sofia government made any concessions in Thrace or in Dobrudzha to the Ottomans.[32] The devotion of the ordinary Bulgarian soldier to nationalist goals by this time, however, was by no means clear. A little later in July, the Bulgarian legation in Constantinople reported that the Turks were on the verge of collapse, and without German help for their forces in Palestine would have to settle with the British.[33] An Ottoman withdrawal from the war would have had catastrophic consequences for the Bulgarians, because it would have opened up their virtually unguarded southeastern frontier to Entente forces. The Bulgarians distrusted and detested the Ottoman Turks but needed them in the war. The concern about the Ottomans, widely reported in the Bulgarian press, was a source of encouragement for the Serbian troops in the trenches in front of the Bulgarian positions.[34] The two old enemies of the Serbs were becoming hostile once again toward each other. For the Serbs this Bulgarian-Ottoman antagonism heralded a possible collapse of the Central Alliance.

Not surprisingly, by the summer of 1918 many Bulgarians had serious reservations about their main ally, Germany. There were several reasons for this. Although Bulgarian soldiers admired German culture, organizational skill, and efficiency, they loathed the haughtiness and superior manner the Germans assumed toward their Bulgarian allies.[35] Such attitudes caused deep resentment among Bulgarian troops.

Another problem resulted from Bulgarian disappointment over the results of the Treaty of Bucharest of 1918, imposed by the Central Pow-

ers on Romania. The Bulgarians were especially infuriated that the Ottomans claimed a role in Dobrudzha because Ottoman soldiers had participated in the campaign. The Bulgarians realized that the Ottomans were
using claims to Dobrudzha as leverage for Thrace. For the time being the
Ottomans did not realize their expectations there. Nevertheless, contrary
to Bulgarian expectations, the treaty of Bucharest of 1918 had not secured
for them the northern part of the Dobrudzha. Instead, it was consigned to
a joint Austro-Bulgarian-German administration. To many Bulgarian soldiers this appeared proof that the Germans did not support Bulgarian national aspirations. If the Germans would not recognize Bulgarian claims
to northern Dobrudzha, would they uphold Bulgarian national goals in
Macedonia?[36] All Bulgarian war objectives appeared to be in jeopardy.

Nor did the Treaty of Bucharest consign to Bulgaria a proportional
share of the Romanian material assets. According to the division of spoils
among the Central Powers allies, the Bulgarians received only a 15 percent
share of these assets, and this only after protest that the original 10 percent was too meager.[37] The Bulgarians badly needed Romanian foodstuffs
and raw materials. By this time even Tsar Ferdinand was becoming increasingly frustrated with his allies. He cabled Colonel Ganchev, the Bulgarian representative to the German command, "I am sick from the anger
that creeps over me because of German behavior on every issue, and have
no trust in them, especially in the Emperor's circles and in the scoundrels
in the Imperial Chancellery."[38] The tsar seems to have become infected by
the same war weariness that had appeared at the front.

Bulgarian soldiers greatly resented German economic domination of
their country. Some asked themselves, "Isn't Bulgaria in the hands of foreign interests?"[39] After the alliance agreement of 1915 between Germany
and Bulgaria, Germans had begun to dominate the Bulgarian economy.
German currency circulated in Bulgaria, and German soldiers, better paid
than their Bulgarian comrades, bought up much of the available food.[40]
German purchases of Bulgarian produce also contributed to the high food
prices and general inflation within Bulgaria. Also the better rations enjoyed by German soldiers at the Macedonian Front were a cause of great
disgruntlement for the Bulgarians.[41] Compounding this was the supply
problem within Germany. In his June 1918 report to the tsar, General
Zhekov noted that the Bulgarians had not received any kind of military
supplies from the Germans since April.[42] While the Bulgarians resented

many things about their German allies, continued persecution of the war was unthinkable without them.

The morale problems caused by Bulgaria's allies were not confined to the soldiers at the front. German policies also caused concern among the Bulgarian senior military leadership. As early as 1916, the Germans realized that Bulgarian chief of staff Zhostov openly opposed the Germans and their policies. General Zhostov forthrightly informed the German military attaché in Sofia, von Masow, that the Germans were worse than the Russians had been in regards to meeting Bulgarian expectations for military material.[43] Only General Zhostov's death later in 1916 ended this source of opposition to the Central Alliance among senior Bulgarian officers.

When a Bulgarian delegation traveled to Berlin in April 1918 to press for the delivery of war materials, General Zhekov urged its members to remind the Germans of a resentment that still rankled after almost three years. This was the German refusal in the autumn of 1915 to permit the Bulgarian offensive that had driven an Anglo-French force out of Serbia to proceed into Greece as far as Salonika to expel the Entente troops based there. At that time, the Germans were averse to undermining the pro-German position of Greek King Constantine, who also was the brother-in-law of Kaiser Wilhelm. In the summer of 1918, Zhekov pointed out that "we contain and continue to hold in Macedonia a 350 thousand man enemy army, which if the operation there was terminated, would be utilized on the French or Palestinian Fronts."[44] Moreover, the Bulgarians thought that they would not be fighting at all in southern Macedonia in 1918 if they continued their 1915 offensive against the French and British all the way into Greece and had taken Salonika.[45] The German disinclination to declare war on Greece was also a source of difficulty for the Bulgarians. The failure of Germany to adopt a hostile position toward Greece seemed to emphasize the lack of German commitment to the Bulgarian cause.

Particularly alarming to the Bulgarian high command was the possibility that the Germans would withdraw their remaining forces in Macedonia for use on the Western Front. This would leave the Bulgarians largely alone to confront the better-fed and better-clothed and better-equipped Entente forces. The German concentration on the Western Front threatened to deprive the Bulgarians of not only German soldiers but also German equipment. On 5 February 1918, Zhekov wrote to von Hindenburg to complain that Germans had not fulfilled their obligations to provide the Bulgarian army with artillery materials.[46] By this time the material and morale situation in the Bulgarian army was becoming serious.

The situation became critical in 1918 during the great German spring offensive on the Western Front. The Bulgarians understood that the outcome of the war depended upon the success of Ludendorff's offensive. Colonel Ganchev reported on 20 February 1918 that "the fortunes of Germany and the command of the German army are in the hands of General Ludendorff."[47] By implication the fortunes of Bulgaria were also in Ludendorff's hands. Zhekov understood that he had to deal with Ludendorff, despite his personal inclinations.

In the spring of 1918, the Germans began to withdraw the greater part of their heavy artillery from the Macedonian Front, despite the dire evaluation of the situation by the Bulgarian General Staff. Ludendorff, "sincerely or not," indicated that the enemy was not in a position to launch an offensive on the Macedonian Front, and if it did it would fail.[48] The German troops and equipment were desperately needed to sustain the ongoing efforts on the Western Front.

Hindenburg stressed to Zhekov that the war would be decided on the Western Front and that he wanted all German infantry and artillery units on the Macedonian Front to go to the west.[49] Zhekov already understood this.[50] Nevertheless he insisted to Tsar Ferdinand, "On a political and military basis the Germans have not adopted a point of view, that would have brought about an end to the war for us on that front, since on such a basis we hold and continue to hold in Macedonia a 350 thousand man army, which if that operation was finished, would be used on the fronts in France and Palestine."[51] He pointed out that preparations for the removal of German troops from Macedonia would undermine morale in Bulgaria. "These measures, without contributing to the improvement of provisions, will cause the feeling in the army and among the Bulgarian people, that our front is being abandoned at the moment when we are encountering new enemies and when serious problems are imminent on the Macedonian Front."[52] Zhekov made a strong case for the continuation of a German presence in Macedonia. In January he argued that "the war with Serbia is still not finished, it continues in a much wider extent than envisioned beforehand, but consequently the allies are not able to deny us the agreed upon aid owed us."[53] Zhekov persisted in his opinion that the Bulgarians needed German troops to maintain the defensive posture on the Macedonian Front. "From the point of view of the factual situation on the southern front, from considerations of clear natural right that ensue from the obligations of German and Austria from the convention, and finally from a moral basis, I cannot agree to the desire of the German High Command to withdraw German soldiers from Macedonia."[54] He also pointed out, "I consider that any such weakening of power in Macedonia would be dangerous for the secure defense of the positions, since all information indicates that the Entente is increasing its forces in Macedonia with the Greek Army and with sections of volunteers, formed in America and Russia."[55] The Greeks had joined the Entente on 30 June 1917. They had added their forces to those already on the Macedonian Front, increasing the Entente's numerical superiority there.

Zhekov did accomplish some modification of the German plans through his persistent objections to their withdrawal from the Macedonian Front. He had wanted them to maintain in Macedonia at least one division of ten to twelve battalions, to be at the front, not left as reserve.[56] Nevertheless, of the twenty-two German battalions and seenty-two artillery batteries on the Macedonian Front at the end of 1917, only three battalions and thirty-two batteries remained in Army Group Scholtz by the summer of 1918.[57] Units of the Bulgarian Third Army, transferred from Dobrudzha after the signing of the Treaty of Bucharest, replaced the departing German troops. The Germans did agree to leave some troops and equipment behind. These amounted to only three *jaeger* (light infantry) battalions, thirty-two batteries, and several machine gun and mortar sections. Including the German Eleventh army, which consisted of seven Bulgarian divisions and one German division commanded by General von Scholtz and with a German staff, there remained 18,000 German officers and men on the Macedonian Front.[58] The realization that a German commander with a German staff was directing Bulgarian soldiers in the defense of Bulgaria can hardly have been a source of great comfort to the majority of solders in the German Eleventh Army. In any event, these German soldiers were insufficient to bolster the increasingly demoralized Bulgarian forces.

The Germans considered that Bulgarian strength in Macedonia sufficient to meet any enemy attack. They were eager to shift their forces to the Western Front to sustain the ongoing offensive there. General Zhekov's evaluation of the Bulgarian situation led him to a different conclusion. In July he warned von Hindenburg, "I am seriously concerned whether we, with our weakened forces and paltry means, are in condition to resist to the end a powerful attack from our more numerous enemies."[59] The reversals the German army began to suffer on the Western Front in July had to concern the Bulgarians.[60] Nevertheless, Zhekov did not attempt to hide the poor material and morale condition of the Bulgarian army from his ally.

The German High Command was aware of the difficult conditions in the Bulgarian army.[61] They had known of Bulgarian supply problems for some time, but tended to blame the Bulgarians for these problems, especially for the difficulties in procuring foodstuffs.[62] Bulgarian responsibility evoked little German sympathy. After the war, von Hindenburg claimed that German victories on the Western Front and "what help as we could" of food and clothing increased Bulgarian morale.[63] At the time, however, he was blunt about rejecting Bulgarian supply demands. He used the ongoing offensive on the Western Front to rebuff Bulgarians' complaints that they needed more military supplies.[64] There is no indication of any increase in Bulgarian morale in the summer of 1918 due to the activities of the German army, rather the contrary.

Zhekov himself did not view the German army solely in the context of its leadership. He understood that in a successful military alliance, the relationship between the two sides extended all the way through the ranks. Zhekov realized that the German and Bulgarian soldiers were fundamentally different in their perspectives on the war.

> The Germans were not able to easily estimate objectively such a truthful interpretation of the spirit of our soldiers. They measured everything with their own concepts and their own standards, and were not able to take into account our people and our army. But cultural and military superiority of the Germans should have been able to suggest to them how to understand and value a valiant ally like Bulgaria and the conditions for its fighting abilities and physical endurance.[65]

Zhekov also reported, "The (Bulgarian) soldiers are amazed by German culture, organization and efficiency, but they also immediately discovered cold haughtiness, and egotism in the behavior of their ally."[66] These are criticisms that Zhekov might have raised himself about his own treatment by his German colleagues.

The Austro-Hungarians also infringed on Bulgarian interests. In the summer of 1918 they assumed control over the Bulgarian-administered region around the Serbian town of Vranje.[67] The Austrians and Bulgarians also clashed over control of the railroad line in the Morava River valley in occupied Serbia. The Germans encouraged Bulgarian pretensions to a frontier on the Morava as a way to deflect Bulgarian claims in Dobrudzha.[68] These issues tainted the successful conclusion of the Romanian campaign and undermined Bulgarian confidence in maintaining their war goals.

During the summer of 1918, yet another factor emerged to further undermine the Bulgarian war effort. In July, the consequences of the American entry into the war for the first time appeared to have a noticeable effect on Bulgarian morale. Although the United States and Bulgaria were not at war with each other, concerns about American material and financial contributions to the Entente war effort began to undermine the Bulgarian soldiers' faith in ultimate victory.[69] Some Bulgarians had worked in the United States, and as a result had developed some awareness of the agricultural and industrial productive capacities there.

During the summer the Bulgarians also made overtures to the new Ukrainian state.[70] This entity was a German satellite, but potentially a Bulgarian ally in the struggle for Dobrudzha and a source of foodstuffs. The disarray in Ukraine, as nationalists, communists, anarchists, and others contended for power, prevented any real connection between Kiev and Sofia from developing.

Amidst the gloom, one positive event briefly improved the morale of the Bulgarian soldiers. This was a change of government in Sofia. Vasil Radoslavov, who as prime minister had led Bulgaria into the war on the German side in October 1915, resigned on 20 June. Radoslavov's resignation was mainly due to his failure to secure all of Dobrudzha for Bulgaria at the negotiations for the Treaty of Bucharest. The new prime minister, Aleksandŭr Malinov, was not as closely tied to German interests as his predecessor. He inspired hopes among Bulgarian soldiers that the corruption and inefficiency associated with the previous government might finally recede.[71] The change of civilian leadership seemed to be a step in the right direction. Zhekov himself had in June emphasized that "only an authoritative, popular and honest government" could hope to address the morale problems of the country.[72] Entente intelligence in southern Macedonia noted that the number of Bulgarian deserters had diminished after the change of government, "no doubt caused by the hopes for peace that Malinov's coming to power has aroused."[73] In July, only 140 Bulgarians deserted to the Entente, as compared to 201 in June.[74] Crown Prince Boris noted at the end of July that the worst of the crisis was over and that morale seemed to be improving.[75] Nevertheless, most of those who did desert did not go over to the enemy, but left for the interior of Bulgaria, presumably to their homes. From 1 March to 10 August 1918, 264 soldiers deserted from the 2nd Thracian Infantry Division, of whom 52 crossed enemy lines.[76] The others presumably made their way to their homes or hid out in the mountains. The morale crisis was far from over. Cases of insubordination increased, and in mass meetings soldiers denounced the war. Demonstrations against the war also grew throughout Bulgaria, where the food and clothing situation was as bad as that at the front. War weariness pervaded both home and the front.

While any one of these factors was sufficient to undermine morale, the combination of concerns about food and material shortages at home and at the front and the lack of confidence in Bulgaria's allies seriously undermined the ability of the Bulgarian army to remain in the field. Insubordinate behavior and desertions increased throughout the summer of 1918.[77] Nevertheless, during the summer of 1918, no major mutinies developed in the Bulgarian ranks on the order of those that had previously broken out in the French, Italian, or Russian armies. Significantly, at this point Bulgarian reports on morale made little mention of the material superiority and the fighting abilities of the Entente troops in Macedonia.

During the spring of 1918, the Entente forces received an important augmentation with the arrival of the Greek army 1st and 2nd Corps, six divisions in all. These six divisions added 7,889 officers and 286,047 men to the Entente forces.[78] These forces had been in training since the abdication of King Constantine the previous summer. Entente command now considered them ready for combat. They soon obtained an opportunity to prove themselves. Beginning on 30 May these Greek units, together with elements of the French Eastern Army, attacked the 5th Danubian Division of the Bulgarian First Army's defensive positions at Yerbichna (Gk: Skra di Legen) and neighboring Kititsa ridge. The Yerbichna position was essentially a fortified ridge spur west of the Vardar River, south of the

Greek frontier. The Bulgarians had fortified positions on a ridge southwest of Lake Dorian and northwest of Salonika. A triple line of trenches surrounded the rocky crest of Yerbichna, 1,096 meters high. In the first significant fighting on the Macedonian Front in 1918, mainly Greek and some French troops succeeded in taking the Bulgarian positions. An Entente report on the battle claimed 1,805 Bulgarians and a certain number of German specialists as prisoners, and admitted 300 French and Greek dead and 1,500 wounded.[79] The Greek soldiers from the Cretan Division and the Archipelago Division of the refurbished Greek army had been preparing to fight since the abdication of King Constantine and the resolution of the national rift the previous summer. Their success was a tremendous morale boost for the Greeks. It recalled the Greek success against the Bulgarian Second Army in the Second Balkan War five years earlier. The Greek victory also inspired the Serbs to get back into the fight.[80] They were eager to renew offensive actions against the Bulgarians.

Bulgarian troops were unable to respond with their usual counterattacks, due to their low morale and poor material condition. There were "numerous cases of going over to the enemy, of desertion to the rear, self inflicted wounds and numerous expressed indications that the infantry would not attack."[81] The Greek success was especially disquieting to the Bulgarians because it indicated the renewal of the conflict that had begun in the summer of 1913, to the initial detriment of the Bulgarians. A German report of 15 June identified poor provisions, poor clothing, officers' lack of concern for the welfare of their troops, and war weariness as the causes of the general malaise in the Bulgarian army.[82] General von Scholtz noted the situation in the Bulgarian army after the Yerbichna defeat. In a letter to General Zhekov he expressed concern about Bulgarian morale, but stated, "I am convinced, that above all senior Bulgarian officers will work to ameliorate conditions and that all Bulgarian officers, who have tirelessly worked to maintain order in the ranks, will continue to impose rigorous discipline."[83] Von Scholtz offered encouragement but little material aid. The newly promoted Major General Ganchev at headquarters in Pless attempted to make the best of the situation. He pointed out after the Yerbichna defeat that "if the French and English are defeated (on the Western Front), which is highly likely, then any success of the Salonika Army will come to nothing."[84] Even with the loss of Yerbichna and the disturbances in the Bulgarian army, the Bulgarians succeeded in inflicting heavy losses on the attacking Entente forces. The Entente captured 1,812 Bulgarians, some of whom presumably were deserters, and lost 2,795 men.[85] After the war, General Zhekov did admit that a successful French and Greek attack on the Yerbichna position on the Macedonian Front on 30 May had been a serious blow, not because of the tactical abilities of the Entente troops, but because the Bulgarian morale was already too low to attempt a counterattack.[86] The defeat at Yerbichna indicated that the state of morale in the Bulgarian army undermined its ability to fight even on defense.

The morale crisis exacted a toll even among senior officers. After the Bulgarian First Army failed to counterattack at Yerbichna because of material and morale factors, General Zhekov relieved its commander, Lieutenant General Dimitŭr Geshov, and ordered him to take leave. Zhekov appointed the "more healthy, more lively and more steadfast" Lieutenant General Stefan Nerezov in his place.[87] Geshov's situation was unenviable, but Nerezov's was impossible. He was expected to inspire his troops and to hold his positions without the material and psychological means to do so. Indeed General Zhekov himself had reported on the same problems that had demoralized General Geshov. He had exhibited some sense of demoralization when he reported to Tsar Ferdinand on 2 April: "For Bulgaria the continuation of the war is not our fault and is not in our interest, and it could continue for a long time."[88] This was during the time of the German successes on the Western Front. Zhekov apparently perceived little hope at this point for Bulgaria in those German victories. In any event, this change of command did little to improve the morale of the soldiers in the First Army.[89] Discontent remained rife.

The Yerbichna defeat worried the government. Radoslavov lamented on 5 June in Sofia that the unrest at the front was directed against the government.[90] This was a rather narrow perspective on the demoralization of the army. Radoslavov's despair, however, aptly demonstrated the state of demoralization that had pervaded the entire country.

The Yerbichna defeat was a precursor for the Dobro Pole catastrophe in September. In both cases poor material conditions and morale compounded a military setback and prevented an effective response. Because of Yerbichna, the September military rebellion cannot have come as a surprise to the Bulgarian command and the Bulgarian government. While the Entente noted the morale problem in the Bulgarian army, it failed initially to connect this to the Yerbichna battle. A French report after the Yerbichna battle noted only that the "the counterattacks on our new positions were weak and without result."[91] A later report, however, did acknowledge that the morale problem diminished the capacity of the Bulgarian army to fight.[92] The Entente could not afford to ignore the opportunity the Bulgarian morale crisis presented.

The army and government made some effort to reverse the decline of morale. Already in 1917 a periodical intended to raise the spirits of the soldiers began publication. Entitled *Field Army Bookshelf,* it included articles on the history, geography, and literature of Bulgaria to explain Bulgarian war aims.[93] The next year the army established a school to train officers and soldiers to spread pro-war propaganda in the ranks. Neither of these efforts met with much success.

Bulgarian deserters kept Entente intelligence well informed about conditions in the Bulgarian army and in Bulgaria. Around 2,200 Bulgarians deserted from the Second Army to the Entente from February to August 1918.[94] This was from a formation that had experienced little combat since 1916. The reasons for desertion varied. Entente authorities recognized that the Bulgarian army faced a morale crisis. Nevertheless, they regarded the fighting abilities of their enemies with respect. In July an Entente report stated, "In spite of the crisis that seems to span Bulgaria, the Bulgarian army appears determined to energetically defend its front against an enemy offensive."[95] Even this late in the war, Entente forces in Macedonia anticipated strong Bulgarian resistance against any attack.

By August, a combination of factors had rendered the Bulgarian army extremely war weary. Beginning in July a rumor had begun to circulate among the troops that the alliance agreement with the Central Powers was valid for only three years and was about to lapse on 15 September, the third anniversary of the announcement of mobilization. If the Bulgarian government did not take measures to conclude peace by 15 September 1918, the Bulgarian soldiers would refuse to fight anymore.[96] This rumor proved to be a portent of things to come. Also, a report from the headquarters of Army Group Scholtz in Skopie cited instances of desertion and insubordination and war weariness among units of the German army and navy and the civilian population. It stated, "The feeling that force of arms may not be able to attain peace more and more is arising in the masses."[97] This information belied Ganchev's optimistic reports from German Army Headquarters. It cannot have encouraged the Bulgarian command that the war could still be won on the Western Front. If the Germans could not win the war, then surely Bulgaria had lost it.

Prime Minister Malinov attempted to address some of these problems by sending a note to the German government on 12 August. In this note, Malinov asked for talks on three issues: military equipment, financial help, and more German troops for the Macedonian Front.[98] He pointed out that the military convention of 6 September 1915 obligated Germany to provide Bulgaria with military equipment. He also noted that the arrival of the Greek army at the Macedonian Front placed the Bulgarians at a severe numerical disadvantage. The Germans took the Bulgarian prime minister's request seriously and attempted to mollify him. Material, including 13,000 uniforms, 120,000 pairs of boots, 50,000 gas masks, and artillery munitions were "already expedited," and additional quantities of these items were "on order."[99] Some artillery batteries were said to be "on the way." With their own material resources diminishing and their own troops in retreat, however, the Germans had little real help to offer.

The Bulgarians were not the only army on the Macedonian Front to suffer declining morale. It was pervasive, on all fronts. A French report of 21 April 1918 noted that the Serbian army, after seven years of war, the Romanian peace, and the "Russian treason," had undergone a crisis of morale.[100] The Entente soldiers, however, had major advantages not available to those of the Central Powers. They had the material and food resources provided by the Americans, and the promise of the American army. Even as the German offensive raged on the Western Front, these helped to alleviate some of the war weariness in Entente positions on the Macedonian Front. By this time the Russian contingent on the Macedonian Front had already departed, the victim of collapsed morale. Finally, a big German success in the west carried with it the implication that the numbers of troops on the Macedonian Front might have to be shifted to meet the emergency there.

The success at Yerbichna, however, energized the Entente forces, especially the new Greek army. It compensated to some degree for the Greek humiliation at Fort Rupel two years earlier; it served as a validation of the travails of the Greek national schism and its resolution by the Entente; and it extended the national rivalry between the Bulgarians and the Greeks. The arrival of a new energetic commander, General Franchet d'Espérey, in Salonika on 17 June 1918 also buoyed Entente morale. He replaced General Louis Guillaumat, who had devoted much effort to the reorganization of the Entente armies and to overcoming some of the problems caused by his quarrelsome predecessor.

In the summer of 1918 the Bulgarian army was in a difficult position. Having scarcely recovered from the substantial human and material losses of the Balkan Wars of 1912–13, it faced the much more numerous and better-equipped Entente army snugly ensconced in southern Macedonia and well supplied from Salonika. Bulgarian material resources were exhausted, and many Bulgarians had become deeply suspicious of the motivations of their allies. At the same time, Bulgaria remained completely dependent on Germany to resolve the war. The Central Powers could not win the First World War on the Macedonian Front, but they could lose it there.

Unlike the armies of France, Italy, and Russia, demoralization of the Bulgarian army did not occur because of military defeat or high combat casualties. Bulgarian soldiers were chronically hungry, miserably clad, worried about their families, and suspicious of their allies. One Bulgarian non-commissioned officer bluntly explained the situation to General Zhekov on 20 July 1918:

> We are naked, barefoot, and hungry. We will wait a little longer for clothes and shoes, but we are seeking a quick end to the war. We are not able to last much longer. And here (at the front) it is difficult, but we shall endure it; however, we are not able to endure what is happening in our villages. There they are ransacking and confiscating everything, and we are going barefoot and hungry.[101]

Ironically, Zhekov had warned the Bulgarian government in much the same sense the previous spring:

> I consider it my highest responsibility to the Fatherland to emphasize that the army will make the utmost effort and will give everything it can, to protect the gains we have made up to now, but the government must keep in mind, that for success in the present war our brave

army must have the necessary technical means and military material that corresponds in quantity and quality of that which our enemies have at their disposal.[102]

The government itself lacked the means to provide the army with the necessary materials. For the Bulgarian army fighting on the Macedonian Front in the summer of 1918, the real enemy, whether greedy Bulgarian war profiteers, grasping Ottoman diplomats, or arrogant German generals, was behind them.

As one Bulgarian commentator later wrote, General Zhekov had to fight on three fronts: against the German High Command, against the Bulgarian government, and against the Entente.[103] Zhekov was in an especially difficult situation in his relationship with his German allies. Bulgaria depended upon the Germans for virtually all its war materials except for foodstuffs. To a considerable degree, Bulgarian concerns about the purposes of the other Central Powers allies reflected the Bulgarian experience in the Balkan Wars. Bulgaria had gone to war allied with Greece and Serbia against the Ottoman Empire. Soon after the victory over the Ottomans, disagreements led to war between Bulgaria and its former allies. The disputes with the Ottomans during the First World War might have easily led to hostilities. For the Bulgarians, alliances did not guarantee the resolutions of disputes.

General Zhekov and the Bulgarian government understood that only Germany could win the war. Increasingly, however, he realized that Bulgaria could lose it. Under these circumstances, he endeavored to represent the best interests of his country, as he understood them. Zhekov's tragedy during the summer of 1918 was that he saw Bulgaria's defeat coming, but he could not persuade his allies to assist him to avoid it.

FIGURE 10.

*Bulgarian artillery in action at the Macedonian Front.*

COURTESY BIBLIOTELESCOPE

FIGURE 11.

*Bulgarian telephone operators
at the front line 1917.*

COURTESY BIBLIOTELESCOPE

**FIGURE 12.**
*Downed French plane.*
COURTESY BIBLIOTELESCOPE

FIGURE 13.

*German officers awarding Iron
Cross to Bulgarian soldiers.*

COURTESY BIBLIOTELESCOPE

FIGURE 14.

*Bulgarian officers and soldiers
at the Krivolak front line.*

COURTESY BIBLIOTELESCOPE

**FIGURE 15.**

*Tsar Ferdinand (right) and the*
*German Emperor Wilhelm II.*

COURTESY BIBLIOTELESCOPE

FIGURE 16.
*British outpost on the
Macedonian Front*

FIGURE 17.
*Serbian soldiers at the
Macedonian Front*

# BREAKTHROUGH

By the end of the summer of 1918, conditions on the Macedonian Front had worsened considerably for the Central Powers. The great influenza epidemic had caused some physical and morale problems among the Bulgarian soldiers.[1] Much to the dismay of the Bulgarian command, the Germans had withdrawn considerable numbers of troops and weapons to use in the great offensives on the Western Front. At the same time, the material condition of the Bulgarians deteriorated to an appalling degree.

The morale problem in the Bulgarian army did not escape the notice of the Entente forces in Macedonia. A French report dated 15 September noted, "the Bulgarian people and army are overcome with a desire for peace, increased by a determined hatred of the Germans and Turks."[2] Deserters reported that many soldiers believed that the Bulgarian government would make peace on 15 September. This was the anniversary of the initial mobilization in 1915. Nor were the Germans oblivious to the morale problems in the Bulgarian army. A German report of 10 August indicated that the influence of Aleksandŭr Stamboliski's antiwar Agrarian Party had grown very strong at the front. The same report noted, however, that despite the overwhelming war weariness, neither the tsar nor the government intended at that point to seek a separate peace. The reported cautioned, "The picture could change, if the Tsar and government, despite their good intentions, face opposition and lose courage to continue the war. Unfortunately we need to keep such an eventuality in mind, so that we do not have to reorient our affairs at the last possible moment."[3] The war-weary situation on the Macedonian Front and throughout Bulgaria was obvious to the Germans. The report implied that an Entente military effort could knock Bulgaria out of the war. By the end of the summer of 1918 Bulgaria, like all the other Central Powers, was at the end of its ability to wage war.

By September 1918, the Bulgarian government recognized that the war was drawing to an end. In particular it became aware of German attempts to secure a peace settlement. Major General Petŭr Ganchev, the Bulgarian representative at German military headquarters in Pless, reported on 2 September that the Germans were prepared to go to a peace conference in Washington, D.C., but were waiting for a success on the Western Front to make proposals.[4] Their allies, who had already demonstrated a lack of military support for Bulgaria, were now considering a diplomatic resolution to the conflict, without any consultation. These peace attempts made the failure of the German offensives on the Western Front obvious. The Bulgarians could not be certain that their interests would receive consideration at any such conference. Nevertheless, despite their disagreements with their German allies, the Bulgarians did not seriously consider a separate peace at this point. The Germans recognized that the Bulgarian government and military thus far remained loyal.[5] This was more than could be said about the Austro-Hungarians after the fiasco of the Sixtus Affair.[6] The realization that the Germans were considering an end to the conflict, however, could only have undermined Bulgarian efforts to see the war to a victorious conclusion.

The Bulgarian army remained hopeful that the continued fighting elsewhere might end in an overall settlement of the war. A report prepared for Crown Prince Boris, dated 14 September, on the eve of the battle of Dobro Pole, stated, "It is important for us to hold the Macedonian Front at all cost until the results from the battles of the Western Front are clear, after which we will need to reorient our policy."[7] The report suggested in particular an arrangement with Britain directed against the Ottoman Empire. This report indicated that by September the German defeat in the west was becoming obvious. In any event one way or another, the end of the present conflict was approaching.

Similar concerns about the peace process undermined Bulgarian relations with Austria-Hungary. On the eve of the Entente offensive in Macedonia, 13 September, Emperor Karl telegraphed Tsar Ferdinand: "It seems to me that we can no longer rely upon a continuing German resistance on the Western front."[8] The next day, Austro-Hungarian foreign minister Count István Burián proposed a general peace conference.[9] Initially, Prime Minister Aleksandŭr Malinov seemed to back this effort.[10] To Burián's request for support, however, the Sofia government replied that while it wanted peace, it could not abandon the goals for which Bulgaria was fighting.[11] This Austrian initiative emphasized to the Bulgarians that their Habsburg ally pursued its own agenda, to the detriment of Bulgaria. It also indicated that the Austro-Hungarians understood that the Germans had suffered defeat on the Western Front and that a military victory by the Central Powers was no longer possible.

Another serious distraction on the eve of the Entente offensive was the almost total breakdown of relations between the Bulgarians and their Ottoman allies. This arrangement was always tentative. The Bulgarians and Ottomans had fought each other in the Balkan Wars of 1912–13. Five years later, the Ottomans were pressuring the Bulgarians to return the Maritsa valley, ceded at the beginning of the war to the Bulgarians, and western Thrace, conquered by the Bulgarians during the First Balkan War. Relations between the Bulgarians and their Ottoman allies were so bad that a report for Crown Prince Boris issued on the eve of the Bulgarian collapse recommended that after results of the Western Front battles became clear, the Bulgarians should orient their policy toward Britain to seek help against the Ottomans.[12] Had the Bulgarians and Ottomans both managed to hold out much longer against their Entente enemies, they might well have opened hostilities against each other. While both were utterly exhausted, their deep mistrust of each other could have spurred them to further efforts. Amidst all these problems, the renewal of Entente activity on the Macedonian Front was by far the most serious facing the Bulgarians.

The Entente had contemplated an offensive in Macedonia for some time. Conditions at the end of the summer of 1918 were propitious for such action. Bulgarian morale was poor, and the Germans, already in retreat in the west, were unlikely to provide significant assistance to their ally. The area between the Cherna Bend and Lake Doiran, held by the German Eleventh Army and the Bulgarian First Army, offered the most promising location for the proposed offensive. Located just south of the post-1913 Greek-Serbian frontier in Greek territory, Dobro Pole and the neighboring high points of Sokol on the west and Veternik on the east were fortified ridges of considerable height in the Moglena Mountains lying between the Cherna and Moglenica Rivers. Most of these high ridges were stony and lacked significant vegetation. They were the extension of the same ridge system where to the southwest at Kaimakchalan in the autumn of 1916 the Serbs had gained a significant victory. Dobro Pole was over 1,800 meters at its highest point, the so-called Pyramid, and Sokol was 1,885 meters high. Behind Dobro Pole was a large open, somewhat marshy area, the eponymous "good field." This was really a large drainage basin. If the Entente units could succeed in taking the ridge positions, they could rapidly spread out in this area and from there surge into the area of the inverted V between the Cherna and Vardar Rivers. With the seizure of Dobro Pole, Entente forces could advance into on Macedonia up to the Vardar valley and from there on to Skopie. This advance could divide the German Eleventh Army from the Bulgarian First Army.

The region to the west was not promising for the Entente offensive because of the extremely difficult terrain and the distance from the main command and supply position at Salonika. Any break through the Central Power's lines to the west was unlikely to produce a decisive result because Entente troops would find themselves in the wilds of Macedonia and Albania. An attempt to traverse the Central Powers' lines to the east would come up against the mountain barrier of the Rhodopes. Dobro Pole afforded direct access to the Vardar-Morava River system and the Serbian heartland.

The Bulgarians had begun to establish defenses at Dobro Pole in the autumn of 1916. These defenses, like those elsewhere along the lines, included a primary emplacement of infantry trenches with traverses every 50 to 200 meters, and a secondary emplacement 1.5 to 3 kilometers to the rear, with artillery batteries located 1.5 to 3 kilometers further behind the front line.[13] Between the infantry positions and the artillery was a system of obstacles and permanent barbwire emplacements. Crown Prince Boris had reported to his father in the autumn of 1917 that the front had been "strengthened and could resist attack."[14] The Bulgarians had labored throughout the previous winter to build up their fortified positions. They enhanced their trenches and shelters and set up observation points. The lack of materials, difficult winter conditions, and poor roads made hampered their efforts. With some improvisation, however, the Bulgarians succeeded in improving the positions.[15] These fortifications still had weaknesses in their barbwiring, trenches, and especially artillery.

The initial idea for an attack at Dobro Pole seems to have originated in Serbian staff discussions immediately after the end of the fighting in November 1916. Colonel Živko Pavlović, a Serbian General Staff officer who at the time commanded the Šumadija Division of the Serbian Second Army, first recognized that an attack on the Bulgarian positions at Dobro Pole presented the Entente with the chance to break through the Central Powers' defenses and advance north into pre-1913 Serbia.[16] His commander, General Stepa Stepanović, thought that the Bulgarian positions at Dobro Pole offered a good opportunity for an attack, "when we have greater strength."[17] The Serbs continued to contemplate an attack in front of their positions at Dobro Pole throughout the next year. In 1918 another memorandum from the Serbian General Staff pointed out that a breakthrough at Dobro Pole would be "the first step toward the goal of cutting the Berlin-Constantinople road. A good portion of the Bulgarian army would be completely demoralized. Our own morale would grow."[18] Based on superiority in numbers in Macedonia, General Guillaumat had urged the Entente command to sanction action in Macedonia in March 1918.[19] A French report of 5 June 1918 indicated the Bulgarian defensive positions at Dobro Pole in front of the Serbian Second Army as offering a promising location for an Entente offensive. The report pointed out that Entente artillery could bring flanking fire on the Dobro Pole positions, that access to the approaches to Dobro Pole was easy, and that the seizure of the positions at Dobro Pole would open up the entire line. The report concluded presciently, "A successful operation there would have consequences of the highest importance for the general situation on the Macedonian Front."[20] General Louis Franchet d'Espérey, who had replaced General Guillaumat in June, submitted a plan for an attack at Dobro Pole to Paris for approval on 13 July 1918. His subsequent order issued on 31 August gave instructions for the exploitation of the anticipated success in rupturing the Bulgarian lines.[21] He envisioned a two-phase operation, a first phase intended to break through the Bulgarian lines and a second phase meant to rapidly spread out behind them through the Cherna valley north to the Vardar valley. From there Veles and Skopie would be in reach. Each attacking force had a specific objective; The French First Army to Skopie and beyond to Kumanovo and Niš, the Serbian Second Army to Veles and Shtip, the British Third Army to Strumitsa, and the Greek Fourth Corps to Demir Hissar, Fort Rupel, and Petrich. The Serbian Second Army would undertake the initial assault. After the initial breakthrough, the Serbian First Army would rush through into the Cherna-Vardar triangle. The Serbian antagonism toward the Bulgarians from the Balkan Wars, together with their success against the Bulgarians two years earlier in the fighting at Cherna Bend and Bitola, were important factors in their eagerness for the fray.[22] The national aspirations for the Greeks and Serbs obviously played a role in the formulation of these objectives. The Greeks could demonstrate their commitment to the Entente after the national division of 1915–17 and overcome the embarrassment of the surrender of Fort Rupel to the Bulgarians two years earlier. The Serbs could set foot again on the home territory they had evacuated three years before.

The initial French concept was based upon surprise. This was later abandoned as being impractical, because of the need to concentrate forces in front of the elevated Bulgarian positions. Nevertheless, the French still hoped to achieve some measure of shock. Secondary attacks by British and Italian forces would be made northeast of Bitola, and at Doiran and Syar.[23] The Italian forces extending across southern Albania west of Lake Ohrid to the Adriatic Sea did not participate in the offensive. After consultation with the British and Italians, French headquarters sanctioned the offensive. Final authorization from the French government, with the concordance of London and Rome, arrived in Salonika on 10 September.

Since midsummer, the Entente had recognized that the Bulgarian army was undergoing a crisis of morale. "In the current situation, the allied armies in Macedonia have for the moment a freedom of action that allows them to impose their will on the enemy."[24] Low Bulgarian morale would give the offensive at Dobro Pole a clear advantage. At the same time the morale situation in the Entente armies was improving. The victory at Yerbichna had buoyed the spirits of the new Greek army. Also the Serbs sought revenge, not against the Austrians or Germans, but against their hereditary Bulgarian enemies.[25] Underlying this quest for revenge were dim memories of the Serbo-Bulgarian War and more clear ones of the Balkan Wars.

On the Bulgarian side at Dobro Pole were the 2nd Thracian Division commanded by Major General Ivan Rusev, which defended the Sokol and Dobro Pole positions, and the 3rd Balkan Division, commanded by Lieutenant General Nikola Ribarov, which defended the Veternik position. They were assigned to the German Eleventh Army, the mainly Bulgarian formation with a German staff and under the command of the German General Kuno von Steuben. Bolstering the Bulgarian infantry were several squads of German machine gunners. The lines of responsibility between the two Bulgarian divisions met between Dobro Pole and Veternik, presenting a challenge to command. They were outnumbered in men and guns. The position was astride both banks of the Vardar valley, which hampered communication between the divisions of the army. The material situation in both Bulgarian divisions was miserable.

The Bulgarian army command recognized the relative weakness of its position in Macedonia. During the Entente attacks in June 1918, the Bulgarians had noted the Entente's particular interest in its Dobro Pole positions.[26] A Bulgarian report of 1 September anticipated renewed attacks on this position. It stated, "Overall the attack in the direction of Dobro Pole is just a matter of days."[27] The report was uncertain about the objective of the attack. It noted that a weaker attack could take the Dobro Pole ridge, and a stronger one could break through Bulgarian secondary defense and push on to Prilep.

Some Bulgarian officers even perceived in the anticipated September offensive by the Entente a means to rally the morale of the Bulgarian soldiers.[28] General Zhekov anticipated an Entente offensive against the Bulgarian lines at the end of August or the beginning of September.[29] At the beginning of September, Bulgarians captured a Serbian NCO and three privates, who stated that the huge offensive planned against Dobro Pole included two French divisions.[30] After the war, Major General Hristo Burmov, who had replaced General Zhostov as the chief of staff of the Bulgarian

army, testified that the Bulgarians knew everything about the enemy preparations.[31] Even though the Bulgarians knew the enemy intentions, they
feared they would be unable to counteract them. Their soldiers were under-
fed, underequipped, outnumbered, and demoralized. Their allies were distracted by their own military problems and diplomatic initiatives.

Under these circumstances, an attack on Dobro Pole offered the Entente the opportunity to achieve complete victory with a single successful operation. The Entente had every reason to be confident of success. A
French report issued on the eve of the battle stated, "The Entente armies
are in a very satisfactory condition, especially in morale and material."[32]
After almost three years of frustration in Macedonia, the Entente forces
appeared on the eve of success.

By September 1918, the Bulgarians had reached "the peak" of their general mobilization, with 878,000 men in uniform, of whom 697,000 were in
the military.[33] Of these, 70–73 percent were engaged on the Macedonian
Front in the First or Second Armies.[34] Only a shadow of the Third Army remained in Dobrudzha to enforce Bulgarian claims to this disputed region.
The small Fourth Army covered Bulgaria's Aegean coast. The extent of mobilization meant that when the army suffered military defeat at Dobro Pole
and morale in some units collapsed, there were no additional sources of
manpower to deal with the situation. The demands of the war had overextended Bulgarian manpower.

By mid-September 1918, the Entente forces in Macedonia had a slight
advantage in numbers of soldiers and a pronounced advantage in artillery
and airplanes on the Macedonian Front.[35] According to figures presented
to Tsar Ferdinand, the Entente had 221,000 men and 1,824 artillery pieces
to the Central Powers' 171,000 men and 15,000 artillery pieces.[36] These figures were probably too low. The Entente benefited from the arrival of additional reinforcements at Salonika. The most recent formation to join the
Serbian Second Army at Salonika was a "Yugoslav" contingent composed
of Austro-Hungarian South Slav POWs. The 6,000 men of the Yugoslav Division had crossed Russia on the Trans-Siberian Railroad, had embarked
on transport ships at Dalny and Port Arthur, and after a long sea journey
had arrived at Salonika in April 1918. Upon arrival it joined the Serbian 2nd
Army.[37] The appearance of the "Yugoslav" troops gave a tremendous morale boost to the Serbian soldiers already on the Macedonian Front. Over

the past year the Russian revolutions and the Salonika trial had eroded their enthusiasm for the war. In addition, General Franchet d'Espérey held two British and three Greek divisions in reserve. Other figures give the Entente 717,000 men with 2,609 artillery pieces, 2,682 machine guns, 6,434 automatic rifles, and 200 airplanes, while the Bulgarians had a total of 550,000 men supported by 1,217 artillery pieces, 2,710 machine guns, and 30 airplanes.[38] These Bulgarian soldiers were stretched over a 350-kilometer front from the mouth of the Struma River west to the Shkumba River in Albania. In addition there were two divisions in the 19th Austro-Hungarian Corps in Albania and three German battalions of around 18,000 men serving with the Bulgarians. This discrepancy in manpower undoubtedly was also a basis for low Bulgarian morale. In the summer of 1918, Army Group Scholtz, consisting of the German Eleventh Army and the Bulgarian First Army, had only two infantry regiments in reserve.[39] These weak forces had to cover both the German General of the Infantry Kuno von Steuben's German Eleventh Army, headquartered at Prilep, and General Nezerov's Bulgarian First Army, headquartered at Dedeli near Doiran.

The Entente's advantage in manpower and weapons became more pronounced in front of Dobro Pole itself. The main Entente forces arrayed against the Bulgarians at Dobro Pole were in the Serbian First Army under General Petar Bojović, consisting of the Danube, Drina, and Morova Infantry Divisions, and the Serbian Second Army under General Stepanović, consisting of five divisions, the Serbian Šumadija, Timok, and Yugoslav, and the French 122nd and 17th Colonial Divisions. Concentrating for the attack at Dobro Pole, the French and Serbian First and Second Armies had 36,500 riflemen against 11,600 Bulgarians, 756 machine guns to 245 Bulgarian, 2,610 light machine guns to 0 Bulgarian, 654 artillery pieces against 146 Bulgarian, 18 cavalry squadrons to 3 Bulgarian, and 81 airplanes to 24 Bulgarian.[40] These numbers considerably reduced the advantage the Bulgarians enjoyed in their defensive positions.

In preparation for the Entente attack on Dobro Pole, laborers cut roads and passages to the initial assembly areas. Artillery troops positioned their guns. Much of this work was accomplished under the cover of darkness. Nevertheless, these preparations did not entirely escape notice by the Bulgarians. They could see the preparations from their elevated positions. Air reconnaissance also detected the increased activity in front of Dobro Pole.

General von Scholtz noted clear signs of offensive preparation at Dobro Pole on 27 August.[41] Nevertheless, the Bulgarian command and the German staff of Army Group Scholtz remained confident and failed to perceive the danger that a decisive breakthrough at Dobro Pole could pose.[42] General von Scholtz still believed as late as September that the reserves were in position to cover the anticipated attack at Dobro Pole.[43] On the eve of the Entente attack General von Scholtz wrote, "Even if we cannot attack anymore, we can still defend ourselves diligently."[44] Given the difficulties in the Bulgarian army and the remoteness of any aid from Germany, von Scholtz's certainty about Dobro Pole is difficult to understand. This confidence in the fighting abilities of his forces was not necessarily shared by his Bulgarian allies. They had witnessed throughout the summer the deterioration of the morale of their troops, and the erosion of German support in manpower and material.

On 13 September the Serbian Command informed its soldiers, "All officers and men must bear in mind, the success of the entire offensive depends upon rapid penetration. . . . It is necessary to violently penetrate, without resting to the final limits possible of human and equine ability."[45] This statement encompassed the main concept of the offensive, a quick thrust through the enemy lines and a rapid drive to the rear as far as possible. The Entente offensive began at 0700 hrs on 14 September with heavy artillery shelling of the Bulgarian positions. A Bulgarian observer described the effect of the fire: "The earth in the positions was completely destroyed or collapsed by the concentrated fire. The greater part of the trenches disappeared. In their place appeared huge pits, in which it was impossible to move around."[46] The initial artillery fire also resulted in heavy Bulgarian casualties. Throughout the day, Entente aircraft, which had command of the skies, bombed and strafed the Bulgarian positions. Probing attacks of the Dobro Pole positions began in the evening, but were deflected by heavy Bulgarian machine-gun fire and the use of hand grenades. Alert to the impending danger, General von Scholtz summoned reserves.[47]

French and Serbian infantry attacks began at 0530 hrs the next morning at Dobro Pole against the Bulgarian 2nd Thracian Division. Troops from the Serbian Second Army, including the Šumdija Division, attacked the easternmost defensive positions at Veternik. The French Senegalese from the 17th French Colonial Division attacked west of Veternik, west of them the Yugoslav Division; and the French 122nd Division attacked between Dobro Pole and Sokol. This attack represented the main thrust of the Entente attack.

Insufficient number of guns and quantities of shells limited the ability of the Bulgarians to disrupt the attack with artillery fire. After Entente attackers reached within 500 meters of the Bulgarian trenches, they were effectively safe from Bulgarian artillery.[48] The Bulgarian artillerists lacked the ability to raise their trajectory in order to fire close in their own positions. This meant that once the attacking soldiers had neared the initial Bulgarian positions, they were relatively safe from artillery fire. Despite heavy Bulgarian machine-gun fire and Bulgarian infantry counterattacks, French, French Colonial, and Serbian troops all succeeded early that day in taking Bulgarian positions. French troops from the 122nd Division took the Pyramid, the high point of the Dobro Pole ridge, by 0800 hrs, using flamethrowers to destroy Bulgarian machine-gun nests. This was a critical loss for the Bulgarians early in the battle, because this position gave the French visual control of the battlefield. The seizure of the Pyramid was the first important Entente success in the battle of Dobro Pole.

Around 1330 hrs, the French 17th Colonial Division found its progress thwarted by strong Bulgarian resistance between Veternik and Dobro Pole. General Stepanović sent the Šumadija Division to its assistance.[49] By late afternoon the French and Serbian soldiers had overcome Bulgarian resistance there. The determination of the Bulgarians during the initial phase of the battle demonstrated that their morale problems had not yet undermined their will to fight. Meanwhile, the Serbian First Army attacked and took the Sokol position southwest of Dobro Pole. During the same time at Veternik, the Serbian Second Army captured three hundred Bulgarian soldiers, four howitzers, and two field guns early in the morning of 15 September.[50] French airplanes again attacked the Bulgarian positions with machine-gun fire and bombs that afternoon. The Bulgarians succeeded in bringing down one of them.[51] This small victory was not sufficient to forestall the Entente success the first day.

When the Entente attacks began, the commander of the Bulgarian army, the energetic General Zhekov, was not on hand to deal with the crisis. He had left Bulgaria on 8 September to seek treatment in Vienna for mastoiditis.[52] His deputy commander in chief, General Georgi Todorov, lacked his superior's acumen. Despite clear evidence that an Entente attack was to begin at Dobro Pole in the middle of September, General Todorov too was absent from his headquarters on the 15th. He was in Sofia that day to attend a banquet organized for the visiting King Frederick Augustus III of Saxony. Moreover, 250 of the best soldiers of the 10th regiment of the 2nd Thracian Division went from the front for a parade in honor of the Saxon king.[53] These soldiers might have enabled the 10th Regiment, which held the important Sokol positions on the west approaches to Dobro Pole, to maintain a stronger resistance against the Entente attack. At the very least, General Todorov seems not to have been alert to the danger that most Bulgarians had been anticipating for some time.

Some Entente accounts of the opening battle claim that initial attacks achieved surprise and that the Bulgarians soon ran away.[54] This was not the case. The Bulgarians undertook at least five counterattacks. Evidence of a morale crisis is difficult to find in the performance of the Bulgarian troops in the first day of fighting. Nevertheless, by the afternoon of the 15th, the French troops and the Serbian Drina Division had gained local superiority on the western flank at the Sokol positions. On the eastern flank, the Veternik positions held out against an attack by the Serbian Šumadjia Division until about 1300 on 15 September. The loss of the two flanking ridges made continued resistance at Dobro Pole problematic. That first day the Bulgarians lost 3,000 prisoners and 50 artillery pieces, which were difficult to move in the mountainous terrain. At the same time, the Serbs lost 33 officers and 757 men, while the French Colonial troops lost 30 officers and 1,200 men.[55] These heavy losses on both sides during the first day of the fighting at Dobro Pole testify to its intensity. Even so, it is impossible to know how many of those Bulgarian prisoners willingly surrendered. By the end of the first day of fighting, mainly French, French Colonial, and Serbian troops had seized the three main Bulgarian positions, Sokol, Dobro Pole, and Veternik. In taking these locations, the French and Serbian troops had breached the Bulgarian primary lines of defense. By the evening of that first day, after heavy fighting, on the orders of General von Scholtz the Bulgarians fell back to their secondary positions. They had begun to retreat to the north from their frontline positions off of the Dobro Pole ridge between the Cherna and the Vardar Rivers.

The morning of 16 September, the Bulgarian secondary defensive lines began to come under attack. Entente artillery had continued to fire through the night on these positions. The Danube and Drina Divisions of the Serbian First Army also attacked Bulgarian positions west of Sokol beginning at 0530 hours. By 1230 they had pulled even with the Yugoslav Division.[56] At this time, General von Scholtz ordered General von Reuter, the commander of the amalgamated Bulgarian and German reserve force in Palikura, to the breakthrough. A German reserve battalion from Prilep rushed to Kozyak, the next ridge behind Dobro Pole and the location of secondary defensive positions, to help on 16 September. This effort was to no avail. Another reserve unit, the 49th Regiment, ordered to reinforce the Bulgarian 3rd Balkan Division, only arrived on 19 September.[57] Bulgarian casualties continued to mount. One reason for their heavy losses was their traditional tactic of massing troops in a single line.[58] Also, the Bulgarians continued to counterattack with bayonet charges, which though frightening to the enemy, inevitably cause high casualties among the attackers. By the early evening of 16 September, the Bulgarian positions on Kozyak, a ridge of about 1,850 meters behind Dobro Pole, had also fallen. This loss was fatal to the secondary defensive positions.[59] An initial breach of 11 kilometers on the first day of the attack widened to 25 kilometers by the end of the second day. Had sufficient reserves been nearby, the gap might have been sealed at this point.[60] The Bulgarian army lacked reserves to cover the front. The Germans were not present in sufficient numbers to cover the Macedonian Front.

The situation became worse when General Rusev ordered the withdrawal of the battered Bulgarian 2nd Thracian Division from the Kozyak positions on the evening of the 16th without informing the units to his right and left. He did this evidently to make the difficult crossing of the Cherna River.[61] This enabled the 2nd Thracian Division to gain better access to munitions and other supplies. Meanwhile, because of the withdrawal of the 2nd Thracian Division, the 3rd Balkan Division retreated north retreated toward the Vardar. This opened up the gap between the two Bulgarian divisions that the Serbs were quick to exploit.[62] There were no reinforcements to rescue the situation for the Bulgarians.

The initial German report on 17 September was dire. It stated that after a retreat of 10 kilometers over a 30 kilometer wide, the front was "lost."[63] Within two days of the initial attack, the retreat of the Eleventh Army had become a rout. Another ominous development occurred on 17 September. Some soldiers in the 2nd Division began to refuse orders, and sol-

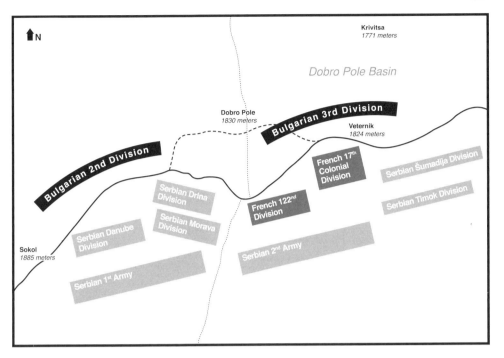

**Dobro Pole 1918**

diers drifted off to the rear without authorization. After the miserable rations, the threadbare uniforms, and the uncertainties about the war, the French and Serbian breakthrough at Dobro Pole was the final ordeal for many Bulgarian soldiers. General von Reuter, moving toward the broken line with his reinforcements, drew his pistol on some of these soldiers in an attempt to impose order. In response, he received threats of bayonets and hand grenades.[64] Given the animosity that had developed toward the Germans in the Bulgarian ranks, General von Reuter was fortunate to escape unscathed from his encounter with mutinous Bulgarian soldiers. North of Kozyak in the third line of fighting, German units held out until the early morning of 17 September. They then retreated under Serbian pressure.

By 18 September, the Entente forces were beginning to understand the extent of their success. They had completely eliminated all enemy resistance from Sokol to Veternik and had taken the secondary positions at Kozyak. A directive of the Serbian command noted on 18 September, "[I]t is necessary now that communications in the Vardar valley be cut;

the success of this maneuver lies in the rapidity of the operation, which at the same time results in continued and progressive energetic attacks."[65] The Entente now had in sight the realization of wider goals.

Heavy fighting developed on 18 September between the advancing Serbian Second Army and the retreating Bulgarian 3rd Balkan Division around the village of Mrezhechko, east of the Cherna and north of Dobro Pole. General Burmov, the Bulgarian chief of staff, identified this location as the "decisive point" in the fighting, but reported that all available reserves were committed.[66] There were no additional Central Powers forces at hand for Mrezhechko. Burmov recommended that the Bulgarian 1st Sofia Division return from the area of Lake Ohrid to participate in the battle. The difficulty of the terrain and the lack of decent roads were certain to delay the arrival of any reinforcements from Albania.

Retreat proved difficult all along the Bulgarian lines. The Bulgarian positions were often on extended ridge lines. Having established these positions in the aftermath of the fighting in the fall of 1916, the Bulgarians in 1918 lacked the means to evacuate them. They did not have the tractors to draw their heavy guns back. Many guns had to be abandoned. Nor did the Bulgarians have the vehicles to move the troops quickly either toward the fighting or away from it.[67] Their ability to rush their limited reinforcements to the front and to retreat suffered. In an effort to stabilize the failing 2nd Thracian Division, Major General Asen Nikolov replaced General Rusev as commander on 18 September. By this time the situation in the 2nd Thracian Division was beyond the ability of one general officer to counteract.

Nevertheless, even after the French and Serbian breakthrough at Dobro Pole, the Bulgarians were still able to achieve some success elsewhere. They won a defensive victory at Doiran, a heavily fortified elevated position immediately west of the ruined village and the lake both named Doiran, about 5–6 kilometers east of the Vardar River. Doiran had been the scene of fighting between British and Bulgarian soldiers on two major occasions earlier in the campaign, in the autumn of 1915 and again in the spring of 1917. Generally the Bulgarians had prevailed in these engagements. As recently as April 1918, the Bulgarians had beaten back a British attempt to storm their positions. These Bulgarian positions were basically similar to those constructed all along the Macedonian Front. They consisted of a primary position of two lines, prepared artillery positions, and a secondary position, all at a depth of about 4 kilometers. In front of the high point of Grand Couronné was a fortified position the British called "the Devil's Eye." From the Grand Couronné, the Bulgarians could observe the entire region over to Lake Doiran. The echelon defensive lines there were more extensive than in many other locations, and included wire netting, ditches, and "wolf pits."[68] The Bulgarians had worked in the summer to strengthen these fortifications. They even formed an antitank platoon with two 53mm guns in anticipation of a British armor attack.[69] Some sources identified the defensive positions at Doiran as the best fortified in the First Army.[70] Against a more numerous enemy that included four British divisions and the Greek Seres Division, which incorporated a regiment of French Zouaves, and the Crete Division, the Bulgarian 9th Pleven Division fielded 17 infantry battalions, 183 machine guns, 136 artillery pieces, 28 light and 14 medium mortars, 1½ cavalry squadron, 1 pioneer battalion, a balloon section, and 11 small and 6 medium searchlights.[71] British sources claimed that the defenders outnumbered the attacking force at Doiran because of the ravages of influenza in the British ranks.[72] If this was true, it indicates an incomprehensible disregard for the abilities of the same Bulgarian troops who had thus far stopped two British offensives at Doiran. As at Dobro Pole, the Bulgarians were able to observe the preparations for the attack from the ground and from the air. These had started a month before the actual assault.

The British and Greek attack was a part of the general offensive already underway at Dobro Pole. The Entente forces had reason for confidence. On 16 September, the British 66th Brigade headquarters' orders stated, "Owing to the very favourable situation which obtains on the Western and other battle fronts, the disturbed political situation in Bulgaria and the low morale of her troops, success in this attack may be looked for with the greatest confidence."[73] The Doiran attack began that same day, with heavy artillery fire and for the first time on the Macedonian Front, some gas shells. Around 0508 hrs on 18 September, as the the French and Serbs poured into the breach in Bulgarian lines to the west at Dobro Pole, the combined British, French, and Greek Entente force attacked at Doiran. Airplanes using bombs and machine guns supported the attack. At first the attack seemed to make some progress, breaking through the first-line Bulgarian defenses.

Nevertheless, the Bulgarians held. Despite all their privations of the previous year, their morale remained intact. Bulgarian counterattacks, impossible at Yerbichna the previous May because of poor material and morale, began almost immediately, and soon six prisoners were in Bulgarian hands.[74] Bulgarian artillery, which included a German battery, was effective at Doiran. The Bulgarian guns responded to the initial British use of gas shells with gas shells of their own. This was the first major use of gas on the Macedonian Front. The British and Greek troops failed to advance in the face of heavy Bulgarian artillery and small arms fire. Those few Entente soldiers who reached the Bulgarian lines were killed.

A mixed British and Greek force, including the Cretan Division, made a supplementary attack northeast of Lake Doiran against Bulgarian secondary defensive positions on the morning of 18 September in an attempt to outflank the main Bulgarian positions at Doiran. This attack forced the British and Greek force to cross a low open area in front of the elevated Bulgarian defenders. Bulgarian artillery set the dry grass in the open area on fire. This caused heavy casualties and helped to foil the attack.[75] Bulgarian bayonet counterattacks soon restored some outer positions lost in the initial attacks. After two days of intense fighting, the British and Greeks failed to make any progress against the determined defenders.

The British and Greek attacks on both fronts dwindled the afternoon of 19 September. One Bulgarian defender later wrote that after this Bulgarian victory, "The morale of the troops at that moment was ten times the number of their forces."[76] The Bulgarians lost 494 killed and 1,208 wounded in the defense of Doiran, while the Entente lost 11,673 dead and 500 prisoners.[77] After the victory, General Vladimir Vasov, who had directed the 9th Pleven Infantry Division's successful defense of the same positions against a British attack in April 1917, stated, "Today all Bulgaria will burst with pride and will retain in their memories the sons and heroes of the 9th Artillery brigade, the heroes from Dorostol, Svishtov, Troyan and Pleven from the 57th and 58th regiments and every other attached unit, who with unimaginable self sacrifice shed their blood in order to preserve their honor and their future."[78] The mention of "honor" in this message implies that General Vasov realized that events were not proceeding well for the Bulgarian army elsewhere on the front.

Once again at Doiran, the Bulgarians had repulsed an Entente attack. This success indicated that even at this late date, and despite low morale, Bulgarian soldiers were still capable of a sustained military effort. The defensive success against units of the Greek army was particularly satisfying. It made up to some degree for the failure against Greek soldiers the previous summer at Yerbichna. It also recalled the defensive victory the Bulgarian army achieved against invading Greeks at Kresna Gorge during the 2nd Balkan War in 1913. Elsewhere Bulgarian forces in western Macedonia did not come under heavy attack and maintained their positions.

The Doiran success raised the question as to why the Bulgarians stopped the British and Greeks but collapsed in front of the French and Serbs. The Bulgarian units involved in both battles had access to the same supplies and were led by officers of about the same quality. They both faced traditional Balkan enemies. One factor was the quality of the defensive works. Another factor was General Vasov himself. He had commanded the 9th Pleven Division since March 1917, and had led it in the victory at Doiran in April of that year. He had taken care to maintain good relations with his subordinates and to demonstrate his concern for their well-being. By contrast, General Rusev, who led the 2nd Thracian Division at Dobro Pole, had been in command only since July. Finally, all the Bulgarian commanders and their subordinates in the 9th Pleven Division received the same training in fighting conditions.[79] This helped to establish a bond among the soldiers. The German commander and staff of the Eleventh Army cannot have inspired great confidence in the Bulgarian soldiers, given the variety of problems that had arisen between the two allies over the course of the war. Both the attackers and defenders suffered from the influenza epidemic, so the importance of this factor remains unclear.

Despite this success, Bulgarian activity at Doiran ceased on 20 September, when the collapse of the center of the lines forced the 9th Pleven Division to join in the retreat to avoid being cut off by the oncoming Entente forces. In contrast to the debacle at Dobro Pole, the Bulgarians were able to withdraw much of their heavy artillery successfully from their positions at Doiran. As they slowly retreated they met disaster. Entente airplanes harassed the retreating Bulgarians with machine-gun fire and bombs, especially at the narrow Kresna and Rupel defiles. They had a powerful effect on the already stressed Bulgarian soldiers.[80] With these attacks, the British were able to exact a measure of satisfaction for their failures at Doiran. The British and Greek attack did represent one important success for the Entente. It prevented the Bulgarians from transferring units from Doiran to plug the gap at Dobro Pole.[81] Some units of the Bulgarian 9th Pleven Division might have been able to rally their comrades in the 2nd Thracian and 3rd Balkan Divisions to withstand the Entente attacks. At the same time, the Bulgarian success at Doiran prevented British and Greek units from accomplishing their mission. Had the Entente forces succeeded at Doiran, they could have inflicted an even greater catastrophe on the Bulgarian Army. By holding on at Doiran, the 9th Pleven Division enabled the remaining elements of the 2nd and 3rd Divisions to successfully retreat.

At Dobro Pole, the Entente achieved complete victory with a single successful operation in a short period of time. Complete breakthrough the Bulgarian positions had taken only four days, from initial artillery barrage to collapse and retreat of the Bulgarian army. At no other time and on no other front did this occur in the First World War. The lack of food and military equipment and the demoralization of the Bulgarian army, the withdrawal of most German units, and the increasing concerns of the Sofia government for the viability of its allies made the Macedonian Front the most dangerous location anywhere for the Central Powers. Through the summer of 1918 the Germans advanced on the Western Front. The fighting in distant Palestine, though going badly for the Ottomans, held little threat for the Ottoman government in Constantinople. At the same time Ottoman forces continued to advance in the Caucasus. The Austro-Hungarians were in poor material condition, but still occupied strong defensive positions in the Alps.[82] The Central Powers had already won the war in the east against Russia and Romania.

The Entente attributed their success to surprise and to the selection of Dobro Pole as the best location for a frontal assault.[83] They also had a well-motivated and well-supplied force. Despite the complexity of its forces, the multinational Entente Army functioned together reasonably well. The Greeks and Serbs were eager to inflict defeat on their Bulgarian adversaries.

There were many reasons for the Bulgarian defeat. They lacked vehicles for withdrawal. They lacked sufficient reserves to plug the gap opened at

Dobro Pole. The Bulgarian army was in the throes of a morale crisis due to the lack of material resources, especially food, and the lack of confidence in Bulgaria's allies. Bulgaria's allies could offer little real support.

The demoralization of the Bulgarian army, the distraction of the Germans on the Western Front, the Austrians' search for peace, and the threat from the Ottomans almost seem to impose a sense of inevitability in the Bulgarian collapse at Dobro Pole. Yet even in these extreme conditions, the same Bulgarian army that collapsed at Dobro Pole mounted a successful defense at Doiran. Only the withdrawal of Bulgarian units to the west in disarray forced an end to this effort. The Bulgarians might still have mounted a successful defense in any of a number of rugged locations in Macedonia but for the collapse of morale in the center of the lines. While Entente military strength was superior to that of the Bulgarians, the years of bad food, shoddy material, and uncertain relations with their allies proved to be as effective weapons as Serbian infantry and French artillery in the defeat of September 1918.

# COLLAPSE

While the fighting raged at Doiran, to the west French and Serbian forces continued to advance through the gap in the Bulgarian lines opened at Dobro Pole. The Serbian First Army captured bridges over the Cherna at Rasim Bey and established positions on the other side of the river on 18 September. This placed the Serbian First Army in position to threaten the eastern flank of German Eleventh Army and its headquarters in Prilep. In the east, a French and Greek force captured the Dzena ridge, which dominated the eastern side of the bulge the Entente breakthrough had forced in the Bulgarian lines.[1] The efforts of General von Reuter's replacement division to plug the gap created by the collapse of the 2nd Thracian Division and to hold the line failed. On 18 September, General Todorov ordered the 3rd Balkan Division to new positions southwest of the Vardar River.[2] This retreat severed the 3rd Balkan Division from its direct connection with the 2nd Thracian Division and from the rest of the Eleventh Army. Meanwhile the Serbian Second Army raced for Gradsko, on the Salonika-Skopie railroad and just above where the Cherna flows into the Vardar. Because of its location astride the lines of communication, the control of Gradsko was critical for both sides. For the Bulgarians and Germans, Gradsko was vital for continued connection between the First and Eleventh Armies. For the Entente, control of Gradsko would provide their forces with access to the Vardar Valley and the railroad that could accelerate their progress toward Skopie and points further north.

Initial reports reaching Sofia about the situation at the front were ominous. Seeking additional information, the Ministerial Council sent a delegation on 19 September to Bulgarian Army Headquarters in Kyustendil to investigate the extent of the apparent disaster. General Burmov reported to them that the situation was "very difficult" but "fixable."[3] He thought that additional Austro-Hungarian and German help would be necessary for the stabilization of the front. This was the Bulgarian government's first indication that the Bulgarian army had suffered a serious reverse.

After the Entente attacks began at Dobro Pole, the Bulgarians turned to their allies for assistance. The Germans had little help to spare. To General Todorov's request on 18 September for ten German divisions, General von Hindenburg responded, "As your Excellency knows, Germany is in the most difficult fight on the Western Front. All strength must be directed there. It must be assumed, that the decisive act of the Great War will occur here."[4] Von Hindenburg could offer the Bulgarians only the undermanned 217th Infantry Division, then in Sebastopol in the distant Crimea. He advised the Bulgarians that they must endeavor not to lose the initiative and that they might have to retreat. Von Hindenburg's advice probably came from experience. The Germans themselves were already retreating on the Western Front. They had few resources that they could direct to the Macedonian Front. They also tended to view the Bulgarian call for help with some condescension. After the war, Ludendorff wrote that the Bulgarians ought to have offered the Germans help in the west, and not demanded aid from them.[5] Given Bulgaria's lack of manpower and material resources, this was out of the question.

Meanwhile the Bulgarian command considered its options. It planned a counterattack based on the success at Doiran against the British and Greek attack. In a meeting with General von Scholtz's staff, together with General von Steuben, commander of the Eleventh Army, and General Reuter, commander of an amalgamated Bulgarian German division in which several units were thrown together, in the headquarters of the German Eleventh Army in Prilep on 18 September, General Todorov proposed an attack by some units of the Bulgarian First and Second Armies on the eastern right flank of the Entente offensive. This attack on the Serbian flank offered some chance of success.[6] A strong Bulgarian thrust might have cut the Serbian advance off and surrounded it. The Bulgarian General Staff did not understand that the breach at Dobro Pole was not the cause of the general unrest in the army, but the consequence of it.[7] The success of any such counterattack was problematic.

Perhaps the Germans understood that the Bulgarian Army was a broken instrument. In any event they preferred to allow supply problems and the rugged terrain to weaken the Entente advance.[8] When advancing units slowed down due to the difficult logistical and command conditions imposed by having to surmount ridges with bad roads or no roads at all, counterattack from the flanks could destroy the Entente advance. The German plan did have some advantages. The French and Serbian troops were advancing into a pocket that could be pinched off and crushed between the German Eleventh Army in the west and the Bulgarian First Army in the east. This was basically the same strategy the Bulgarians proposed. The Germans preferred that the Entente advance further before undertaking the counterattack. The Bulgarians had succeeded with a similar counterattack against the Greek army at Kresna Gorge in July 1913 during the final days of the Second Balkan War. General Todorov agreed to the German plan without insisting on his own. His swift acquiescence to the German plan indicated a lack of confidence in the Bulgarian army at this critical point. Having been acting commander in chief for only two weeks, General Todorov must have been uncertain about his own responsibilities and capabilities. Some Bulgarians regarded the order to withdraw and not counterattack after the successful defense at Doiran as a fatal mistake.[9] This is probably wishful thinking. The eastern units of the Eleventh Army, especially the 2nd Thracian Division, were already disintegrating by this time. The other formations, greatly outnumbered by the Entente, were unlikely to enjoy offensive success.

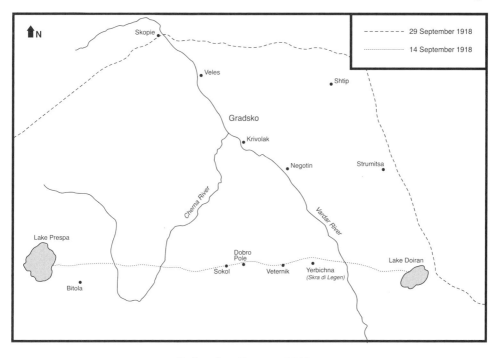

**Bulgarian Retreat 1918**

General Todorov must have had reservations about the German plan. The next day he met with General von Scholtz in Skopie and again proposed the the western flank of the Bulgarian army be reinforced to prevent further Entente advance, and that an attack be launched from the west along a line from Skopie to Veles and from the east at Demirkrapia against the two flanks of the Entente advance.[10] Once again the Germans refused to consider the Bulgarian plan. The Germans had no confidence that the Bulgarians could manage such a complicated operation, especially since by this time disciplinary disarray had erupted in at least two Bulgarian divisions.

The gap in the Bulgarian lines allowed the Serbs to cross the Cherna River on 20 September. At this point Major General Asen Nikolov replaced General Rusev as commander of the failing 2nd Thracian Division. He had to continue the retreat already in progress. A mixed Bulgarian and German force finally arrived to fight on Kozyak. There were no established defensive positions further back. By this time the immediately available reserves were exhausted.

As the Entente offensive continued, the Bulgarian situation deteriorated. On 20 September Crown Prince Boris, who had gone to the front to "save everything that could be saved," reported to his father, Tsar Ferdinand, from the front that the condition of the army was "more serious than I could have believed" and that "given the Bulgarian mentality, I believe that retreat will mean disintegration."[11] Crown Prince Boris meant that in the past on the offensive the Bulgarian army had been a formidable foe, but now hungry, exhausted, and angry, and under heavy attack, it could not maintain defensive positions. Boris drove from unit to unit, sometimes at the wheel himself, in an effort to rally the defeated Bulgarian soldiers. His efforts to stop the Bulgarian retreat and stem the collapse of morale were brave, but like those of General von Reuter, fruitless. That same day, Tsar Ferdinand telegraphed Habsburg Emperor Karl personally to ask his assistance in obtaining German help. "Without quick help we cannot avoid a catastrophe, whose consequences for our collective war would be fatal."[12] He also approached Kaiser Wilhelm: "Immediate help is required, because the connection between Doiran and Niš at Krivolak is in great danger and this threatens the entire front. Without immediate help a catastrophe, whose consequences would be fatal for our common interests, cannot be averted."[13]

The Bulgarian tsar had often in the past displayed a tendency to become overexcited by threats of danger. This tendency had become more pronounced during Bulgaria's defeat in the Second Balkan War in 1913. This time events justified his disconcertion.

On 20 September General Todorov ordered the First Army, just after its victory at Doiran, to retreat.[14] It moved northeasterly in the direction of Strumitsa. Prime Minister Aleksandŭr Malinov sent a government delegation, including finance minister Andrei Lyapchev and General Sava Savov, to army headquarters in Kyustendil to investigate the situation at the front. It reported back to Sofia on 21 September, "A great part of our army has demobilized, and in the rest a determination to retreat in difficult circumstances has set in."[15] The government only now began to comprehend the extent of the military problem. Clearly the Bulgarian army staff failed to deal effectively with the situation.[16] The staff officers were unable to grasp the extent of the collapse in the center. Nor were they able to formulate an effective plan of action.

By 21 September, all opportunity for the counterattack was lost as Entente forces advanced on both flanks. By this time, the Serbs had sustained losses of 680 dead, 3,206 wounded, and 130 missing.[17] Also Entente forces had captured around 5,000 Bulgarians.[18] This somewhat low number of prisoners indicates that the war-weary Bulgarian army was not surrendering in large numbers even in defeat. Many had joined the mobs of disaffected soldiers returning to Bulgaria intending to seek some recourse for their suffering.

On 21 September in Veles, General Todorov again met with the commander of the German Eleventh Army, General von Steuben. The German general informed him that it would be impossible to organize a reserve force at Veles.[19] This meant in effect that the German strategy had failed. The Bulgarians and their German allies did not have necessary forces to stop the Entente advance with the available forces. That same day, the Germans attempted to establish a blocking force between Gradsko and Krivolak, further down the Vardar, with a variety of mainly German and some Bulgarian units under the command of General Dieterich. Tsar Ferdinand visited Gradsko the same day. There he demonstrated some of the same low morale that was afflicting many of his soldiers. His demeanor suggested that he had lost hope that the situation could be saved.[20] The Bulgarian tsar was never one to maintain a cool head in the face of adversity. Nevertheless, he evidently understood that the forces available to the Central Alliance at this point had little chance of holding off the Entente advance.

Meanwhile, the situation in Macedonia continued to worsen for the Central Powers. On 22 September, the Italian 35th Division, in the Cherna Bend northeast of Bitola, began to undertake an attack in support of the ongoing Entente offensive.[21] The Bulgarian defenses on the fortified ridge termed "Hill 1050" had stymied the Italians for over a year. The defeat at Dobro Pole forced the Bulgarian to withdrawal. The Italians then joined in the Entente advance against the retreating Bulgarians.

Some Bulgarian officers continued to hope for the best. On 23 September, General Zhekov, from his sickbed in Vienna, advised Tsar Ferdinand that Bulgaria must fight on as long as possible: "I still retain the hope, that if the Germans understand that without sensible effective support Bulgaria will not be in a position to continue the war, the German High Command either will give us enough soldiers to help, in spite of the overwhelming stubbornness of Ludendorff, or then we will be free to pursue our own interests."[22] Even the pro-German Zhekov recognized that the Germans' failure to help freed Bulgaria from alliance commitments. Realistically, he foresaw a change in Bulgarian policy brought about by military defeat.

That same day General Burmov still expected that massive Austro-Hungarian and German assistance could rescue the situation. In a report to the Bulgarian Foreign Ministry, he compared Bulgaria's condition to that of Italy the previous autumn during the Caporetto disaster. Just as Italy's allies saved her, so today, "Bulgaria can be saved only on the same basis."[23] General Burmov proposed that a Bulgarian counterattack on the western flank of the Entente advance could develop from the area of Skopie.[24] By this time, however, the Bulgarians were beginning to understand that Austro-Hungarian and German help could not arrive in time to stabilize the situation. The Bulgarian army was in retreat on both flanks in order not to be cut off by the breach in the middle of the Bulgarian lines. In the west, the 1st Sofia Division of the Bulgarian First Army, the unit General Burmov had in mind for his proposed counterattack, held out between Struga and Ohrid against a French attacks, but finally had to join the retreat to avoid being cut off by the Entente advance and stranded in western Macedonia. Bulgarian and German forces abandoned Prilep and Ohrid.

The mixed Bulgarian-German force evacuated Gradsko and Krivolak on 24 September, three days after Tsar Ferdinand's visit. The loss of Gradsko broke the line of communication between the German Eleventh and the Bulgarian First Armies. This meant that the gap in the Central Powers line first established at Dobro Pole had widened considerably. Now it would be almost impossible to bridge. The Bulgarian First Army evacuated Shtip on the 25th. A Serbian cavalry unit entered it the same day. Once they had gained access to the roads, the Serbs used British and French trucks to drive into Kochana.[25] The Entente forces demonstrated throughout the campaign a much greater mobility than the Bulgarians and Germans. They had far more vehicles than the Central Powers allies. Buoyed by their success in the initial breakthrough, they also gained momentum of morale against their increasingly demoralized enemies. A Serbian High Command report explained the situation: "Our troops enthusiastically rush to overcome all obstacles."[26] As Bulgarian morale deteriorated, Serbian morale soared.

The Austrians at last offered some help. The Austro-Hungarian military attaché in Sofia, Major Kuenzl, reported on 23 September that the Austrians would send two infantry divisions, the 9th from Italy, considered to be "very good," and the 30th from Ukraine, to arrive in Skopie on 27 or 28 September.[27] The first three Austrian battalions arrived there only on 27 September. About this same time, Kaiser Wilhelm telegraphed Tsar Ferdinand to assure him that the Germans were doing everything possible to help the Macedonian Front, including sending the German unit from Sebastopol. He unhelpfully suggested that the Bulgarians had been precipitant in their retreat.[28] Undoubtedly the difficulties the Germans were experiencing on the Western Front undercut any sympathy they might have had for the Bulgarians on the Macedonian Front. The German 217th Division from Crimea and the Alpine Corps from the Western Front began to arrive in Macedonia on 25 September.

At first Prime Minister Malinov failed to understand the peril of the Bulgarian position. He focused much of his time and effort on the Dobrudzha issue. Acquisition of this territory was clearly an important issue for the government. To the great annoyance of the Germans, the Bulgarians had begun to draft Bulgarian inhabitants of all Dobrudzha for military service.[29] Malinov did acknowledge on 17 September that events on the Macedonian Front had "taken an unfortunate turn."[30] Nevertheless, even as the Bulgarian army was in retreat, Malinov continued to insist on Bulgarian claims to Dobrudzha. On 22 September, he emphasized to General Nikifor Nikiforov, the Bulgarian minister in Berlin, that Bulgarian claims to all of Dobrudzha must still prevail: "You will understand that any other decision in the Dobrudzha question, with our army in retreat, is impossible."[31] Austria-Hungary, Germany, and the Ottoman Empire finally agreed to Bulgarian claims to Dobrudzha, including north Dobrudzha, on 24 September.[32] Bulgaria could have all of Dobrudzha. The Bulgarians were obligated by the agreement, however, to reach an accommodation with the Ottomans in Thrace by the cession of the Maritsa valley as far as the Aegean. At this late date, the German acceptance of Bulgarian rule in all Dobrudzha was likely a ploy to keep Bulgaria in the war. Events on the Macedonian Front prevented the Sofia government from the consideration of this agreement.

The retreat of the Bulgarian First Army forced the German Eleventh Army, already in difficulty because of the collapse of the 2nd Thracian and 3rd Balkan Divisions, to continue its retreat to the north. The Entente advance continued relentlessly. On 23 September, a French unit entered Prilep. A bulletin from Serbian Headquarters on 24 September stated: "Our supply situation becomes more difficult every day, so it is necessary to liberate the Bitola-Prilep road or the Vardar valley, otherwise our advance will probably slow down."[33] As the Entente forces advanced, they captured much material the Bulgarians and Germans could not take with them as they retreated. At Krivolak, on the Vardar River, and on the Salonika–Skopie railroad, they took locomotives, railcars, guns, and two new German airplanes.[34] This demonstrated the haste with which the Bulgarians and Germans evacuated Krivolak. That same day, General von Scholtz moved his headquarters out of Skopie and Macedonia north to Leskovacs on the Morava River in Serbia proper.

Meanwhile the deterioration of discipline in the Bulgarian army worsened. On 24 September, rebellious Bulgarian soldiers seized control of Kyustendil, the location of Bulgarian General Headquarters, about 40 miles southwest of Sofia. Some soldiers even fired on the headquarters. They seemed to be leaderless, and had only a vague sense of purpose. Adding to the sense of disarray was the extreme heat. That day the temperature reached 60 degrees Celsius.[35] A pamphlet from the time gives a sense of the soldiers' frustrations:

> After such sacrifices in men and material we are defeated. For three years we have defended our goals against a more numerous enemy, we have endured misery and misfortune, we have defended our borders naked, barefoot and hungry, we have fought heroically for foreign interests, and pledged that we would fight for the national ideal, for national interest and national unity because we were misled by the newspapers and by everything.[36]

Two days later, as many as 30,000 insurgents moved into Radomir and Gornya Dzumaya in southwestern Bulgaria.[37] The Bulgarian soldiers were determined to obtain some measure of satisfaction from those Bulgarian

military and government officials they deemed responsible for their condition.

The Bulgarian army had few reserves to draw upon to suppress the
soldiers' rebellion. Undoubtedly many Bulgarian soldiers still under discipline likely sympathized with the frustrations of the rebels. If German
soldiers, whose presence was a cause of some of the Bulgarian discontent,
were used to quell the rebellion, they were likely to cause even greater unrest. In any event, General von Reuter, with pistol drawn, had had little success in calming the mutineers back on 17 September.

Despite the Entente advance and the discipline problems within the
Bulgarian ranks, the ever-optimistic General Burmov still hoped on 24 September that the arrival of German and Austrian troops might help stabilize the front and create better conditions in which to ask for an armistice.
Nevertheless, even he understood that Bulgaria's continued participation
in the war was over. Like most of the Bulgarian command, Burmov was
looking for favorable terms by which Bulgaria could leave the war. By the
next day, both General Stefan Nerezov, the First Army commander, and
General Ivan Lukov, the Second Army commander, were urging the government to conclude an armistice.[38] Indiscipline in the army was also increasing. The German minister in Sofia reported on 24 September that
consideration of a separate peace had not started.[39] Clearly he misjudged
Bulgarian military and political opinion.

After the initial Entente breakthrough, even some Bulgarian generals
were demoralized. The commander of the Bulgarian Second Army, General Ivan Lukov, especially seems to have been overwhelmed by the same
poor morale that afflicted the 2nd Thracian and 3rd Balkan Divisions and
other formations. General Lukov never had been a strong advocate for the
Bulgarian alliance with the Central Powers.[40] During the initial phase of
the Entente offensive, his Second Army, holding the Macedonian Front east
of Lake Doiran, did not come under direct Entente attack. Nevertheless,
it failed to move to the southwest in support of the First Army. When on
19 September one of his division commanders asked for orders to advance
against the British and Greeks, Lukov responded, "Don't be in a hurry, because we are anticipating the armistice."[41] Like many Bulgarian soldiers,
he clearly had lost his interest in continuing the fight. When General Lukov advised Tsar Ferdinand to seek an armistice on 25 September, the tsar

bravely responded that the general should go down fighting with his men.[42] Neither man was likely to seek a heroic end. The tsar's courage did not extend much beyond his advice to General Lukov. He feared that an army of 20,000 "Bolsheviks" was marching on Sofia to free the Agrarian Party leader Aleksandŭr Stamboliski, who had been imprisoned for antiwar activities, and proclaim him president of a republic.[43] In an effort to assuage the mutinous soldiers, the government released Stamboliski from prison on 25 September. The peasant leader, after some hesitation, joined the agitation against the war and the tsar.[44] The collapse of the nationalist expectation of a Greater Bulgaria for the second time in six years increased the appeal of the Agrarian Party's pacifist political program to the mostly peasant Bulgarian soldiers.

The deterioration of the military situation, the indiscipline in the army and uncertainty about the actions of the Central Powers allies caused a Crown Council meeting on 25 September to decide to seek an armistice with the Entente. General Todorov informed the council that the military circumstances were "hopeless."[45] Only then did Minister President Malinov finally recognize that the war and with it Dobrudzha were lost. After the council he reported to the Tsar, "The Crown Council has concluded, with deep regret, that the war is lost and that there is no alternative except to ask for peace. Only this way can we protect our country from ruin and from all those evils which Bulgaria could expect if the enemy crosses its borders."[46] The Bulgarians wanted to keep the likely vengeful Greeks and Serbs off of their territory. For the second time in five years, Bulgaria had lost a war inspired by nationalist expectations.

By the time of the Crown Council of 25 September, most of the Bulgarian military and civilian leadership clearly recognized that the war could not continue. A combination of issues led to this decision. The army had clearly lost the battle of Dobro Pole and as a result had to retreat in Macedonia due to low morale from the lowest ranks right up to high command. Part of the army was in a state of open rebellion. No help was immediately at hand from Austria-Hungary or Germany. This entire process from defense to defeat had taken only ten days since the beginning of the Entente offensive at Dobro Pole.

Even Tsar Ferdinand, despite his bluster two days earlier, recognized that Bulgaria could not remain in the war. He also understood the danger for his personal situation. Shortly after the Ministerial Conference, Ferdinand somewhat histrionically telegraphed Emperor Karl:

> The destruction of my unfortunate army proceeds at a rapid pace. The First Army of Nerezov is melting away. The helpless Second Army is threatened by the superior power of the Greeks and English, and unable to move its artillery because of lack of horses and draft animals. Revolutionary troops, burning and murdering everywhere, are already threatening Sofia. The Malinov Government demands an armistice and an immediate peace from me. I have submitted my abdication to the Ministerial Council. I am still alive but maybe not tomorrow. I think it is better to stay here in order to save, what can be saved.[47]

About this same time, Ferdinand claimed in a telegram to General Zhekov that the government had concluded the armistice without his (the tsar's) agreement.[48] The Tsar typically relied on words rather than deeds in this crisis.

The Entente had defeated Bulgaria on the field of battle, and its forces were poised to invade the country. In this situation there was one dim hope for the Sofia government. This was the position of the United States. Bulgaria and the United States were not at war. They retained diplomatic relations throughout the conflict. The Bulgarian government placed great importance on its good relations with the United States. It hoped that American government would actively assist in the conclusion of an armistice.[49] On 25 September, a Bulgarian delegation headed by the minister of finance, Andrei Lyapchev, and accompanied by the writer and diplomat Simeon Radev, the war-weary Second Army commander General Lukov, and the American consul general, D. I. Murphey, traveled down the valley to Salonika to negotiate Bulgaria's exit from the war with Entente representatives. The fate of Bulgaria rested with their efforts.

The Bulgarians immediately informed their German allies on 25 September of their decision to seek an armistice.[50] While this cannot have been a surprise to the Germans, it nevertheless caused deep consternation at German headquarters. The German Supreme Command considered ordering General von Scholtz to assume dictatorial powers in Sofia to keep Bulgaria in the war.[51] They rejected this idea, however, because they understood that the political situation in the country had deteriorated too far. In any event, the Germans lacked the manpower and resources to impose their will on Bulgaria. If sufficient German and Austrian help arrived soon, however, the Sofia government might be induced to break off the Salonika talks.

A few Bulgarians still hoped that the situation at the front could be restored. Chief among these was the Bulgarian representative at German army headquarters, Major General Petŭr Ganchev, who returned to Sofia during the crisis. Baron Kurt von Lersner, the German Foreign Office liaison at German military headquarters, telegraphed General Ganchev denouncing the "suicidal panic" of the Malinov government and urging the appointment of "an energetic Mihail Savov" to command the Bulgarian forces.[52] General Ganchev evidently attempted to act on this suggestion. He was able to find little interest, however, in a plan to replace the Malinov government with one including Savov that would hold out against the Entente and the mobs of soldiers advancing on Sofia.[53] Ganchev assured the Germans that "the activity of the Malinov government should not be perceived as originating with Tsar Ferdinand and directed against the Central Powers."[54] General Mihail Savov did arrive in Sofia on 26 September, probably on the initiative of Tsar Ferdinand or of General Ganchev. After his arrival, General Savov attempted to secure support from the tsar to form a pro-German government to replace that of Malinov.[55] He found little enthusiasm for this project in the palace. Even the Tsar seemed dubious that General Savov could restore the situation. Probably Ferdinand still mistrusted Savov because of his role in the outbreak of the Second Balkan War.[56]

The situation in Macedonia remained opaque in Germany. As late as 27 September, Tsar Ferdinand received an encouraging telegram from Kaiser Wilhelm: "The German and Austrian troops arriving from all sides will bring necessary help to your army and push back the enemy further."[57] The kaiser evidently was unaware that his ally was seeking an armistice. Wilhelm was evidently even more isolated from the ongoing catastrophe than his Bulgarian counterpart.

The decision by the Bulgarian Ministerial Council to seek an armistice did not mean an immediate end to the fighting. While General Lukov was in Salonika, his Second Army finally became involved in the fighting. A sharp combat developed with the Greek 14th Division on the Struma River. The Bulgarians took some Greeks prisoner and captured two artillery pieces and a number of machine guns.[58] The Bulgarian Second Army was more aggressive than its commanding general. This Bulgarian victory recalled their success against the Greeks at Kresna Gorge at the end of the Second Balkan War in 1913 and against the Greek divisions at Doiran. As with these two previous Bulgarian successes, it had little impact on the outcome of the overall situation. Yet it demonstrated that the factors causing poor morale—bad food, tattered uniforms, unreliable allies—did not prevent the Second Army from fighting.

Meanwhile, fighting continued elsewhere in Macedonia between some Bulgarian and German units and the advancing Entente forces. The Central Powers generally maintained an orderly retreat. The battered remains of the Bulgarian 2nd Thracian Division, which had suffered the initial collapse at Dobro Pole, retreated in discipline to Ovce Pole, north of Veles, due to the "relentless personal actions in the front lines" of its new commander, General Nikolov.[59] By this time the 2nd Thracian Division could do little to impede the enemy. A British infantry unit and Greek cavalry entered Strumitsa the morning of 26 September. This was the first important location within the borders of pre-1915 Bulgaria occupied by the Entente. Despite heavy resistance offered by the Bulgarian 4th Preslav Division, Veles fell during the night of 27 September. French troops entered Ohrid the next day. Fighting continued some places until the 29th. Skopie fell to the French on 29 September despite some resistance from German forces there that included an armored train. The Bulgarian 1st Sofia Division of the German Eleventh Army, retreating from the vicinity of Ohrid, attempted to occupy the city in advance of the French. Like the 9th Pleven Division of the Bulgarian First Army, the 1st Sofia Division had managed to maintain discipline after the Dobro Pole disaster.[60] Before it could marshal its forces for a full attack on Skopie, the armistice had come into effect.

The situation in southwestern Bulgaria, where hordes of disgruntled Bulgarian soldiers gathered, now threatened the survival of the regime. Crown Prince Boris told the German military attaché in Sofia, Colonel von Masow, that if the Germans did not arrive soon, revolution would break out in Bulgaria.[61] The 217th Infantry division came by sea from the Crimea to Varna, and from there by train to Sofia. The Germans began to arrive in

Sofia on 25 September. Two German battalions took up positions around the royal palace. Their mission had changed. The Germans now found themselves preparing to fight disgruntled Bulgarian soldiers, not the Entente. The German failure to arrive promptly undoubtedly undermined Bulgarian morale further. This can have been of small satisfaction to those in the Bulgarian military who had decried the transfer of German troops from the Macedonian Front earlier that year and who had repeatedly requested the Germans to strengthen the front.

After the decision of the Ministerial Council on 25 September to seek an armistice, the fate of Bulgaria rested with the efforts of the delegation at Salonika. When it arrived, the Entente commander, General Franchet d'Espérey, sent a note to the Bulgarian delegation, which contained the following reassurance:

> We could justly behave cruelly toward Bulgaria. She no longer has an army and is at our mercy. However, we do not want to ruin [Bulgaria]. Nor do we want to impose humiliating conditions on her. We will not enter Sofia, nor will we compromise your sovereignty. But we require from you certain guarantees, necessary or not, for the security and progress of our operation.[62]

Minister Lyapchev sought mild terms for Bulgaria, even suggesting that Bulgaria could now become a neutral state.[63] They also wanted to retain five divisions under arms in case of an eventual threat from Germany or Romania over Dobrudzha or, more likely, a conflict with the Ottomans.[64] This latter had been escalating for some time. The Bulgarian delegation, however, was in no position to impose conditions. It had to accept all of the Entente demands. General Zhekov, still ailing in Vienna, urged that the armistice negotiations end and the fighting continue in the expectation of help from the Central Powers.[65] This was no longer a realistic option for the Bulgarians. American support had little effect in ameliorating the armistice conditions. Overall these conditions were not especially onerous for Bulgaria. The main provisions were:

1. Bulgarian sovereignty will be maintained;
2. 1915 borders will be maintained;
3. there will be no military indemnity;

4. Germans have four weeks to evacuate Bulgaria;
5. Sofia remains unoccupied;
6. British and French will run the main Bulgarian railroad lines; no Greek or Serb troops will enter Bulgaria;
7. there will be general demobilization of the Bulgarian army except for three infantry divisions and four cavalry regiments, which remain on duty;
8. Entente forces will have unhindered passage through Bulgaria.

The armistice agreement also contained four secret conditions. These included:

1. the eventual passage of Entente troops through Bulgarian territory;
2. British and French troops' occupation of certain strategic points within Bulgarian territory;
3. the Entente command's reservation of the right to demand, if necessary, complete end to relations between Bulgaria and its former allies;
4. repatriation of prisoners of war held by Bulgaria.[66]

Bulgaria avoided foreign occupation, and managed to maintain a small defensive force for suppression of the insurgency or defense against the Ottomans. Nevertheless, the Serbs soon disarmed one of the remaining Bulgarian divisions under arms. The armistice was signed at 2300 hours on 29 September and took effect at noon the next day.

By the time the Bulgarian delegation signed the armistice, what remained of the Bulgarian army was withdrawing over the old Bulgarian frontier toward Kyustendil. Much of the army was still conducting a fighting retreat along with German forces. Some units learned of the armistice from fliers dropped from Entente airplanes that stated, "Bulgarians! You are defeated. We have nothing against you and will not obstruct you on the way back to Bulgaria. Give us the Germans as prisoners."[67] The Bulgarian soldiers used this opportunity to go home, but had little interest in cooperating with the Entente against their erstwhile German allies.

The Bulgarian Second Army had retreated across the old Bulgarian frontier to the Struma River in the vicinity of Vrach (now Sandanski). During the Bulgarian retreat, British and Greek forces had captured 1,300 prisoners, undoubtedly mostly Bulgarian, and 70 guns.[68] Further west, the Serbs detained most men remaining with the Bulgarian 2nd Thracian and 4th Preslav Divisions, including 77,000 soldiers, 15,000 officers, and 3 generals.[69] This number is probably an exaggeration. Much of the 2nd Thracian Division had already deserted. These angry soldiers were on their way to Kyustendil and Sofia.

Meanwhile, on 27 September in Radomir, Raiko Daskalov, a leader of the Agrarian Union, the leading peasant party in Bulgaria, proclaimed Bulgaria a republic with himself as commander of the armed forces and Aleksandŭr Stamboliski, the most prominent Agrarian leader, as chairman. Daskalov stated, "Today, September 27 1918, the Bulgarian people broke the fetters of slavery, toppled the despotic regime of Ferdinand and his aides, pronounced them enemies to the people, declared itself a free people with a republican government and offered a hand to the European peoples for peace and understanding."[70] Groups of soldiers commandeered trains and moved toward the capital. On 28 September, "the first day of the fratricidal Bulgarian civil war," five trains loaded with rebellious soldiers set out from Radomir and Pernik toward Sofia.[71] The disorganized mobs of soldiers began to coalesce under the Agrarian leadership.

For the Bulgarian government, the armistice issue became vital for the resolution of the growing civil disorder. On 29 September insurgents moved toward Sofia in three columns from the southwest. They intended to establish a republic and punish those they considered responsible for the suffering of the troops and the second military catastrophe in five years. Lacking artillery, this motley force hoped to seize the capital by a night attack.[72] That same day, loyal troops, mainly officer cadets and members of the Tsar's bodyguard and recently arrived German units, counterattacked and drove the insurgents from the suburbs of Sofia toward the southwest, whence they had come. The insurgents lost 2,500 dead and over 2,000 prisoners.[73] This was an important victory for the government and the army. As a result of this success, there would be no revolutionary state in Bulgaria as a result of the First World War. Fighting continued on into October in southwestern Bulgaria between government troops and scattered bands of rebels, but the insurgency had lost its momentum. News of the armistice undercut the major cause of the rebellion. Most soldiers returned home.

The insurgents were tired of fighting. Their war-weariness had been a primary motivation for the insurgency in the first place.

With the end of the war, a major motivation for the insurgency was
gone. Despite the end of the rebellion, the resentment among many of the
soldiers over the issues that had caused it lingered for some time. A German report of 23 October noted that the new Bulgarian government, which
now included Socialists and Agrarian Party "republicans" had given up
the old singular policies and now had embarked on a less nationalistic
and more cooperative policy.[74] One diplomatic report from later that year
noted:

> The internal troubles and events at the front have healed quickly
> and rapidly. The abdication of Tsar Ferdinand produced an imme-
> diate easing of tensions. Tsar Boris has managed his duties as a con-
> stitutional monarch with a wisdom which has increased his popu-
> larity trough out the country. The government established from the
> former opposition bloc follows a program in which the main points
> are external peace and defense of the rights of the Bulgarian na-
> tion conforming to the principles proclaimed by the Entente powers
> and within the alleviation and the regulation of the question of pro-
> visions.[75]

A government led by the Agrarian Party came to power in 1919, undoubtedly elected on the basis of the great popular resentment that developed
during the war and had contributed to the Bulgarian catastrophe of September 1918. This government, led by Stamboliski, pursued the leaders of
cabinets going back to the Balkan Wars, including Radoslavov and General
Zhekov, to hold them responsible for the loss of wars in 1913 and in 1918.[76]
Both Radoslavov and Zhekov escaped arrest by remaining outside Bulgaria. Undoubtedly Tsar Ferdinand also would have faced retribution for
his role in the Bulgarian defeat, but for his absence from the country. Other
prominent political figures, including Balkan War leaders Ivan E. Geshov
and Stoyan Danev, did undergo legal proceedings. Only the overthrow of
the Agrarian government and the murder of Stamboliski in June 1923 by
disgruntled military and Macedonian elements ended this process.

The Ministerial Council did not immediately act on Ferdinand's offer
of abdication. Undoubtedly the soldiers' rebellion distracted the govern-

ment. Perhaps Malinov and his ministers feared that a precipitous change of head of state might provoke a reaction from the Germans. In any event, the Tsar retained his royal prerogatives for the time being. In the aftermath of the armistice he seems to have still considered the idea of allowing General Savov a role in the government.[77] After the Salonika armistice was concluded, Ferdinand's position was not viable. He had lost two wars. His country was in civil disarray. He remained tsar of Bulgaria until 3 October, when he stepped down in favor of his son Boris. Ferdinand later said, "The work of a lifetime was destroyed in a single afternoon."[78] This was a gross exaggeration. The defeat of Bulgaria caused by collapse of the Bulgarian army took place over the course of two years. He left Sofia by train the same day, never to return to Bulgaria. Ferdinand, who outlived his son and successor, Boris, spent the remainder of his life in Coburg, Germany, the hereditary seat of his family. Certainly the threat of social revolution posed by the Agrarian-led soldiers and the example of Russia were factors in persuading the moderates in the government to continue to support the monarchy. The abdication of Tsar Ferdinand helped to solidify this support. Boris retained enough personal popularity in the country to remain tsar until his death in 1943.

Even after the armistice was signed, the German ambassador in Sofia, Count Oberndorff, still thought the situation might be saved by a "large, decisive expedition, (also against Salonika?)."[79] This idea demonstrates that the ambassador, isolated in Sofia, was out of touch with conditions in his own country. The German army, in retreat all along the Western Front, was in no position to undertake a "large, decisive expedition" in southeastern Europe. This idea also shows that the ambassador understood the importance of Salonika for some Bulgarians. Had the Germans agreed to the resolution of the Salonika problem proposed by the Bulgarians in December 1915, the events of September 1918 might not have been so critical.

By 29 September, the numbers of the Central Powers allies in Sofia had grown to four understrength German battalions, including the 217th Division and two Austrian battalions, around 6,000 men, all under the command of General von Reuter. The Germans recognized that with their available forces they could not assume control in Bulgaria.[80] The successful intervention of the Germans in battles raging on the Macedonian Front in the autumn of 1916 was not repeated in 1918. While they were too late to prevent the Bulgarian defection, they did secure Sofia against the rebel elements. They also ensured the succession of Prince Boris to the Bulgarian throne.

The end of the war for Bulgaria did not mean the end of the war for the other combatants on the Macedonian Front. After the defeat of the Bulgarian revolutionaries, the Germans departed from Bulgaria according to the stipulations of the Salonika armistice. The German and Austro-Hungarian divisions that had come to aid Bulgaria in the aftermath of the Dobro Pole disaster withdrew to the northwest to Niš. These included the German 217th, 219th, and Alpine Corps, the Austro-Hungarian 30th Division from Ukraine, and the 9th and 59th from Italy.[81] They joined with the German elements of the Eleventh Army and, under pressure from General Franchet d'Espérey's French and Serbian armies, continued to withdraw quickly to the north. General von Scholtz directed the remaining Bulgarians toward Kyustendil in order to clear the roads for the retreat of his German and Austro-Hungarian units.[82] At the same time the Italian XVI Corps, long inert in Albania, began to advance against the remaining Austro-Hungarian forces there. The entire southeastern European front now moved northward as the Germans and Austro-Hungarians withdrew to the Danube. They envisioned this river as a final line of defense. This German and Austro-Hungarian withdrawal from the Balkan Peninsula in the autumn of 1918 would presage a similar German anabasis twenty-six years later, in the autumn of 1944.

The Entente forces moved quickly through the difficult terrain of northern Macedonia and southern Serbia. Franchet d'Espérey's forces reached Niš on 10 October. After a brief fight against the retreating Germans and Austro-Hungarians, they took the town the same day. This provided the Serbian troops with great satisfaction, as Niš had been the capital of wartime Serbia. Serbian forces entered Belgrade on 1 November 1918. On 7 November, Crown Prince Alexander returned to the Serbian capital as the de facto ruler of the new Yugoslav state, which had been proclaimed by the Yugoslav National Council in Zagreb on 29 October. As Austria-Hungary collapsed, the Eleventh Army, already shorn of its Bulgarian elements, was in southern Hungary.

Meanwhile General Milne's British forces split off from the French and Serbs and headed across Thrace to Constantinople. Bad weather, inadequate naval transport, and poor roads hampered their progress.[83] They had only reached Dedeagach, the Bulgarian Aegean port, on 30 October, when the Ottomans signed an armistice with the Entente at Mudros. With Austria-Hungary in collapse, the new Hungarian government finally signed an armistice with the Serbian forces on 13 November after five days of negotiations in Belgrade. Meanwhile, elements of the British and French forces entered Bulgaria and moved to the Danube to cross over into Romania and to clear that country of German and Austro-Hungarian occupation troops. Entente units crossed the Danube at Ruse, Nikopol, and Svishtov on 10 November. That same day Romania reentered the war on the side of the Entente. The next day Germany signed the armistice.

Bulgaria was not the first combatant to leave the First World War. Already Montenegro, Russia, and Romania had collapsed due to external and internal factors. Nor were the Bulgarians the first Central Power in 1918 to experience major defeat. By September 1918, the Germans were retreating in the west, the Ottomans were retreating in Palestine, and the Austrians were barely holding on in Italy. After their defeat at Dobro Pole, however, the Bulgarians were beset by many factors that rendered them unable to continue the war. The material condition of their army was abysmal. Some troops, mainly from the First Army, were in open rebellion. With the Bulgarians bereft of resources and with their army in retreat and disarray, the Austrians seeking peace, the Germans unable to help immediately, and the Ottomans demanding Bulgarian territory, the Central Powers were collapsing. The defeat in 1913 made the decision to end the war particularly wrenching for the Bulgarian government, military, and monarch. Nevertheless, the Bulgarian government and military perceived no other option in these circumstances other than an immediate armistice and exit from the war.

Bulgaria's precipitous withdrawal from the war had important consequences for Southeastern Europe. It brought the Serbian army back to Serbia after an absence of three years. It enabled the British army to threaten Constantinople from Thrace. This reversed the British defeat at Gallipoli and made the continued participation of the Ottoman Empire in the war impossible. The armistice of Salonika also served to restore calm to Bulgaria. War-weariness was a major factor in bringing about the army disorders and the ephemeral Radomir Republic that had threatened the tsarist government in Sofia. After Bulgaria left the war, the reasons for discontent among the soldiers dissipated. In any event, there was little interest in the capital at continuing the war alongside Germany. Only General Zhekov, ill in Vienna, and General Mihail Savov showed any interest in pursuing this course. Not even Tsar Boris wanted to threaten his newly gained throne with such a hopeless cause. Begun without great enthusiasm, the war ended with a collective sigh of relief.

# CONCLUSION

## 9

The First World War continued the cycle of war that had begun in southeastern Europe as the inhabitants of the region attempted to form national states on the western European model. The fighting during this cycle grew to include not only the peoples of southeastern Europe themselves, beginning in 1912, but by 1914 also forces from all of the Great Powers.

At the center of much of the fighting was Bulgaria. Bulgaria's defeat in the Balkan War caused great frustration. Especially galling was the failure to secure the main goal of Bulgarian *irredentia*, Macedonia. Greece and Serbia had divided the Macedonian spoils. When the Great Powers became involved in the fighting in 1914, Bulgaria's strategic location, astride lines of communication for the Central Powers and proximate to Constantinople and the Straits for the Entente, made it a valuable potential ally for both sides. Hoping to realize the nationalist objectives thwarted by their defeat in the Balkan Wars, the Bulgarians entertained proposals from both

sides. Those from the Central Powers, which promised the immediate occupation of Macedonia, proved to be the most appealing. This provided the
most direct means to rectify the injustice of the 1913 Bucharest Treaty. The
Bulgarians eagerly entered the war on 11 October and joined the Austro-
Hungarian and German offensive against Serbia. They quickly overran
Macedonia. To their astonishment and dismay, the Bulgarians found that
the conquest of Macedonia involved them in fighting not only the anticipated Serbian enemy but also Great Power forces from France and Great
Britain. The previous spring these same powers had attempted to offer Bulgaria at least a portion of Macedonia as an incentive to join the Entente.
The Bulgarian army commander, General Zhekov, insisted in the fall of
1915 to his German allies that they should eliminate the threat posed by the
Entente armies in Salonika. The Germans, however, preferred to contain
the Entente armies to prevent their use elsewhere. Also the Germans did
not want to undercut the neutral policies of Greek King Constantine. By
the summer of 1916 the balance of forces had tipped in favor of the Entente.
Additional troops arrived from Italy and Russia. Also the Serbian army,
after being refurbished, joined the Entente forces. Anticipation over the
entry of Romania into the war on the side of the Entente was the catalyst
to provoke simultaneous initiatives from both sides at the end of the summer of 1916. The Bulgarians advanced from the western and eastern flanks
into northern Greece. In the east they occupied western Thrace against
little Greek and Entente resistance. In the west they reached Florina. The
Entente offensive, launched in support of Romania, pushed the Bulgarian
western flank back as far as Bitola. Both sides had made gains and sustained losses. During 1917 both sides remained relatively quiet. The Entente lost effective use of the Russian contingent due to the turmoil of the
Russian Revolutions. It gained, however, the use of a united Greek army
after ousting King Constantine and imposing a Greek unity government
on Athens. Circumstances for the Bulgarian soldiers on the Macedonian
Front began to erode. In the summer of 1918 the Entente prepared again to
achieve a settlement on the Macedonian Front.

Meanwhile, the condition of the forces opposing the Entente had deteriorated considerably. The material situation among the Bulgarian troops,
especially in food and clothing, was abysmal. The Germans had withdrawn
the bulk of their forces and equipment from Macedonia to participate in

the big 1918 offensives on the Western Front. Relations among the Central allies were poor, with the Bulgarians suspicious of the Germans and hostile to the Ottomans. The Entente was determined to use its superiority in manpower, material, and morale to achieve a decisive victory on the Macedonian Front.

The Entente assault on the Bulgarian positions at Dobro Pole began with heavy artillery fire on 14 September 1918. Despite strong resistance from the Bulgarian troops of the 2nd and 3rd Divisions, the Serbian First and Second Armies and the French 122th Division succeeded in establishing control of the most important point of the Dobro Pole positions, as well as the Sokol and Veternik positions. By the next day the Bulgarian lines were breached and the defenders fell back to secondary positions. These fell the next day. The Bulgarians retreated in disarray. Discipline collapsed in some elements of the 2nd Thracian and 3rd Balkan Divisions, brought about by defeat but augmented by material want and morale collapse. By 16 September, French and Serbian troops were making their way over difficult terrain north toward the communication and supply center of Gradsko. As the French and Serbs raced northward, a mixed British and Greek force attacked to the east of the breach at the Bulgarian defenses at Doiran. Here the Bulgarians held and inflicted heavy casualties on the attackers. This effort was too late to stop the oncoming Entente forces. They reached Gradsko on 25 September and Skopie on 29 September. Even before this disorders grew in the Bulgarian ranks. A large troop of disaffected soldiers converged on Kyustendil, the location of Bulgarian army headquarters. With the army in retreat and with discipline breaking down, the government in Sofia decided on 25 September to seek an armistice. This was signed in Salonika on 29 September. For the second time in five years Bulgaria had lost a war.

The Bulgarians had difficulty in understanding the defeat at Dobro Pole combined with their success at Doiran. Why did the troops break at Dobro Pole but hold at Doiran? Both suffered from the same lack of material and food resources. In both locations soldiers suffered from the same frustrations concerning Bulgaria's war effort and Bulgaria's allies. All the soldiers were tired of fighting that had begun in 1912. In some sense they were not unlike the Germans at the end of the First World War, who had triumphed in the east but lost in the west. While French and Serbian troops had defeated two famished, naked, and exhausted divisions, another division, existing in the same miserable conditions, had defeated British and Greek units. In recognition of his success at Doiran, the British Legion, a First World War veterans organization, invited General Vazov to London in 1936. There he met personally with British General Milne, his foe at Dorian.

Several theories arose to explain this inconsistency in the resistance of the Bulgarian army to the September 1918 Entente offensive. One was betrayal, either from domestic sources or by the Germans. The later communist regime in Sofia often exaggerated the influence of the Russian Revolution on dissident soldiers. The establishment of a "Radomir Republic" under the Agrarian leader Aleksandŭr Stamboliski suggests, however, that domestic issues were a stronger motivation for the mutinies than the appeal of international socialism. The failure of the Germans to respond as quickly and thoroughly as they did in the autumn of 1916 with troops and supplies, and the ongoing disputes with the Central Powers allies, lend credence to the issue of external betrayal. Also the decision of German command to permit the Entente advance after the breakthrough at Dobro Pole contributed to this concept.

Many Bulgarian sources blame the defeat on the superiority of the Entente in men and material. The Entente forces were said to have a 1:2.5 advantage in manpower, 1:7.1 in infantry weapons, and 1:2.7 advantage in machine guns.[1] Undoubtedly the numerical edge was a factor in the Entente success. Another obvious cause of the Bulgarian collapse was the problem of morale. On 30 September 1918, the day after the signing of the armistice, Bulgarian chief of staff Major General Burmov stated unequivocally, "The main cause of our failure was because of shaken spirits of the soldiers and the complete collapse of morale in the units."[2] The morale of the Bulgarian officer corps had also become problematic. Obviously Generals Lukov and Nerezov had little stomach for fighting after the Entente breakthrough at Dobro Pole and the outbreak of indiscipline in the Bulgarian ranks.

The problem of poor morale affected other participants in the First World War. Poor morale played an important role in the Austro-Hungarian defeat in Galicia during the Brusilov offensive in 1916 and the Italian defeat at Caporetto in 1917. Both the Austro-Hungarian and Italian armies were able to recover from their defeats, to a great degree due to the efforts of their allies to resupply them. By September 1918 the Bulgarians' allies had no material resources left to distribute.

Still, the poor morale problem among the Bulgarian soldiers was severe. According to one source, the Bulgarian army court-martialed 40,000 soldiers, NCOs, and officers on the Macedonian Front during the First World War. Of these 2,500 were shot.[3] These execution numbers are probably too high. If correct, they would make Bulgaria one of the most Draconian belligerents in the execution of its own soldiers in the war.[4]

The failure of Bulgarian morale after the Entente breakthrough at Dobro Pole was not unique in the First World War. Yet Bulgaria was the only major belligerent that lost the war at a single battle. The major reason for this was the terrible state of morale in the Bulgarian army. As Napoleon said, "In war, morale counts for three quarters, the balance of material force only makes up the remaining quarter." When the Entente forces broke through the Bulgarian positions at Dobro Pole, Bulgarian morale, already battered by years of bad food, poor equipment, and doubts about the purposes of the other Central Powers, collapsed. Yet even after this disaster, some formations retained cohesion and discipline.

Bulgarians made efforts to understand causes for the defeat in the First World War. An easy target was their relations with their allies. Most Bulgarians thought that throughout the war their interests were subordinate to those of the Germans. Some faulted the Bulgarian military and government for their failure to advocate for Bulgarian interests. As one Bulgarian historian later wrote, "The Bulgarian high command from the beginning of the war to its fatal end was unable to maintain Bulgarian interests."[5] German interests trumped Bulgarian interests. General Zhekov strove to maintain Bulgarian goals, but often with little result. One Bulgarian general noted that in this respect General Zhekov was a "one eyed man leading the blind."[6] Besides the enigmatic Colonel, later General, Ganchev, stationed at German headquarters, Zhekov was the main point of contact with the allies.

How could they have succeeded at Doiran when they collapsed at Dobro Pole? Was the nationalist goal of unification with Macedonia in fact a chimera? One result was the supposition that officers and enlisted men in the Bulgarian army had different perceptions of the war and its goals. The Bulgarian officer corps to a considerable degree were the bearers of the nationalist ideal. Reserve officers were frequently schoolteachers who directed nationalist sentiments to their students. The majority of enlisted personal, however, were peasants. They experienced the privations of the war, and understood the nationalist objectives only in vague terms. After the war many officers blamed the largely peasant soldiers' lack of patriotism or focus on self-interest for the Bulgarian morale collapse and the Bulgarian defeat.[7] After the war the gap between officers and enlisted manifested itself in the Agrarian government of Aleksandŭr Stamboliski, which had the support of many of the enlisted soldiers. Among those who participated in its bloody overthrow in 1923 were officers. Perhaps the Bulgarian soldiers' experiences in the war were among the reasons that fascism failed to take hold there in the interwar period. Nevertheless, as one demobilized Bulgarian soldier pointed out after the war about the fate of Bulgarian prisoners of the Greeks and Serbs, "There is not much difference between officers and men, the suffering, the hard labor, insufficient food, struggle and death."[8] This could probably serve as an overall statement for the experience of the Bulgarian army in the First World War.

The Germans tended to apportion blame to Bulgaria for the defeat at Dobro Pole and even for the loss of the war itself. The title of the official German history hints at this blame; *Weltkriegsende an der mazedonischen Front* (The end of the World War on the Macedonian Front) is somewhat accusatory. The Germans frequently decried the poor Bulgarian supply system. In retrospect they also condemned the Bulgarians for harboring overreaching nationalist claims to Greek, Serbian and Romanian, territories.[9] The Germans' own wartime aspirations lend little credibility to their complaints against the Bulgarians.

Zhekov understood that Bulgarian relations with the Germans were rife with complication. Vaguely echoing Thucydides, Zhekov wrote after the war, "The alliance of the small with the large has a high degree of discomfort for the former."[10] Wisely, he realized that Bulgaria's relationship with the German allies as well as his relationship with German command was not based on equality.

The Battle of Dobro Pole was among the most decisive battles of the First World War. The breakthrough that French and Serbian soldiers achieved over the course of three days knocked Bulgaria out of the war in less than two weeks and ended most serious fighting in southeastern Europe. The magnitude of this success is a testament to the courage of these soldiers as well as the war-weariness of their Bulgarian opponents. After the French and Serbian troops succeeded in breaching the Bulgarian lines, many Bulgarian soldiers gave way to anger and despair over the conditions in which they had lived and fought over the previous two years. Rather than continue the increasingly hopeless resistance to the Entente advance, they sought at military headquarters in Kyustendil and in Sofia rectification for their suffering.

The verdict of the First World War provided southeastern Europe with little resolution. Bulgaria sought to fulfill claims to Macedonia again under German aegis in 1941. Because Bulgarian soldiers did not participate in the invasion of Macedonia, nor did they assist the Germans in other theaters, the cost was comparably smaller to Bulgaria than in the First World War. Nevertheless, Bulgarian control of Macedonia lasted only until 1944, about as long as it had in the First World War.

The Greeks and Serbs had only slightly better luck. Greek hopes of realizing great nationalist goals soon came to naught. Encouraged by the grandiose vision of a "Greater Greece" and by Venizelos, the Greek army advanced into Anatolia. There a revived Turkish army inflicted on it a catastrophic defeat. Three thousand years of Hellenic culture in Asia Minor was ended by this disaster. A more recent attempt to extend the control of a nationalist government in Athens in 1974 in Cyprus ended in the Turkish occupation of a third of the island.

Serbian nationalist dreams also ended in disaster. The Serbian-dominated first Yugoslavia lasted twenty-three tumultuous years. The second Yugoslavia collapsed in part because of Serbian nationalist excesses in Kosovo and Bosnia. The resulting conflicts again brought into southeastern Europe the military forces of great powers. The remaining Serbian state is little larger than it was in 1912, before the Balkan Wars.

Bulgaria's participation in the First World War was costly in lives and material. In 1915, 10,939 killed and 30,062 wounded; in the heavy fighting on two fronts in 1916, 41,889 killed and 82,700 wounded; in the relative lull of 1917, 19,039 killed and 24,017 wounded; and in the final catastrophic year 1918, 29,357 killed and 18,247 wounded; in total, 101,224 killed and 155,026 wounded.[11] These are very high losses from a total population of around 5 million.

Compared to the peace conditions the victorious Entente imposed on the other members of the defeated Central Powers, those Bulgaria endured were mild. At the Treaty of Neuilly, signed on 27 November 1919, Bulgaria lost all the territories taken during the war, including Macedonia and Dobrudzha. In addition Greece received western Thrace, including the Aegean coast. The new Kingdom of the Serbs, Croats, and Slovenes took four enclaves along Bulgaria's western frontier, including Bosilegrad, Strumitsa, Tsaribrod, and some territory south of Negotin. In addition, the Bulgarian army was limited to 20,000 long-term volunteers. Finally Bulgaria had to pay reparations of coal, livestock, and other materials, plus over 2 billion gold francs. This sum was later reduced to 5.5 million gold francs. These territorial and material losses, in addition to the human toll of the war, left a legacy of bitterness in Bulgaria. During the interwar period Bulgaria experienced political instability. The Stamboliski government perished in a bloody coup. Another coup in 1934 brought to power a cabal of military leaders. Finally, in 1935, Tsar Boris imposed a mild royal dictatorship, which led Bulgaria into the Second World War, again on the German side. This time the material and human loses were much lower than in the Balkan Wars or the First World War. The Bulgarians once again occupied Macedonia and parts of Serbia, but avoided participation on the Eastern Front. Bulgaria switched sides after the appearance of the Red Army on the Danube in September 1944. During the Cold War, the Bulgarian communist regime remained a staunch ally of Soviet Russia. The issue of Macedonia occasionally surfaced during the time of Soviet displeasure with Tito's Yugoslavia, but never aroused much enthusiasm. Nor did the nationalist fires ever really rekindle after the collapse of communism in 1989. The excesses that ravaged the western Balkans during the Yugoslav wars did not involve Bulgaria. The casualties of the fighting of 1912–18 are not forgotten, but they are no longer a basis for politicians to seek further conflict.

# *Notes*

## Introduction

1. On Salonika see Mark Mazower, *Salonica, City of Ghosts* (New York: Vintage, 2004).

2. *"We"* and *"we"* [*sic*]. Archive of Tsar Ferdinand of Bulgaria, Hoover Institute, Stanford, California (hereafter referred to as Ferdinand), 53-7 1915, Dorbrovitch palais Sofia za General Gekoff [*sic*] (this was evidently a mistransliteration of Zhekov), 22/12 Dec. 1915, pp. 2–3.

## 1. Balkan Politics

1. Instityt za voenna istoriya pre Generalniya shtab na BNA, *Srŭbsko-bŭlgarskata voina 1885 sbornik dokumenti* (Sofia: Voenno izdatelstvo, 1985), no. 16. Manafest na knyaz Aleksandŭr I Batenberg za priznavaneto sŭedinenieto, p. 26.

2. Karel Durman, *Lost Illusions, Russian Policies towards Bulgaria in 1877–1887* (Uppsala: Acta Universitatis Upsaliensis, Sweden, 1987), pp. 122–23.

3. *Srŭbsko-bŭlgarskata voina,* no. 242. Dogovor za mir mezhdu Knyzhestvo Bŭlgariya i Kralstvo Sŭrbiya, pp. 334–35.

4. F. R. Bridge, *From Sadowa to Sarajevo: The Foreign Policy of Austria-Hungary 1866–1914* (London: Routledge, 1972), Document 24, Memorandum by Legationsrat Count von Rhemen, on the agreement made between Austria-Hungary and Russia concerning Bosnia and the Herzegovina (1873–1902), secret, January 1903, pp. 429–30.

5. Ferdinand 63-6 1916, Convention draft, 31 March 02 os; see also E. C. Helmreich and C. E. Black, "The Russo-Bulgarian Military Convention of 1902," *Journal of Modern History* 9 (1937): 471–82.

6. On the genesis of this organization and uprising, see Duncan Perry, *The Politics of Terror, The Macedonian Revolutionary Movements 1893–1903* (Durham, N.C.: Duke University Press, 1988).

7. Bridge, pp. 265–66.

8. Ibid., p. 303.

9. Petŭr Goranov, "Tŭrnovskiyat akt ot 5 oktomvri 1908 g.," in *Obyavyavane na nezavisimostta na Bŭlgariya prez 1908 g.*, ed. Mito Isusov et al. (Sofia: Bŭlgarskata akadmeiya na naukite, 1989), p. 17.

10. The treaty is available in several Bulgarian and Serbian sources. For an English translation, see Ivan E. Geshov, *The Balkan League* (London: John Murray, 1915), pp. 112–17.

## 2. Balkan Wars

1. Richard C. Hall, *The Balkan Wars 1912–1913: Prelude to the First World War* (London: Routledge, 2000), pp. 16–18.

2. Edward J. Erickson, *Defeat in Detail: The Ottoman Army in the Balkans 1912–1913* (Westport, Conn.: Greenwood, 2003), p. 59.

3. Hellenic Army General Staff, *A Concise History of the Balkan Wars 1912–1913* (Athens: Army History Directorate, 1998), p. 56.

4. Ivan Fichev, *Balkansata voina 1912–1913 Prezhiveltsi, belezhki i dokumenti* (Sofia: Dŭrzhavna pechatitsa, 1940), p. 231.

5. Alfred Rappaport, "Abaniens Werdegang," *Die Kriegsschuldfrage* 5 (September 1927): 824.

6. Feroz Ahmad, *The Young Turks* (Oxford: Oxford University Press, 1969), p. 115.

7. Edouard Driault and Michel Lhéritier, *Histoire diplomatique de la Grèce de 1821 à nos jours* (Paris: Les Presses universitaires de France, 1926), p. 85.

8. Alex N. Dragnich, *Serbia, Nikola Pašić and Yugoslavia* (New Brunswick, N.J.: Rutgers, 1974), p. 101.

9. E. C. Helmreich, *The Diplomacy of the Balkan Wars 1912–1913* (New York: Russell and Russell), pp. 353–54.

10. Djordje Dj. Stankovich, *Nikola Pashich i Jugoslovensko pitanje* (Belgrade: Beogradski izdavachko-grafichkkizavod, 1985), vol. 1, p. 134.

11. Vladimir N. Kokovtsov, *Out of My Past: The Memoirs of Count Kokovtsov* (Stanford, Calif.: Hoover Institute Press, 1935), p. 344.

12. Hall, *Balkan Wars*, p. 101.

13. For the peace agreement see Helmreich, p. 331.

14. Ministerstvo na voinna shtab na voiskata, voenno-istoricheski komisiya, *Voinata mezhu Bŭlgariya i drugite balkanski dŭrzhavi prez 1913 god.* (Sofia: Dŭrzhavna pechatitsa, 1941), vol. 1, p. 301.

15. Hellenic Army General Staff, pp. 236–43.

16. Simeon Radev, *Konferentsiyata v Bukyresht i Bukureshtkiyat mir ot 1913 g.* (Sofia: Tinapres, 1992), p. 67.

17. Hall, *Balkan Wars,* pp. 135–36.

18. N. Petsalis-Diomidis, *Greece at the Paris Peace Conference of 1919* (Thessaloniki: Institute for Balkan Studies, 1978), pp. 31–32.

19. One historian pointed out that the situation in the summer of 1914 essentially duplicated that of the autumn of 1913. Helmreich, *Balkan Wars,* p. 426.

20. Petsalis-Diomidis, p. 34.

21. Georgi Markov, *Golyamata voina i Bŭlgarskiyat klyuch za Evropeiskiya porgreb 1914–1916 g.* (Sofia: Prof. Marin Drinov, 1995), p. 50.

22. Andrej Mitrović, *Serbia's Great War 1914–1918* (West Lafayette, Ind.: Purdue University Press, 2007), p. 68. On the Serbian army, see J. Lyon, "'A Peasant Mob': The Serbian Army on the Eve of the Great War," *Journal of Military History* 11 (1997): 481–502.

23. On the confused Austro-Hungarian mobilization in August 1914, see Graydon A. Tunstall, *Planning for War against Russia and Serbia* (Boulder, Colo.: Social Science Monographs, 1993), pp. 159–88.

24. John R. Schindler, "Disaster on the Drina: The Austro-Hungarian Army in Serbia 1914," *War in History* 9, no. 2 (2002): 191.

## 3. The Establishment of the Macedonian Front

1. Driault and Lhéritier, p. 84.

2. Markov, *Golyamata voina i Bŭlgarskiyat klyuch za Evropeiskiya porgreb 1914–1916,* p. 133.

3. See James M. Potts, "The Loss of Bulgaria," in *Russian Diplomacy and Eastern Europe 1914–1917,* ed. Alexander Dallin et al. (New York: King's Crown, 1963), p. 222.

4. See Richard C. Hall, *Bulgaria's Road to the First World War* (Boulder, Colo.: East European Monographs, 1996), p. 269.

5. For terms of the agreement, see Gerard Silberstein, *The Troubled Alliance: German-Austrian Relations 1914–1917* (Lexington: University Press of Kentucky, 1970), pp. 173–74. The 1912 Serbo-Bulgarian alliance assigned southeastern Macedonia to Bulgaria as the "uncontested" zone and left northwestern Macedonia, the "contested zone," to the ultimate arbitration of Russian Tsar Nicholas.

6. Hristo Hristev, ed., *Bŭlgarska voenna istoriya, Podbani izbor i dokymenti,* tom 3 (Sofia: Voenna izdatelstvo, 1986) (hereafter referred to as *BVI*), no. 32 Voenna konventsiya mezhdu Germaniya, Avstro-Ungariya i Bŭlgariya 24 August 1915, pp. 59–60. See also Silberstein, pp. 170–71.

7. For the terms of this convention, see Nikola T. Zhekov, *Bŭlgarskoto voistvo 1878–1928 g.* (Sofia: Bratya mladinovi, 1928), pp. 346–347.

8. Gencho Kamburov, "Voennopoliticheskite otnosheniya mezhdu Bŭlgariya i Germaniya prez Pŭrvata svetovna voina," in Bŭlgarska akademiya na naukite, *Bŭlgarsko-Germanski otnozheniya i vŭzki* (Sofia: Bŭlgarska akademiya na naukite, 1972), vol. 1, pp. 246–47.

9. Markov, *Golyamata voina i Bŭlgarskiyat klyuch za Evropeiskiya porgreb 1914–1916 g., p.* 53. Dimitriev commanded the Russian Third and later the Twelfth Armies during the war. In 1918 in Rostov the Communists shot him as a hostage.

10. Tsar Ferdinand, the nominal commander of the Bulgarian army during the defeat of the Balkan Wars, did not again assume direct command of the Bulgarian army. Nevertheless he retained strong influence in the command of the Bulgarian army. Stilyan Noykov, "The Bulgarian Army in World War I, 1915–1918," in *East Central European Society in World War I,* ed. Béla K. Király and Nándor F. Dreisziger (Boulder, Colo.: Social Science Monographs, 1985), p. 405.

11. Dimitŭr Azmanov, *Bŭlgarski visi voennachalnitsi prez Balkanskata i Pŭrvata svetovna voina* (Sofia: Voenno izdatelstvo, 2000), pp. 174–75.

12. For a breakdown of Bulgarian artillery and infantry weapons at the beginning of the First World War, see Stancho Stanchev, Ignat Krivorov, and Todor Petrov, eds., *Bŭlgarskata armiya v Pŭrvata svetovna voina (1915–1918)* (Sofia: Voenno izdatelstvo, n.d.), pp. 78–80.

13. Ferdinand 54-6 1915, Military Reports, Report of Gen. Savov, 2 February 1915 os., p. 19.

14. Iordan Milanov, "Bŭlgarskata armiya prez Pŭrvata svetovna voina (1915–1918)," *Voennoistoricheski sbornik* 59, no. 4 (1990): 91.

15. Stanchev, Krivorov, and Petrov, p. 70.

16. *BVI* no. 50, Manifest kŭm Bŭlgarskiya narod za obyavyavane voina na Sŭrbiya, p. 77.

17. The figures are from Stanchev, Krivorov, and Petrov, pp. 81–82.

18. Tushe Vlahov, *Otnosheniyata mezhdu Bŭlgariya i tsentralnite sili po vreme na voinite 1912–1918 g.* (Sofia: Bŭlgarskata komunisticheska partiya, 1957), pp. 220, 231.

19. Dimitŭr Histov, "Mobilizatsiyata na Bŭlgarskata voiska prez 1915," *Voennoistoricheski sbornik* no. 1 (1972): 211–12.

20. *BVI* no. 43, Poveritelen doklad no. 205, p. 70.

21. Mitrović, p. 147.

22. David Dutton, *The Politics of Diplomacy: Britain and France in the Balkans in the First World War* (London: Tauris Academic Studies, 1998), pp. 22–30.

23. Ministère de la Guerre, Ètat-Major de L'Armée-Service historique, *Les Armées françaises dans la Grande Guerre* (hereafter referred to as *AFGG*) (Paris: Imprimerie nationale, 1936), VIII vol. annex 1, 2nd vol. no. 7 (hereafter indicated thus: VIII 1, 2), Capacité de transport de la ligne Salonique Belgrade dans l'éventualité de renforts en Serbie, 13 April 1915, p. 24.

24. E. Adamov, ed., *Die Europäischen Mächte und Griechenland während des Weltkrieges* (Dresden: Carl Reissner, 1932), nos. 20, 21; *AFGG* VIII 1, 2 no. 96, Note au sujet de l'intervention française dans les Balkans 2 October 1915, p. 129.

25. Général [Maurice] Sarrail, *Mon commandement en Orient (1916–1918)* (Paris: Ernest Flammarion, 1920), p. xiv.

26. Ibid., annexes no. 2, Note no. 4/3 du 3 octobre 1915 au sujet de l'intervention française dans les Balkan, p. 306.

27. Albert Pinguad, "Le second ministrère Venizelos (24 août–5 octobre 1915) et les origins de l'expédition de Salonique," *Revue d'histoire de la guerre mondiale* 12 (1934): 143–44.

28. Ministerstvo na vŭnshnite raboti I na izpovedaniyata, *Diplomaticheski dokumenti po uchastieto na Bŭlgariya v Evropeiskata voina* (Sofia: Dŭrzhavna pechatitsa, 1921) (hereafter referred to as *DD*) I 88, pp. 44–45.

29. Ibid., Rezolyutsiya.

30. Ibid., I 93, p. 48. Tonchev reported that the Greeks attempted to persuade the Germans to award them the Serbian Macedonian town of Bitola. The Bulgarians strongly opposed this idea.

31. Markov, *Golyamata voina i Bŭlgarskiyat klyuch za Evropeiskiya porgreb 1914–1916 g.,* p. 124.

32. Zhekov, p. 446.

33. Ferdinand 54-5 1915 Reports, Military, Byuletin, 5 and 6 October, p. 2.

34. *AFGG* VIII 1, 2 no. 358, "Note au sujet l'armée bulgare," 3 November 1915, p. 371.

35. Sarrail, p. 20.

36. Alan Palmer, *The Gardeners of Salonika* (New York: Simon and Schuster, 1965), p. 39.

37. *AFGG* VIII 1, 2 no. 373, Telégram, Général Sarrail a Guerre cabinet, Paris, 4 November 1915, p. 385.

38. Anatolii Prokpiev, "Belomorski chast na Bŭlgaski flot prez Pŭrvata svetovna voina," *Voennoistoricheski sbornik* 4 (2004): 29.

39. Erich von Falkenhayn, *The German General Staff and Its Decisions, 1914–1916* (New York: Dodd, Mead, 1920), pp. 206–207; Zhekov, p. 375, Azmanov, p. 185. The dates for the Parachin conference vary. Zhekov indicated it took place on 1 November.

40. Azmanov, p. 184.

41. Von Falkenhayn, p. 207.

42. Noykov, pp. 407–408.

43. Von Falkenhayn, p. 213.

44. Ferdinand 58-3 1915 correspondence, Ganchev, Colonel. Reports date obscure. Telegram of Dobrovich to Gen. Gekoff (Zhekov).

45. Vasil Radoslawoff (Radoslavov), *Bulgarien und die Weltkrise* (Berlin: Ulstein, 1923) pp. 198–99.

46. Ferdinand 54-2 1915, Reports, Military 30 October 1915 os.

47. M. Larcher, *La Grande guerre dans les Balkans* (Paris: Payot, 1929), p. 80.

48. Vasil Radoslavov, *Dnevni belezhki 1914–1916* (Sofia: Sv. Kliment Ohridski, 1993), p. 171.

49. Ferdinand 56-1 1916 General Correspondence, telegram of Ferdinand to the Prince of Tŭrnovo 29 October 1915 os., pp 2–3.

50. *DD* I no. 142, p. 86.

51. Vlahov, 231.

52. Dimitŭr Hristov, "Osnovni voennostrategicheski problemi na Bŭlgarskoto komandyvane prez Pŭrvata svetovna voina 1915–1918 г.," *Izvestiya na Voennoistoricheskoto nauchno dryzhestvo* 17–18, no. 3–4 (1974): 37.

53. Ferdinand 54-5, Reports, Military, Byuletin, 21 November 1915 os., p. 2.

54. Lieutenant-Colonel Nédeff, *Les operations en Macédoine, L'épopée de Doïran 1915–1918* (Sofia: Armeyski Voeno-Isdatelski Fond, 1927), p. 20.

55. Markov, *Golyamata voina i Bŭlgarskiyat klyuch za Evropeiskiya porgreb 1914–1916*, p. 223.

56. Palmer, p. 43.

57. Zhekov, p. 373.

58. Borislav Dichev, *General Georgi Tanovski; Voin, patriot, grazhdanin* (Sofia: Zaharii Stoyanov, 2003), p. 120; Nédeff, p. 21.

59. Radoslavov, p. 175.

60. *DD* I no. 174, p. 106.

61. *"We"* and *"we"* [*sic*]. Ferdinand 53-7 1915, Dorbrovitch palais Sofia za General Gekoff [*sic*] 22/12 Dec 1915, pp. 2–3.

62. *AFGG* VIII 1, 2 no. 693, Général Sarrail à minister Guerre cabinet, Paris, 27 November 1915.

63. Ibid., 3 no. 820 Procès-verbal de la conférence tenue à Chantilly, 8 December 1915, p. 73.

64. Ferdinand 54-5 1915, Reports, Military, Raport of Mayuor Pavlov 7 December 1915 os., pp. 1–2.

65. *AFGG* VIII 2, 3 no. 1058, à general commandant en chef, 30 December 1915. A joint British and French detachment arrested 20 Austrians, 17 Turks, 12 Bulgarians, and 5 Germans. The Bulgarians were taken to France and released in Switzerland. Ferdinand 69-6 1918 Bulgarian Foreign Policy, Doklad of T. Nedkov, 12 February 1916, os.

66. Ferdinand 54-5 1915, Reports, Military, Raport of Mayuor Pavlov 7 December 1915 os., p. 2.

67. Radoslawoff, *Weltkrise*, p. 199.

68. Markov, *Golyamata voina i Bŭlgarskiyat klyuch za Evropeiskiya porgreb 1914–1916, p.* 227. Ferdinand called him a "russophile and a democrat." Ibid. This was damnation indeed from the Bulgarian tsar.

69. Radoslavov, *Dnevni belezhki*, p. 174.

70. Ferdinand 56-11 1916, correspondence, Bulgarian legation in Athens, p. 2.

71. *DD* I no. 220, p. 143.

72. Nédeff, pp. 34–35.

73. Zhekov, p. 370.

74. Von Falkenhayn, p. 216.

75. Mihail Bunardiev, *Ima li predatelstvo na Dobro Pole* (Sofia: Armeiskiya voen.-izdatelski fond, 1921), p. 5.

76. Ferdinand 53-7 1915, Col. Ganchev, reports, von Falkenhayn to Gen. Gecov (Zhekov), 22 December 1915.

## 4. Development of the Macedonian Front

1. Azmanov, p. 184.

2. Zhekov, p. 376; see also p. 432.

3. Milcho Lalkov, *Balkanskata politika na Avstro-Ungariya 1914–1917* (Sofia: Nauka i izkustvo, 1983), p. 364.

4. *AFGG* VIII 1, 3 no. 1170, Compte rendu des opérations de l'armée d'Orient du 16 au 31 janvier 1916, p. 398; no. 1290, Compte rendu des opérations de l'armée d'Orient du 16 au 30 avril 1916, p. 599; Jacques Ancel, *Les Travaux et les jours de l'Armée d'orient* (Paris: Bossard, 1921), p. 81.

5. See, for example, *AFGG* VIII 1, 2 no. 619, Note sur l'occupation de la région de Salonikque, 21 november 1915, pp. 609–11; no. 641, Exposé de la situation dans les Balkans, 22 November 1915, p. 636; Palmer, p. 44.

6. Ferdinand 60-6 1915, Incoming correspondence, Report of Bulgarian Military Attaché Athens, 28 January 1916 os.

7. *AFGG* VIII 1, 3 no. 938, Le général Moschopoulos, commmandant le 3e corps d'armée hèllénique, à Monsieur le general Sarrail, commandant l'armée française d'Orient, 29 décembre 1915.

8. Ferdinand 63-3 1916, Miscellaneous, pp. 1–2. Vereinbarung zwischen der Deutschen und der Bulgarischen Oberstenheeresleitungen. Generals von Falkenhayn and Tappen signed for Germany and General Zhekov and Colonel Ganchev signed for Bulgaria.

9. Von Falkenhayn, p. 214.

10. Ferdinand 53-7 1915, Correspondence, Ganchev, Col., reports, Colonel Gantschev (Ganchev) to general Gekoff (Zhekov), n.d. (Winter 1916), p. 3.

11. Zhekov, p. 374, Nédeff, pp. 23, 30.

12. Vlahov, p. 232.

13. Markov, *Golyamata voina i Bŭlgarskiyat klyuch za Evropeiskiya porgreb 1914–1916, p.* 235.

14. Von Falkenhayn, p. 214.

15. Milanov, pp. 98–99.

16. *BVI* no. 67, pp. 103–105.

17. Nédeff, p. 24.

18. Dimitŭr Minchev, *Uchastieto na naselenieto ot Makedoniya v Bŭlgarskata armiya prez Pŭrvata svetovna voina 1914–1918 g.* (Sofia: Sv. Georgi pobedonosets, 1994), p. 180.

19. Markov, *Golyamata voina i Bŭlgarskiyat klyuch za Evropeiskiya porgreb 1914–1916, p.* 237.

20. *AFGG* VIII 1, 3 no. 1002, Le général commandant en chef de l'armée française à Monsieur le président du counseil, minister des Affaires Étrangères, p. 242.

21. H. James Burgwyn, "Italy's Balkan Policy 1915–1917: Albania, Greece and the Epirus Question," *Storia delle Relazioni Intermazionoli* 2, no. 1 (1986): 8.

22. Aneliki Sfika-Theodosiou, "The Italian Presence on the Balkan Front (1915–1918)," *Balkan Studies* 36, no. 1 (1995): 70–71.

23. *AFGG* VIII 1, 3 no. 1367, Général commandant en chef à général commandant en chef armée d'Orient, Salonique, p. 725.

24. Richard B. Spence, "Lost to the Revolution: The Russian Expeditionary Force in Macedonia, 1916–1918," *East European Quarterly* 19, no. 4 (January 1986): 418.

25. Petar Opačić, "Evakuacija Srpske vojske na Krf i diplomatska borba za opstanak Solunskog front krajem 1915 i početkom 1916. godine," *Vojnoistoijski glasnik* 25, no. 2–3 (1974): 81–82.

26. *AFGG* VIII 1, 3 no. 1318, Compte rendu des opérations de l'armée d'Orient du 16 au 31 mai 1916, p. 655.

27. Ancel, p. 111, n. 1.

28. *AFGG* VIII 2, 1 no. 25, Général Sarrail, à Jogal, Paris, 22 August 1916, p. 24.

29. Stanchev, Krivorov, and Petrov, p. 148.

30. Zhekov, p. 380.

31. Ferdinand 60-5 1916, Incoming correspondence, German military attaché in Athens, signature illegible, to Mirbach, 17 January 1916, p. 3.

32. *DD* II no. 645, Ot Komandira na 2-a Pehota Brigada—v. Lerin do Komandir 1-a Otdelna Armiya v Bitola, 14 July 1914, pp. 416–17.

33. Milen Kumanov, ed., *Bŭlgarsko-Turski voenna otnosheniya prez Pŭrvata svetovna voina (1914–1918) Sbornik ot dokumenti* (hereafter referred to as *BTVO*) (Sofia: Gutenberg, 2004), no. 31, gen. von Falkenhain do gen. Zhekov, 27 June 1916, p. 75.

34. Ferdinand 54-9 1916, Bulgarian Military Affairs, "Telegram von General v. Falkanhayn an General Jekoff am 9. 7. 1916," pp. 1–2.

35. Tsvetlana Todorova, ed., *Bŭlgariya v Pŭrvata svetovna voina, Germanski diplomaticheski dokumenti* (hereafter referred to as *GDD*) (Sofia: Arhivite govoryat, 2005), vol. 2, no. 33, 28 June 1916, p. 99.

36. Ibid., no. 42, 18 June 1916, p. 109.

37. Ferdinand 62-6 1916, Ganchev, Col., Telegram of Gen. Gecoff (Zhekov) to von Falkenhayn, n.d. (August 1916).

38. Zhekov, p. 380.

39. Ferdinand 58-7 GDA 1916, Zhekov to Conrad 23 July 1916, p. 1.

40. Ibid., 62-6 1916, Ganchev, Col., Telegram of Col. Ganchev to Tsar Ferdinand, 28 August 1916, p. 6.

41. Azmanov, p. 223.

42. Markov, *Golyamata voina i Bŭlgarskiyat klyuch za Evropeiskiya porgreb 1914–1916*, pp. 250–251.

43. Iliya Iliev, "Voinite deistviya na 1 (11) armiya na yuzhniya front prez lyatoto i ecenta na 1916 godina," *Izvestiya na Voennoistoricheskoto nauchno dryzhestvo* 6, no. 5 (1968): 81.

44. Milovoje Alimpich, *Solunski front* (Belgrade: Vojnoizdavachki zabod, 1967), p. 140.

45. Stanchev, Krivorov, and Petrov, p. 177.

46. *BVI* nos. 79, 19 August 1916; 80, 20 August 1916.

47. Prokopiev, p. 31.

48. Ferdinand 62-7 1916, Ganchev, Colonel, Telegram Ganchev to Zhekov, 4 September 1916, p. 2.

49. Ancel, p. 89; Sarrial, p. 142.

50. Cyril Falls, *Military Operations Macedonia* (Nashville: Battery Press, 1996), vol. 1, p. 157.

51. Erich Ludendorff, *Ludendorff's Own Story* (New York: Harper and Bros., 1919), vol. 1, p. 298.

52. Von Falkenhayn, p. 329.

53. Zhekov, p. 457.

54. Paul von Hindenburg, *Out of My Life* (London: Cassell, 1920), p. 183.

55. Ibid., p. 248.

56. Ludendorff, vol. 1, pp. 299–300.

57. Glenn E. Torrey, "Romania and the Belligerents, 1914–1918," in *Romania and World War I* (Iaşi: Center for Romanian Studies, 1998), p. 123.

58. See Falls, vol. 1, p. 117.

59. Sarrial, pp. 83, 135.

60. Ibid., p. 138.

61. Ancel, p. 111.

62. *AFGG* VIII 2, 1 no. 89, Joffre to Sarrail, 30 August 1916, p. 71.

63. See, for example, *GDD*, vol. 2, no. 88, 23 September 1916, p. 161.

64. Azmanov, p. 227.

65. Iliev, "Voinite deistviya," p. 87; Azmanov, p. 223.

66. *GDD*, vol. 2, no. 116, 24 November 1916, p. 190.

67. Ibid., no. 33, Shifrovana telegram no. 900, 28 Yuni 1916 g., p. 99.

68. Edward J. Erickson, *Ordered to Die: A History of the Ottoman Army in the First World War* (Westport, Conn.: Greenwood, 2001), p. 148.

69. *BTVO* no. 69, Poveritelen raport no. 7 ot nachalnika na Operatina sektsiya pri Shtab na II armiya do komandivashtiya II armiya s izvestie za pristignalite na chasti ot 50-a turska diviziya, 2 October 1916, p. 121; no. 36, Zhekov to Ganchev, 2 July 1916, p. 84.

70. Ferdinand 62-7 1916, Ganchev, Colonel, Telegram of Col. Ganchev to Tsar Ferdinand, 18 September 1916, pp. 1–2.

71. Ibid., 62-7 1916, Col. Ganchev, reports, Telegram of Col. Ganchev to Tsar Ferdinand, 19 September 1916, pp. 2–4.

72. Alimpich, p. 180.

73. Mitrović, p. 165.

74. See Zhekov, pp. 410–11.

75. Iliev, "Voinite diestviya," p. 107.

76. Georg Girutz, *Herbstschlacht in Macedonien Cernabogen 1916* (Berlin: Gerhard Stalling, 1925), p. 27.

77. Georgi Markov, *Golyamata voina i Bŭlgariata strazha mezhdu Sredna Evropa i Orienta 1916–1919 g.* ( Sofia: Prof. Marin Drinov, 2006), p. 50.

78. Ancel., p. 117.

79. See for example *GDD*, vol. 2, no. 100, 24 October 1916, pp. 174–75.

80. Alimpich, p. 186.

81. Ferdinand 56-2 1916, General correspondence, telegram Rylski (Crown Prince Boris) to the Tsar, 19 November 1916, pp. 1, 3.

82. See Alimpich, p. 236.

83. Sarrail, p. 181.

84. Markov, *Golyamata voina i Bŭlgariata strazha mezhdu Sredna Evropa i Orienta 1916–1919 g.*, p. 54.

85. Girutz, p. 112.

86. Zhekov, p. 383.

87. Girutz, p. 112.

88. Archive of Mladen J. Zujovic, Hoover Institute, Stanford, Calif., folders 1–2, "General Zivko Pavlovic i proboj Solunskog fronta," p. 4.

## 5. The Lull

1. *DD* II no. 993, Ot Pŭlnomoshtniya Ministŭr Bern Do Ministra Vŭnshnite Rapoti, 14 January 1917, p. 649.

2. See Palmer, pp. 110–12.

3. *BVI* no. 116, 14 March 1917, p. 161; *GDD*, vol. 2, no. 189, 6 June 1917, p. 298. See also Elisavata Dimitrova, "Voennoplennicheskata sluzhba v bŭlgarskite lageri prez Pŭrvata svetovna voina," *Voennoistoricheski sbornikник,* 2003–2004, p. 26.

4. Mitrović, p. 257.

5. *GDD*, vol. 2, no. 142, 20 January 1917, p. 222.

6. See, for example, ibid., vol. 2, no. 251, Doklad, 23 October 1917, p. 396.

7. Archive of Racho Petrov, Hoover Institute, Stanford, Calif., 60, note of Gen. Racho Petrov, 11 June 1916.

8. Ludendorff, vol. 1, p. 297.

9. Ferdinand 63-2 1916, World War I, Reports, telegram of von Hindenburg to Zhekov, 7 February 1917.

10. Milanov, p. 108.

11. Ferdinand 59-1 1916, Correspondence, GDA, telegram of Gen. Jekoff (Zhekov) to Col. Gantschew (Ganchev), 20 November 1916.

12. Ibid., 63-5 1916, Miscellaneous, Telegram of Rylski (Crown Prince Boris) to the Tsar, 16 November 1916.

13. Zhekov, p. 458.

14. Azmanov, pp. 189–90.

15. *GDD*, vol. 2, no. 165, 24 March 1917, p. 262.

16. Azmanov, p. 204.

17. Georgi Drenikov, "'S zhelezni ili dŭrveni krŭstivi no ne inache…' Spomeni za Shturmovo napadenie sreshtu pozitsiya 'Sezar III' 13. XII. 1917 g.," *Voennoistoricheski sbornik* 3 (2005): 32.

18. Ferdinand 68-4 1917, Ganchev, Col., Reports, Erglisse der Bersprechung zwischen deutscher und bulgarischer Obersten Heeresleitung, 4 January 1917.

19. Zhekov, p. 415.

20. Palmer, p. 113.

21. Ferdinand 65-2 1917, General correspondence, Telegram of Ferdinand to Prince Tyrnovski, 17 March 1917, p. 2.

22. *AFGG* VIII 2, 3 no. 1729, Compte rendu des opérations des armées alliées en Orient, pour la période du 16 au 31 mars 1917, 3 April 1917, p. 502.

23. Markov, *Golyamata voina i Bŭlgariata strazha mezhdu Sredna Evropa i Orienta 1916–1919 g.*, p. 99; Falls, vol. 1, p. 296.

24. Azmanov, p. 342.

25. Falls, vol. 1, p. 314; Nedev, p. 103.

26. Nedev, pp. 116, 123.

27. Ferdinand von Notz, *General v. Scholz, ein deutsches Soldatenleben in grosster Zeit*, (Berlin: Karl Siegismund, 1937), p. 132.

28. David MacKenzie, *The "Black Hand" on Trial, Salonika 1917* (Boulder, Colo.: East European Monographs, 1995), p. 376.

29. Mitrović, pp. 182–83.

30. Villari, p. 134.

31. *AFGG* VIII 2, 4 no. 2032, Compte rendu des opérations des armées alliées en Orient, (Période du 15 au 31 mai 1917) 5 June 1917, p. 21.

32. Ferdinand 65-4 1917, Comte Rylski to Sa Majesté le Roi, 12 May 1917, p. 2.

33. Markov, *Golyamata voina i Bŭlgariata strazha mezhdu Sredna Evropa i Orienta 1916–1919 g.*, p. 120.

34. *AFGG* VIII 2, 1 no. 505, Général Bousquier attaché militaire près la légation de France en Grèce, à Monsieur le ministre de la Guerre, 25 October 1916, p. 462.

35. Ibid., VII 2, 2 no. 1126.

36. Sarrail, p. 222; Ancel, pp. 141–45.

37. Sarrail, p. 240.

38. Dennis E. Showalter, "Salonika," in *The Great War,* ed. Robert Cowley (New York: Random House, 2003), p. 245.

39. Ferdinand 64-7, Correspondence, general, Ferdinand to Prince of Turnovo, n.d.; 70–6 1918, Correspondence, general, Letter of Crown Prince Boris, 8 July 1917.

40. *GDD*, vol. 2, no. 197, 19 July 1917, p. 320.

41. *DD* II no. 731, Ot Glavnakomanduyushtiya Do Ministra Vŭnshnite Raboti, 22 August 1916, pp. 482–83.

42. Ferdinand 74-1 1918, Incoming correspondence, Report of Korvette Kaptian von Arnim, 12 April 1917, pp. 1–3.

43. Ibid., 69-1 1917, Miscellaneous, Telegram of von Hindenburg to Oberstleutnant von Masow, 19 July 1917.

44. *BVI* no. 31, Taina sbogodba mezhdu Bŭlgaiya i Germaniya, 24 August 1915 (old style) note, p. 59.

45. Ferdinand 68-4 1917, Ganchev, Col., Reports, Shifrovana telegrama of Polkovnik Ganchev to Dorovich, 7 April 1917. Tsar Ferdinand commented in the margin, "C'est ignoble!"

46. Ibid., 68-6 1917, Miscellaneous, Report of General-Maior Aleksandŭr Protogerov, Direktor, 14 October 1917, p. 3.

47. *GDD*, vol. 2, no. 225, 24 September 1917, p. 361; no. 226, 24 September 1917, pp. 363–64.

48. *DD* II 1159, Ot Ministra Vŭnshnite Raboti Do Ministŭr v Berlin, 21 April 1917, p. 743.

49. Petko M. Petkov, "SASHT i Bŭlgariya 1917–1918," *Godishnik na Sofiiskiya universitet, Istoricheski fakultet* 73 (1979): 71.

50. Ferdinand 74-1 1918, Incoming correspondence, D. I. Murphey, (American) Counsel General, "The Situation in Bulgaria," 25 May 1917, p. 2.

51. *BVI* no. 23, Koventsiya po retifiakatsiyata Bŭlgaro-Turskata granitsa, 24 August 1915; Silberstein, pp. 124–25.

52. F. G. Weber, *Eagles on the Crescent* (Ithaca, N.Y.: Cornell University Press, 1970), p. 211.

53. Erickson, *Ordered to Die,* pp. 142–47.

54. Radoslawoff, *Weltkrise,* p. 297.

55. Ferdinand 65-6 1917, Correspondence, Bulgarian Legation in Berlin, no. 156 Pripis na doklad no 477 geheim, 3 March 1917, p. 251.

56. Ibid., 65-6 1917, Correspondence, Bulgarian Legation in Berlin, Shifrovana telegrama Pŭlnomoshtniya Ministr—Berlin to Ministr Predsedetel, 2 January 1917, p. 2.

57. Radoslawoff, *Weltkrise*, p. 264. The German chancellor, Bethmann Hollweg, had initiated this meeting. Rizov's ostensible mission was to investigate the prospects of a general peace or a separate peace between Germany and Russia. Ibid., p. 266.

58. *DD* II no. 1344, Ot Glavnakomanduyushtiya Do Ministra Vŭnshnite Raboti, 13 September 1917, p. 847.

59. *GDD*, vol. 2, no. 223, 22 September 1917, p. 359.

60. Ibid., no. 172, 15 April 1917, p. 272.

61. Ferdinand 67-3, Shtab na DA Telegram General Maior Protogerov, 31 October 1917.

62. *BVI* no. 135, Poveritelno donesnie no. 3958 ot komanduvashiya 1–va otdelna armiya General-Leitenant Dimitŭr Geshov do nachalnik na voennosŭdebnata chast pri shtaba na deistvyvashtata armiya za nezhelanieto na voinitsite da voyuvat i za izpaena sipatiya kŭm bolshevikite 17 Nov. 1917, pp. 195–96.

63. *GDD*, vol. 2, no. 289, 15 December 1917, p. 441.

64. Ferdinand 67-5, Shtab na Deistvuiushtata Armiya, Shtab Sholts, 28 October 1917.

65. Ibid., 67-5, Correspondence, Predsedatel na Ministerski svet, Col. Lykov to General Headquarters-Col. Ganchev, 25 April 1917.

66. Ibid., 64-1 1916, Miscellaneous, Telegram der Obersten Heersleitung an Oberstleutnant von Massow.

67. Ibid., 74-3 1918, Incoming correspondence, Ministerstvo na voinata, Direktsiya na Stopanski Gizhi to Predsedatelya na Ministerski sŭvet.

68. See for example *BVI* no. 118, 17 March 1917, p. 163.

69. *GDD*, vol. 2, no. 165, 24 March 1917, p. 262.

70. *BVI* no. 121, Shifrovana telegrama no. 353 ot Ministŭra na voinata General Maior Kalin Naidenov do Glavnakomanduyushtiya deistvuvashata armiya General-Leitenant Nikola Zhekov za negoduvanie sred voinitsite i podrotvyana na 1 mai, 21 April 1917, p. 168.

71. *DD* II no. 1419, Ot Glavnakomanduyushtiya Do Ministra Vŭnshnite Raboti, 26 December 1917, p. 885.

72. Ferdinand 67-5 1917, Correspondence, Predsedatel na Ministerskii Svet, Shifrovana telegrama of General-Leitenant Zhekov to Negovo Velichestvo Tsarya, 26 December 1917, p. 2.

73. See, for example, *DD* II no. 1302, Ot Pŭlnomoshtniya Ministr v Berlin Do Minisitr Vŭnshnite Raboti, 15 July 1917 Rezolyutsiya.

74. Ferdinand 73-4 1918, Incoming correspondence, Letter of General-Leitenant Zhekov to von Hindenburg, 26 Dec. 1917, pp. 2–4.

75. Markov, *Golyamata voina i Bŭlgariata strazha mezhdu Sredna Evropa i Orienta 1916–1919 g.*, p. 154.

76. *GDD*, vol. 2, no. 259, 1 November 1917, p. 411; no. 265, 10 November 1917, p. 416; no. 266, 10 November 1917, p. 418.

77. *AFGG* 2, 3 no. 1945, Le général Diterichs, commandant la 2e brigade russe, au général Sarrail, commandant les armées alliées, Salonique, 18 May 1917.

78. Spence, p. 426.

79. *AFGG* VIII 2, 4 no. 2275, n. 18, November 1917.

80. Ibid., no. 2274, Situation des armées alliées d'Orient, 8 November 1917, p. 374.

## 6. The Erosion of the Bulgarian Army

1. *GDD*, vol. 2, no. 30, 17 June 1916, p. 93.

2. Iono Mitev, "Voinishkoto vŭstanie v Bŭlgariya prez Septembri 1918 g. i uchastieto na germanski voisk v negovoto poushavane," in Bŭlgarska akademiya na naukite, *Bŭlgarsko-Germanski otnozheniya i vŭzki* (Sofia: Bŭlgarska akademiya na naukite, 1972), vol. 1, p. 280.

3. Petar Stojanov, "Antiratno raspoloženje na frontu u Makedoniji krajem 1917 i tokim 1918 godine," *Vojnoistorijski glasnik* 18, no. 3 (1967): 38.

4. *GDD*, vol. 2, no. 298, 5 January 1918, p. 451; no. 452, 6 January 1918, p. 453.

5. Ferdinand 70-1 1918, Military Affairs, "Doklad do Negovo Velichestvo Tsariya" of Gen. Zhekov, 12 June 1918, p. 5.

6. See Mariya Veleva, "Voinishkite buntove prez 1913 g.," *Istoricheski pregled* 14 (1958): 14–24.

7. Sevo Yavashchev, "Moralnoto sŭstoyanie na Bŭlgarskata armiya v zaklyuochitelniya period na Pŭrvata svetovna voina," *Voennoistoricheski sbornik* 7, no. 2 (1999): 121.

8. Ferdinand, "Doklad," p. 6.

9. Ibid., 70-1 1918, Military Affairs, "Izlozhenie za duha na chastite ot Deistvuyushtata Armiya prez mesets Yuni 1918 god," p. 2.

10. Ibid., p. 4.

11. *BVI* no. 118, "Shifrovana telegrama no. 5802 ot nachalnika na shtaba do glavnokomanuvashtiya Deistvuyushtata Armiya General-Leitenant Nikola Zhekov za

voennite deistviya na 6-a Vidinska i 8-a Tundzhanska diviziya," 17 March 1917, p. 163.

12. Ferdinand 70-1 1918, Military Affairs, "Izlozhenie za duha na chastite ot Deistvuyushtata Armiya prez mesets Yuli 1918 g.," p. 5.

13. *BVI* no. 77, "Poveritelna telegrama no. 3410 na glavnokomandushtiya General-Maior Nikola Zhekov do Ministra na Finansite za katastrofalnoto polozhenie po prehranata na armiyata," 17 July 1916, p. 114.

14. Ferdinand 59-3 1916, Incoming correspondence, Ludendorff to Oberstleutnant von Masow, 30 March 1917.

15. Richard Crampton, "Deprivation, Desperation and Degradation: Bulgaria in Defeat," in *At the Eleventh Hour: Reflections, Hopes and Anxieties at the Closing of the Great War, 1918*, ed. Hugh Cecil and Peter Liddle (Barnsley, South Yorkshire: Leo Cooper, 1998), p. 256.

16. *BVI.*, no. 134, "Taina zapoved no. 1146 na glavnokomanuvashtiya na deustvyvashtata armiya General-Leitenant Nikola Zhekov za namalyavaneto na daxhbata voinitsite," 5 November 1917, p. 193.

17. Ferdinand, "Doklad," p. 3.

18. Ibid., p. 4. Underlining in the original.

19. *GDD*, vol. 2, no. 387, 12 June 1918, p. 573.

20. Ferdinand, "Yuni," p. 2.

21. Ibid., "Yuli," p. 1.

22. Bunardizhiev, p. 18.

23. Ignat Krivorov, "Taktikata na Bŭlgarskite voiski prez Pŭrvata svetna voina," *Voennoistoricheski sbornik* 7, no. 2 (1999): 95.

24. Ferdinand, "Doklad," p. 4.

25. Stiliyan Noikov, "Probivŭt pri Dobro Pole prez 1918 godina," *Izvestiya na Voennostoricheskoto nauchno druzhestvo* 6, no. 5 (1968): 60.

26. Ferdinand, "Yuli," p. 1.

27. Noikov, "Probivŭt pri Dobro Pole prez 1918 godina," p. 61.

28. Dikov, p. 155. This was Captain Georgi Tanovski, who later became a general in the Bulgarian army. He was executed in 1944 after the arrival of the Red Army in Bulgaria.

29. *GDD*, vol. 2, no. 323, 5 March 1918, p. 487.

30. Ferdinand 69-7 1918, Bulgaria, Foreign Relations with Turkey, Report of 18 May 1918. Underlining in the original.

31. Ibid., report of 13 July 1918.

32. *GDD*, vol. 2, no. 358, 17 April 1918, p. 539. From the distance of German Headquarters Colonel Ganchev suggested that the Bulgarians attack and take Sa-

lonika as a bargaining chip against Dobrudzha. This indicated how little Ganchev understood conditions on the Macedonian Front. Ferdinand 72-3 1918, Telegram Ganchev to Dobrovich, 14 March 1918, p. 2.

33. Ferdinand 75-9 1918, Miscellany Report from Constantinople, 23 July 1918 (unsigned, probably minister Nedyalko Kolushev). Also 72-8 1918, Incoming correspondence, Telegram of Gen. Stanchov to Bulgarian High Command, 4 July 1918.

34. *AFGG* VIII 3, 2 no. 822, Compte rendu mensuel des opérations des armées alliées en Orient, période du 1$^{er}$ au 31 août 1918, p. 416.

35. Ferdinand., "Yuni," p. 7.

36. Ibid., "Yuli," p. 5.

37. Kamburov, p. 273.

38. Ferdinand 72-3, Telegram of Tsar Ferdinand to Colonel Ganchev, 2 April 1918.

39. Ibid., "Yuli," p. 5.

40. Richard J. Crampton, *Bulgaria, 1878–1919 A History* (Boulder: East European Monographs, 1983), pp. 454–55.

41. *GDD*, vol. 2, no. 409, 7 July 1918, p. 596.

42. Ferdinand, "Doklad," p. 10.

43. *GDD*, vol. 2, no. 42, 18 June 1916, p. 108. Up through the time of the Balkan Wars, Russia had been Bulgaria's main source of military material.

44. Ferdinand 70-1 1918, Military Affairs, telegram of Gen. Zhekov to Tsar Ferdinand, 2 April 18, pp. 2–3.

45. On this point, see Zhekov, pp. 375–76; Aleksandŭr Ganchev, *Voinite prez tretoto bŭlgarsko tsarstvo* (Sofia: Rodna misŭl, n.d.), pp. 402–407; Kamburov, pp. 252–53.

46. Ferdinand 73-4 1918, Incoming correspondence, General-Leitenant Zhekov to von Hindenburg, 5 February 1918.

47. Ibid., 72-3 1918, Correspondence, Ganchev, Col. Shifrovana telegrama Polkovnik Ganchev to g. Dobrovich, 20 February 1918, p. 1.

48. Zhekov, p. 417.

49. Ferdinand 72-3 1918, Correspondence, Ganchev, Col. Telegrama Polkovnik Ganchev to Gen. Zhekov, 6 April 1918.

50. Zhekov, p. 454.

51. Ferdinand 70-1 1918, Bulgarian Military Affairs, telegram, Glavnokomanduyushtia na Deistvuyushtata Armiya to Negovo Velichestvo Tsariya, 2 April 1918, pp. 2–3.

52. Ibid., 72-3 1918, Correspondence, Ganchev, Col., General-Leitenant Zhekov to Polkovnik Ganchev, 12 April 1918, p. 2.

194

194

NOTES TO PAGES

110–113

53. Ibid., 72-3 1918, Correspondence, Ganchev, Col., General-Leitenant Zhekov to Polkovnik Ganchev, 23 January 1918, p. 1.

54. Ibid., 73-1 1918, Incoming correspondence, Collected telegram, General-Leitenant Zhekov to Ministra na Voinata, 24 May 1918, p. 2.

55. Ibid., pp. 1–2.

56. Ibid., 72-3 1918, Correspondence, Ganchev, Col., General-Leitenant Zhekov to Polkovnik Ganchev, 23 January 1918, p. 2.

57. D. Dieterich, *Welkriegsende an der mazedonischen Front* (Berlin: Gerhard Stalling, 1928), n. p. 17.

58. Asen Karaivanov, "Otbranata na Doiranskata pozitsiya prez Septemvi 1918 godina," *Voennoistoricheski sbornik* (1988): 122; Kamburov, p. 265.

59. Ferdinand 70-1 1918, Military Affairs, Telegram of Gen. Zhekov to Tsar Ferdinand, 15 July 1918, p. 3; *GDD*, vol. 2, no. 393, 19 June 1918, pp. 579–80.

60. See Markov, *Golyamata voina i Bŭlgariata strazha mezhdu Sredna Evropa i Orienta 1916–1919 g.*, pp. 250, 266, 271.

61. Dieterich, p. 17.

62. Ferdinand 59-3 1916, "Entziffertes Telegram, An Oberstleutnant von Massow für General Jekow (Zhekov)," from Ludendorff, 30 March 1917; Dieterich, p. 12.

63. Hindenburg, p. 401. Ludendorff made similar claims. See Ludendorff, vol. 2, p. 275.

64. *GDD*, vol. 2, no. 330, 16 March 1918, p. 503.

65. Zhekov, p. 450.

66. Ferdinand, "Yuni," p. 7.

67. Crampton, Bulgaria, p. 465.

68. Ferdinand 72-3, Ganchev, Col., Telegram of Ganchev to Dobrovich, 14 March 1918.

69. Ibid., "Yuli," p. 6.

70. Markov, *Golyamata voina i Bŭlgariata strazha mezhdu Sredna Evropa i Orienta 1916–1919 g.*, p. 269.

71. Ferdinand, "Yuli," p. 4. The alleged Russophile sympathies of Malinov's Russian-Jewish wife concerned the Germans. See von Notz, p. 147.

72. Ibid., "Doklad," p. 12.

73. *AFGG* VIII 3, 1 no. 371, "Compte rendu mensuel des armées alliées en Orient, Période du 1er au 30 juin 1918," 5 July 1918.

74. Ibid., no. 620, "Compte rendu mensuel des armées alliées en Orient, Période du 1er au 31 juillet 1918," 6 August 1918.

75. *GDD*, vol. 2, no. 420, 28 July 1918, p. 609.

76. Noikov, p. 63.

77. Crampton, "Deprivation," p. 259.

78. Colonel F. Feyler, *La Campagne de Macédoine (1917–1918)*, (Geneva: d'Art Boisonnas, 1921), p. 9.

79. *AFGG* VIII 3, 1 no. 227, Compte rendu bi-mensuel des operations des armies allies en Orient, 5 June 1918, p. 398. The Greek losses were probably higher. Feyer claimed 600 Greek dead and 1,700 wounded, p. 18. The enthusiasm of the Greek troops undoubtedly contributed to their heavy loses.

80. Savo Skoko and Petar Opachich, *Vojvoda Stepa Stepanovich u ratovima Srbije 1876–1918* (Belgrade: Beogradski izdavachko-grafichki zavod, 1984), vol. 2, p. 245.

81. Ferdinand 74-6 1918, Incoming, Report from Army Group Scholtz to O. H. L., 19 June 1918.

82. Ibid., 74-6 1918, Incoming, Telegram of Oberkommando der Heersegruppe v. Scholtz to Kaiserlich deutschen Militärbvollmächtigen fűr Bulgarien, 15 June 1918, p. 1. The report noted, "The present discontent is more directed against the government and superior officers than against the Germans."

83. Ibid., 75-9, Miscellany, Letter of General von Scholtz to Generalleutnant Jekow (Zhekov), 4 June 1918, p. 2.

84. Ibid., 72-3 1918, Ganchev, Col., Telegram of Major General Ganchev to Dobrovich, 2 June 1918, p. 2.

85. Falls, vol. 2, p. 90. Ganchev's promotion, which skipped a rank, was indicative of his favor with Tsar Ferdinand.

86. Palmer, p. 179; Zhekov, p. 415. About the same time the Germans vetoed a Bulgarian attack near Lake Prespa because of the poor condition of the Bulgarian troops. Dieterichs, p. 17.

87. Ferdinand 70-1 1918, Military Affairs, Telegram of Gen. Zhekov to Tsar Ferdinand, 23 June 1918, pp. 1–2. In this document General Geshov is identified as Geshev. On Geshov see Azmanov, pp. 253–60. On General Nerezov see ibid., pp. 283–89.

88. Ferdinand., 70-1, Military Affairs, telegram of Gen. Zhekov to Tsar Ferdinand, 2 April 1918, p. 3.

89. Yavashchev, p. 124.

90. Markov, *Golyamata voina i Bŭlgariata strazha mezhdu Sredna Evropa i Orienta 1916–1919 g.*, p. 240.

91. *AFGG* VIII 3, 1 no. 240, Compte rendu de renseignements n. 9 (période du 20 mai au 5 juin 1918), 9 June 1918, pp. 433, 437.

92. Ibid., no. 253, Note sur une offensive éfentuelle des armées alliées d'Orient en 1918, 13 June 1918, p. 452.

93. Yavashchev, p. 123.

94. Stojanovich, p. 37.

95. *AFGG* VIII 3, 1 no. 415, "Notes sur le moral bulgare," 13 July 1918.

96. *BVI* no. 170, Poveritelno pismo no. 11153 na glavnokomandushtiya deist-vuvashtite armiya General-Leitenant Nikola Zhekov do komanduvashtite armiite i komadyvashtite na diviziite i brigadite za organichavane i antivoennata agitatsiya na BRSDP (t. s.) i BZNS sred voinnitsite na fronta, 26 August 1918, p. 235; *GDD,* vol. 2, no. 409, 7 July 1918; Mitev, p. 292.

97. Ferdinand 72-8 1918, Incoming, Report: "Otnositelno duha na germanskite voiski i naselenie," 3 August 1918, p. 2.

98. *GDD,* vol. 2, no. 432, 12 August 1918, pp. 628–29. See also nos. 432, 433.

99. Ibid., no. 437, 22 August 1918, pp. 634–36.

100. *AFGG* VII 3, 1 no. 76, Note sur les armies allies d'Orient, 21 April 1918, p. 134.

101. S. Toshev, *Pobedeni bez da bŭden biti* (Sofia: Armeiskiya voen-izdatelski fond, 1924), p. 198. General Zhekov ordered the outspoken NCO, Sergeant Stefan Ivanov, arrested and court-martialed for this outburst. Crown Prince Boris, however, interceded for him. Consequently, Sergeant Ivanov returned to his unit with thanks from General Zhekov for his honesty and instructions to keep him informed about conditions in his unit.

102. Ferdinand 70-1, Military Affairs, telegram of General Zhekov to Tsar Ferdinand, 19 April 1918, p. 2.

103. Toshev, p. 50.

## 7. Breakthrough

1. Nédeff, p. 212. The influenza epidemic also incapacitated the Entente forces at Salonika. See Palmer, p. 196.

2. *AFGG* VIII 3, 2, no. 971, Note sur la situation en Macédoine, 15 September 1918, p. 700.

3. *GDD,* vol. 2, no. 428, 10 August 1918, p. 622.

4. Ferdinand 75-6 1918, Telegram of Major General Ganchev to the Minister President, 2 September 1918, p. 1.

5. *GDD,* vol. 2, no. 440, August 1918, pp. 638–39; see also no. 428, 10 August 1918, p. 623.

6. The Sixtus Affair was a failed attempt in 1917 by Emperor Karl to conclude a separate peace with the Entente through his brother-in-law, Prince Sixtus of Bourbon-Parmo, an officer in the Belgian army.

7. Ferdinand 76-1 1918, Miscellany, Izlozhenie, 14 September 1918.

8. Ibid., 73-1 1918, Incoming correspondence, Telegram K. u K. Karl zu Ferdinand, 13 September 1918.

9. Ibid., 72-8 1918, Incoming correspondence, Telegram Col. Tantilov to Gen. Stoyanov, 14 September 1918; 73-1 1918, Incoming correspondence, K. u K. Karl to Ferdinand, 13 September 1918.

10. Petkov, p. 97. Emperor Karl informed Tsar Ferdinand about this initiative on 13 September. Ferdinand 73-1 1918, Incoming, Telegram from Seiner kasierlichen und königlich Apostolischen Majestät Kaiser und könig Karl an Seine Majestät König Ferdinand der Bulgaren, 13 September 1918.

11. Ferdinand 71-5, Correspondence, Bulgarian Legation in Vienna, Telegram of Toshev to Minister President, 14 September 1918, p. 1. See also 72-8 1918, Incoming correspondence, Telegram of Col. Tantilov to Gen. Stoyanov, 14 Sept 1918; Petkov, p. 98.

12. Ibid., 76-1 1918, Miscellany, Izlozhenie, 14 September 1918.

13. Krivorov, pp. 103–104.

14. Ferdinand 64-5 1917, Correspondence, General, Rylski to the Tsar, 4 October 1917.

15. Bunardzhiev, p. 9.

16. See Archive of Mladen J. Zujovic, pp. 1–10.

17. Petar Opačić, "Pedeset godina od proboja Solunskog fronta" *Vojnoistorijski glasnik* 19, no. 3 (1968): 13.

18. Ibid., p. 17.

19. Ancel, p. 180.

20. *AFGG* VIII 3, 1 no. 228, Examen des possibilities d'un operation offensive sur le front du Dobro Polje, 5 June 1918, pp. 408–14.

21. Ibid., VIII 3, 2 no. 816 Instruction générale pur l'exploitation, 31 August 1918, pp. 384–91.

22. J. Revol, *La Victorie de Macédoine* (Paris: Charles-Lavauzelle, 1931), p. 60.

23. Noikov, p. 45.

24. See for example, *AFGG* VIII 3, 1 no. 298 Le président du Couseil, minister de la Guerre, à Monsieur le général commandant en chef les armées alliées en Orient 23 June 1918, p. 522; no. 3666 Notre sommaire sur les possibitiés d'une offensive en Orient et sur les résultats qu'on est droit d'en attendre, pp. 637–41; annex 2 no. 583 Rappart sur the situation dans les Balkans, 3 August 1918, pp. 31–32.

25. Ibid., VIII 3, 1 annex no. 313 Compte rendu mensuel au sujet de l'armée serbe (25 mai au 25 juin), p. 539.

26. Ferdinand 70-1 1918, Bulgarian Military Affairs, Doklad Do Negovo Velichestvo Tsariya, 12 June 1918, p. 2.

27. Milanov, p. 113; Petko Peev, *Ot Pleven prez Nish do Doiran* (Sofia: Stopansko razvitie, 1932), pp. 176–77.

28. *GDD*, vol. 2, no. 428, 10 August 1918, p. 622.

29. Toshev, p. 103; see also Nédeff, p. 209.

30. Noikov, p. 57.

31. Azmanov, p. 355. See also Dieterichs, p. 25.

32. *AFGG* VIII 3, 2 no. 971, Note sur la situation en Macédoine, 15 September 1918, p. 695.

33. Markov, *Golyamata voina i Bŭlgariata strazha mezhdu Sredna Evropa i Orienta 1916–1919 g., p.* 288. Railroad employees and other vital groups were considered to be mobilized.

34. Iordan Avramov, "Voennostrategicheski prichini za Solunsoto primirie ot 1918 godina," *Voennoistoricheski sbornik* 7, no. 2 (1999): p. 116. This amounted to twelve out of a total of seventeen divisions.

35. Petkov, pp. 111–12; Dimitar Nedialkov, *Air Power of the Kingdom of Bulgaria* (Sofia: Fark Ood, 2001), vol. 2, pp. 55–56. Bulgarian sources tend to emphasize the Entente advantage in numbers. See for example, Toshev, pg. 114; Milanov, p. 112.

36. Ferdinand 76-1 1918, Miscellany, telegram of Tsar Ferdinand to Emperor and King Karl, 23 September 1918, p. 1. According to French figures the Entente had 202,061 men in twenty-nine divisions and 2,070 artillery pieces. See Bruno Hamard, "Quand la victoire s'est gagnée dans les Balkans: L'assaut de l'Armée d"Orient de Septembre a Novembre 1918," *Guerres mondiales et conflits contemporains* 184 (1996): 30.

37. Falls, vol. 2, p. 69. According to one source, Bosnian Serbs composed the majority of the Yugoslav Division. Few other South Slavs participated. Villari, p. 194.

38. Karaivanov, p. 120. Nedéff gives slightly lower figures for the Bulgarians and Germans, p. 181.

39. Karaivanov, pp. 122–23. These included six battalions, forty-eight machine guns, twenty-four howitzers, a storm battalion, and a bicycle company.

40. Feyler, p. 36; Revol, p. 12; Ancel, p. 190. Dieterich stated that there were about 56,000 French and Serbian troops with 566 artillery pieces against 33,000 Bulgarian and German troops with 158 artillery pieces "between the Cherna and the Moglencia." Dieterich, p. 24. The Serbs also had some 2,600 automatic rifles, and the Bulgarians had none. Alimpich, p. 326. French and Serbian sources tend to imply that the numbers of both sides were relatively equal, while Bulgarian and German sources emphasize that the Entente forces far outnumbered their own in men and material.

41. Von Notz, p. 148. The report on 14 September by a British prisoner of cholera among Entente forces may have relaxed the Bulgarians and Germans on the eve of the assault. Ibid., p. 149.

42. Hristov, "Osnovni voennostrategicheski problemi," p. 52.

43. Von Notz, p. 148.

44. Ibid., p. 150.

45. Skoko and Opachich, vol. 2, p. 260.

46. Noikov, p. 65; Bunardzhiev, p. 23.

47. Dieterichs, p. 27.

48. Bunardzhiev, p. 24.

49. Skoko II, p. 264.

50. Feyler, p. 47.

51. Noikov, p. 68.

52. Ferdinand 72-6 1918, Incoming, Sanitaren Podpolkovnik Slavov to Dobrovich, 10 September 1918.

53. Azmanov, p. 237.

54. See for example, Borislava Lilić, "The Soldiers from Pirot at the Salonika Front," *Serbian Studies* 12, no. 2 (1998): 63.

55. Hamard, p. 31; Feyer, pg. 52.

56. Opačić, "Pedeset godina," p. 35.

57. Noikov, p. 71.

58. Falls, vol. 2, p. 153.

59. Noikov, p. 73.

60. Bunardzhiev, pp. 21–22.

61. Palmer, p. 206; Dieterichs, pp. 37, 45.

62. Generalpukovnik Velimir Tezich, "Uloga Srpske vojske u Solunskoj ofanzivi," *Istoriski chasopis* 9/10 (1959): 526.

63. *GDD,* vol. 2, no. 449, 17 September 1918, p. 649.

64. Dicterichs, p. 38.

65. Alimpich, p. 373.

66. Ferdinand 73-1 1918, Incoming, Telegram of Nachalnik shtab na Deistvuyushtata Armiya to voennata Kantseariya, 19 September 1918, pp. 1–2.

67. Noikov, p. 78.

68. Dichev, p. 153.

69. Peev, p. 149.

70. Karaivanov, pp. 126, 136.

71. Dimitŭr Hristov, "Otbranata na Doiranskata pozitsiya, (16–19. 9. 1918 g.)," *Izvestiya na Voennoistoricheskoto nauchno druzhestvo* 6, no. 5 (1968): 6.

72. Palmer, p. 208; Falls, vol. 2, p. 187.

73. Alan Wakefield and Simon Moody, *Under the Devil's Eye* (Stroud, Glouchestershire: Sutton, 2004), p. 203.

74. Peev, p. 182.

75. Falls, vol. 2, p. 177.

76. Nédeff, p. 225.

77. Ferdinand 75-8 1918, World War I daily reports, 19 September 1918; Bozhidar Dimitrov, *Voinite za natsionalno obedinenie 1912–1913, 1915–1918* (Sofia: Sv. Kliment Ohridski, 2001), p. 121; Karaivanov, p. 134; Nédeff, pp. 225, 233, 256. Karaivanov gives slightly different figures for Bulgarian loses at Dorian: 454 killed, 857 wounded, and 1,209 missing. Given the state of morale in the Bulgarian army, some of the missing undoubtedly deserted, either surrendering to the enemy or simply going home. Falls gives the total Entente loses at Doiran as 7,103; Falls, vol. 2. p. 186.

78. Penka Angelova, "Spomeni na General Vladimir Vazov za bitkata na Doiranskata pozitsia (16–20 Septemvri 1918 godina," *Voennoistoricheski sbornik 7*, no. 1 (1999): 99. Dorostol, Svishtov, Troyan, and Pleven are all cities in northern Bulgaria where the 9th Pleven Division was raised.

79. Karaivanov, p. 136.

80. Peev, p. 191.

81. Falls, vol. 2, p. 190.

82. The material condition of Austro-Hungarian soldiers in Italy was similar to that of Bulgarian soldiers in Macedonia. See Holger Herwig, *The First World War: Germany and Austria-Hungary 1914–1918* (London: Arnold, 1997), p. 434.

83. Feyler, p. 89.

## 8. Collapse

1. Falls, vol. 2, pp. 196–98.

2. Markov, *Golyamata voina i Bŭlgariata strazha mezhdu Sredna Evropa i Orienta 1916–1919 g.,* p. 293.

3. Ibid., pp. 295, 297.

4. Ferdinand 72-8 1918, Telegram of von Hindenburg to Gen. Todorov, 18 Sept. 1918; *GDD*, vol. 2, Prilozhenie no. 3, 26 September 1918, p. 715.

5. Ludendorff, vol. 2, p. 368.

6. See Hristov, "Osnovni voennostrategicheski problemi," p. 54.

7. Markov, *Golyamata voina i Bŭlgariata straxha mezhdu Sredna Evropa i Orienta 1916–1919 g.,* p. 292.

8. Azmanov, pp. 238–39. See also Palmer, p. 214.

9. Peev, pp. 187–88; Bunardzhiev, pp. 27–28.

10. Azmanov, p. 239.

11. Ferdinand 74-5 1918, Telegram of Rylski (Crown Prince Boris) to Tsar Ferdinand, 20 Sept 1918, pp. 1, 3. The purpose of Boris's visit to the front is quoted from von Hindenburg, p. 408. Von Hindenburg was an admirer of the Bulgarian crown prince.

12. Ibid., 74-4 1918, Telegram of Ferdinand to the Emperor and King, 20 Sept. 1918.

13. *GDD*, vol. 2, no. 453, 20 September 1918, p. 652.

14. Markov, *Golyamata voina i Bŭlgariata straxha mezhdu Sredna Evropa i Orienta 1916–1919 g., p.* 299.

15. Ibid., p. 300.

16. Hindenburg, p. 408.

17. Zhivojin Mishich, *Moje uspomene,* 2nd ed. (Belgrade: Beogradski izdavachko-grafichki zavod, 1980), p. 421.

18. Falls, vol. 2, p. 217.

19. Azmanov, p. 240.

20. Dieterichs, p. 71.

21. Villari, pp. 235–36.

22. Ferdinand 73-6 1918, Incoming correspondence, Shifrovana telegrama ot Glavnokomanduyushtiya na Deistvuyushtata Armiya-Viena za g. Dobrovich, 23 September 1918, pp. 3–4.

23. *DD* II no. 1619, Ot Glavnata Kvartia Do Ministra na Vŭnshnite Raboti, 23 September 1918, p. 1055.

24. Markov, *Golyamata voina i Bŭlgariata strazha mezhdu Sredna Evropa i Orienta 1916–1919 g., p.* 308.

25. Villari, p. 241.

26. Opačić, "Pedeset godina," p. 40.

27. Ferdinand 74-2 1918, Correspondence, telegram of Major Kuenzl to Dobrovich, 23 September 1918; 73-4 1918, Incoming correspondence, Telegram Dobrovich to Ferdinand, 21 September 1918; 73-1 1918, Incoming, Telegram Col. Tantilov to Dobrovich, 21 September 1918.

28. Ibid., 76-4 1919, General, Telegram of Wilhelm to the tsar, n.d., pp. 1–4.

29. *GDD*, vol. 2, no. 445, 6 September 1918, p. 645.

30. Markov, *Golyamata voina i Bŭlgariata strazha mezhdu Sredna Evropa i Orienta 1916–1919 g., p.* 292.

31. *DD* II no. 1612, Ot Ministra na Vŭnshnite Raboti Do Pŭlnomoshtniya Ministŭr v Berlin, 22 September 1918.

32. Ibid., 1613, Ot Pŭlnomoshtniya Ministŭr Koushev v Berlin do Ministra na Vŭnshnite Raboti September 1918; *GDD,* vol. 2, no. 463, 25 September 1918, p. 660.

33. Alimpich, p. 416.

34. Feyer, p. 73.

35. Von Notz, p. 157.

36. *BVI* III no. 184, Pozir za vŭstanicheski voiski v Radomir kŭm voinitsite za vdigane na borba protiv burzhoaziyata i monarhizma, September 1918, p. 253.

37. Mitev, p. 283.

38. *DD* II no. 1628, Ot Ministra na Vŭnishnite Raboti Do Negovo Velichestvo Tsarya, 25 September 1918, p. 1062.

39. *GDD,* vol. 2, no. 459, Telegram, 24 November 1918, p. 657.

40. Azmanov, p. 249.

41. Ibid., pp. 250–51.

42. Ferdinand 74-5 1918, Incoming correspondence, Telegram of the Tsar to Oberst von Masow, 25 September 1918.

43. Ibid., 74-5 1918, Incoming correspondence, Telegram of the Tsar to Oberst von Masow 25 September 1918.

44. On Stamboliski's motives see John D. Bell, *Peasants in Power: Alexander Stamboliski and the Bulgarian Agrarian National Union 1899–1923* (Princeton, N.J.: Princeton University Press, 1977), pp. 131–32.

45. Ferdinand 73-6 1918, Incoming, Note to the Tsar from the Président of the Couseil des Ministres, 25 September 1918, p. 2.

46. *DD* II no. 1628, Ot Ministra na Vŭnishnite Raboti Do Negovo Velichestvo Tsarya, 25 September 1918, p. 1062.

47. Ferdinand 74-2 1918, Incoming correspondence, Telegram of Ferdinand to Emperor Karl, 25 Sept 1918. At the same time, Ferdinand wrote in the same sense to Kaiser Wilhelm. *GDD,* vol. 2, no. 471, Telegram, 25 September 1918, p. 668.

48. Mitev, p. 285.

49. Petkov, p. 99.

50. *GDD,* vol. 2, no. 468, 25 September 1918, p. 665. German Ambassador von Oberndorf reported that Malinov was "in despair."

51. Dieterich, pp. 140–41.

52. Ferdinand 74-2 1918, Incoming, Telegram of Lersner to Gen. Gantscheff, 26 September 1918, pp. 1–2. See also *GDD,* vol. 2, no. 484, 27 September 1918, p. 678. General Ganchev told the German ambassador in Sofia, Alfred von Oberndorf, that Ferdinand summoned General Savov, the Balkan War deputy commander in chief. He arrived on 26 September.

53. See *GDD,* vol. 2, no. 465, 25 September 1918, p. 663.

54. Ibid., no. 470, 25 September 1918, p. 667.

55. See ibid., nos 488, 490, 491, 492, 29 September 1918, pp. 681–84.

56. Savov had issued the fatal orders to attack the Serbs that incited strong Greek and Serbian counterattacks. After Savov's dismissal in June 1913, he had spent most of his time outside of Bulgaria

57. Ferdinand 74-2 1918, Incoming, Telegram of Kaiser to King, 27 September 1918, p. 1. Among Wilhelm's many conceits was his pose as an expert on Balkan issues. He signed this telegram, as he did others to Tsar Ferdinand, as "Balkanski."

58. Dieterich, p. 139.

59. Ibid., p. 127.

60. Azmanov, p. 319.

61. GDD, vol. 2, no. 481, September 1918, p. 676. At this time both Boris and von Masow were in Germany.

62. Ferdinand 73-6 1918, incoming, Telegram of Lyapchev to Foreign minister, 29 September 1918.

63. Villari, p. 247.

64. DD II no. 1669, Doklad ot pŭrviyadelegatpo sklyuchvaneto primirie s Glavnokomuyushtiya Iztochnata Armiya na Sŭglashenieto v Solun, 18 October 1918, p. 1090.

65. Ibid., 1642 Ot Glavnokomuyushtiya v Viena, Do Nachalnik Shtaba na Deistvuyushtata Armiya, 29 September 1918, p. 1072.

66. GDD, vol. 2, Prilozhenie no. 1, 29 September 1918, pp. 714–15; no. 505, 1 October 1918, p. 703.

67. Dieterichs, p. 131.

68. Falls, vol. 2, pp 235, 251.

69. Mishich, p. 423.

70. Lyubomir Ognyanov, "The 1918 Soldier's Insurrection in Bulgaria," Revue Internationale d'Histoire Militaire 60 (1984): 141.

71. Markov, Golyamata voina i Bŭlgariata strazha mezhdu Sredna Evropa i Orienta 1916–1919 g., p. 323.

72. Mitev, p. 285.

73. Ognyanov, p. 142.

74. Ferdinand 74-5 1918, Incoming, Telegram of the K. Geshäftistragers in Sofia, 23 October 1918.

75. Ibid., 76-3 1919, General telegram, 24 December 1918, p. 1.

76. See Todor Galunov, "La Bulgarie d'après-guerre à recherché des responsables de la deuxième catastrophe nationale," Bulgarian Historical Review 3–4 (2002): 182–87.

77. *GDD*, vol. 2, no. 498, 30 September 1918, p. 698.

78. Markov, *Golyamata voina i Bŭlgariata strazha mezhdu Sredna Evropa i Orienta 1916–1919 g., p. 337.*

79. *GDD*, vol. 2, no. 498, 30 September 1918, p. 699.

80. Ibid., no. 499, telegram 678, 30 September 1918, p. 699.

81. See Falls, vol. 2, p. 256 n. 1; Dieterich, sketch (map) 2.

82. Falls, vol. 2, p. 273.

83. Ibid., p. 263.

## 9. Conclusion

1. Avramov, p. 117.

2. *BVI* III, no. 180, Pismo no. 11722 na Nachalnik na shtab na deistvuvashtata General-maior Hristo Burmov na komanyashtite 1-va, 2-ra и 4-armiya i nachalnika na zhelezopŭtnite sŭobshteniya za nastŭplenie sreshtu vŭstanitsite v raiona na Kyustendil, Radomir i Pernik, 30 September 1918, p. 249.

3. Stoyanov, p. 42.

4. See James J. Sheehan, *Where Have All the Soldiers Gone?* (Boston: Houghton Mifflin, 2008), p. 77.

5. Iliev, p. 104.

6. Azmanov, p. 211. This was General Mihail S. Sapunarov, who served in the military bureaucracy and on the Macedonian Front during the war.

7. See Snezhana Dimitrova, "'My War Is Not Your War': The Bulgarian Debate on the Great War," *Rethinking History* 6, no. 1 (2002): 19.

8. Geo. I. Chacharov, *Pod sinkata na angliiskiyat flag iz Makedoniya sled nashata demobilizatsiya* (Sofia: Balkan, 1919), p. 13.

9. See, for instance, Dieterich, p. 16.

10. Zhekov, p. 430.

11. Markov, *Golyamata voina i Bŭlgariata strazha mezhdu Sredna Evropa i Orienta 1916–1919 g.,* p. 383. Zhekov's figures, 120,000 dead and 180,000 wounded, are a little higher. Zhekov, appendix (Prilozhenie) 1. He indicates that these losses were killed, 16% of those mobilized; wounded, 24% of those mobilized.

# Bibliography

## Abbreviations

*AFGG: Les Armées françaises dans la Grande Guerre*
*BTVO: Bŭlgarsko-Turski voenna otnosheniya prez Pŭrvata cvetovna voina
    (1914–1918)*
*BVI: Bŭlgarska voenna istoriya, Podbani izbor i dokymenti*
*DD: Diplomaticheski dokumenti po uchastieto na Bŭlgariya v Evropeiskata voina*
Ferdinand: Archive of Tsar Ferdinand of Bulgaria, Hoover Institute, Stanford
    California
*GDD: Bŭlgariya v Pŭrvata cvetovna voina,Germanski diplomaticheski dokumenti*

## Archives

Hoover Institute, Stanford, California
    Archive of Tsar Ferdinand of Bulgaria
    Archive of Racho Petrov
    Archive of Mladen J. Zujovic, folder 1–2, General Zivko Pavlovic i Proboj Sol-
    unskkog Fronta.

## Primary Sources

### BOOKS

Adamov, D., ed. *Die Europäischen Mächte und Griechenland während des Welt-
    krieges.* Dresden: Carl Reissner, 1932.

Chacharov, Geo. I. *Pod sinkata na angliiskiyat flag iz Makedoniya sled nashata demobilizatsiya.* Sofia: Balkan, 1919.

Falkenhayn, Erich von. *The German General Staff and Its Decisions, 1914–1916.* New York: Dodd, Mead, 1920.

Fichev, Ivan. *Balkansata voina 1912–1913 Prezhiveltsi, belezhki i dokumenti.* Sofia: Dŭrzhavna pechatitsa, 1940.

Geshov, Ivan E. *The Balkan League.* London: John Murray, 1915.

Hindenburg, Paul von. *Out of My Life.* London: Cassell, 1920.

Hristev, Hristo, ed. *Bŭlgarska voenna istoriya, Podbani izbor i dokymenti.* Tom 3. Sofia: Voenna izdatelstvo, 1986.

Instityt za voenna istoriya pre Generalniya shtab na BNA. *Srŭbsko-bŭlgarskata voina 1885 sbornik dokumenti.* Sofia: Voenno izdatelstvo, 1985.

Kokovtsov, Vladimir N. *Out of My Past: The Memoirs of Count Kokovtsov.* Stanford, Calif.: Hoover Institute Press, 1935.

Kumanov, Milen, ed. *Bŭlgarsko-Turski voenna otnosheniya prez Pŭrvata svetovna voina (1914–1918) Sbornik ot dokumenti.* Sofia: Gutenberg, 2004.

Ludendorff, Erich. *Ludendorff's Own Story.* 2 vols. New York: Harper, 1919.

Ministère de la Guerre, Ètat-Major de L'Armée-Service historique. *Les Armées françaises dans la Grande Guerre.* Paris: Imprimerie nationale, 1933–36.

Ministerstvo na vŭnshnite raboti i na izpovedaniyata. *Diplomaticheski dokumenti po uchastieto na Bŭlgariya v Evropeiskata voina.* Sofia: Dŭrzhavna pechatitsa, 1921.

Mishich, Zhivojin. *Moje uspomene.* 2nd ed. Belgrade: Beogradski izdavachko-grafichki zavod, 1980.

Peev, Petko. *Ot Pleven prez Nish do Doiran.* Sofia: Stopansko razvitie, 1932.

Radoslavov [Radoslawoff], Vasil. *Bulgarien und die Weltkrise.* Berlin: Ulstein, 1923.

———. *Dnevni belezhki 1914–1916.* Sofia: Sv. Kliment Ohridski, 1993.

Sarrail, Général [Maurice]. *Mon commandement en Orient (1916–1918).* Paris: Ernest Flammarion, 1920.

Todorova, Tsvetlana, ed. *Bŭlgariya v Pŭrvata svetovna voina,Germanski diplomaticheski dokumenti.* Sofia: Arhivite govoryat, 2005.

Zhekov, Nikola T. *Bŭlgarskoto voistvo 1878–1928 g.* Sofia: Bratya mladinovi, 1928.

ARTICLES

Angelova, Penka. "Spomeni na General Vladimir Vazov za bitkata na Doiranskata pozitsia (16–20 Septemvri 1918 godina)." *Voennoistoricheski sbornik* 7, no. 1 (1999): 95–100.

# Secondary Sources

Ahmad, Feroz. *The Young Turks.* Oxford: Oxford University Press, 1969.

Alimpich, Milovoje. *Solunski front.* Belgrade: Vojnoizdavachki zabod, 1967.

Ancel, Jacques. *Les Travaux et les jours de l'Armée d'orient.* Paris: Bossard, 1921.

Azmanov, Dimitŭr. *Bŭlgarski visi voennachalnitsi prez Balkanskata i Pŭrvata svetovna voina.* Sofia: Voenno izdatelstvo, 2000.

Bell, John D. *Peasants in Power: Alexander Stamboliski and the Bulgarian Agrarian National Union 1899–1923.* Princeton, N.J.: Princeton University Press, 1977.

Bridge, F. R. *From Sadowa to Sarajevo: The Foreign Policy of Austria-Hungary 1866–1914.* London: Routledge, 1972.

Bunardiev, Mihail. *Ima li predatelstvo na Dobro Pole.* Sofia: Armeiskiya voen.-izdatelski fond, 1921.

Crampton, Richard J. *Bulgaria, 1878–1919: A History.* Boulder, Colo.: East European Monographs, 1983.

Dichev, Borislav. *General Georgi Tanovski; Voin, patriot, grazhdanin.* Sofia: Zaharii Stoyanov, 2003.

Dieterich, D. *Weltkriegsende an der mazedonischen Front.* Berlin: Gerhard Stalling, 1928.

Dimitrov, Bozhidar. *Voinite za natsionalno obedinenie 1912–1913, 1915–1918.* Sofia: Sv. Kliment Ohridski, 2001.

Dragnich, Alex N. *Serbia, Nikola Pašić and Yugoslavia.* New Brunswick, N.J.: Rutgers, 1974.

Driault, Edouard, and Michel Lhéritier. *Histoire diplomatique de la Grèce de 1821 à nos jours.* Paris: Les Presses universitaires de France, 1926.

Durman, Karel. *Lost Illusions, Russian Policies towards Bulgaria in 1877–1887.* Uppsala, Sweden: Acta Universitatis Upsaliensis, 1987.

Dutton, David. *The Politics of Diplomacy: Britain and France in the Balkans in the First World War.* London: Tauris Academic Studies, 1998.

Erickson, Edward J. *Defeat in Detail: The Ottoman Army in the Balkans 1912–1913.* Westport, Conn.: Greenwood, 2003.

———. *Ordered to Die: A History of the Ottoman Army in the First World War.* Westport, Conn.: Greenwood, 2001.

Falls, Cyril. *Military Operations Macedonia,* 2 vols. Nashville: Battery Press, 1996.

Feyler, F. *La Campagne de Macédoine (1917–1918).* Geneva: d'Art Boisonnas, 1921.

Ganchev, Aleksandŭr. *Voinite prez tretoto bŭlgarsko tsarstvo.* Sofia: Rodna misŭl, n.d.

Girutz, Georg. *Herbstschlacht in Macedonien Cernabogen 1916*. Vol. 5 of *Schlachten des Weltkrieges*. Berlin: Gerhard Stalling, 1925.

Hall, Richard C. *The Balkan Wars 1912–1913: Prelude to the First World War*. London: Routledge, 2000.

———. *Bulgaria's Road to the First World War*. Boulder, Colo.: East European Monographs, 1996.

Hellenic Army General Staff. *A Concise History of the Balkan Wars 1912–1913*. Athens: Army History Directorate, 1998.

Helmreich, E. C. *The Diplomacy of the Balkan Wars 1912–1913*. New York: Russell and Russell, 1966.

Herwig, Holger. *The First World War: Germany and Austria-Hungary 1914–1918*. London: Arnold, 1997.

Lalkov, Milcho. *Balkanskata politika na Avstro-Ungariya 1914–1917*. Sofia: Nauka i izkustvo, 1983.

Larcher, M. *La Grande guerre dans les Balkans*. Paris: Payot, 1929.

Ludendorff, Erich. *Ludendorff's Own Story*. 2 vols. New York: Harper and Bros., 1919.

MacKenzie, David. *The "Black Hand" on Trial, Salonika 1917*. Boulder, Colo.: East European Monographs, 1995.

Markov, Georgi. *Golyamata voina i Bŭlgarskiyat klyuch za Evropeiskiya porgreb 1914–1916 g*. Sofia: Prof. Marin Drinov, 1995.

———. *Golyamata voina i Bŭlgariata strazha mezhdu Sredna Evropa i Orienta 1916–1919 g*. Sofia: Prof. Marin Drinov, 2006.

Mazower, Mark. *Salonica, City of Ghosts*. New York: Vintage, 2004.

Minchev, Dimitŭr. *Uchastieto na naselenieto ot Makedoniya v Bŭlgarskata armiya prez Pŭrvata svetovna voina 1914–1918 g*. Sofia: Sv. Georgi pobedonosets, 1994.

Ministerstvo na voinna shtab na voiskata, voenno-istoricheski komisiya. *Voinata mezhu Bŭlgariya i drugite balkanski dŭrzhavi prez 1913 god*. Sofia: Dŭrzhavna pechatitsa, 1941.

Mitrović, Andrej. *Serbia's Great War 1914–1918*. West Lafayette, Ind.: Purdue University Press, 2007.

Nédeff, Lieutenant-Colonel. *Les opérations en Macédoine, L'épopée de Doïran 1915–1918*. Sofia: Armeyski Voeno-Isdatelski Fond, 1927.

Nedialkov, Dimitar. *Air Power of the Kingdom of Bulgaria*. Vol. 2. Sofia: Fark Ood, 2001.

Notz, Ferdinand von. *General v. Scholz, ein deutsches Soldatenleben in grosster Zeit*. Berlin: Karl Siegismund, 1937.

Palmer, Alan. *The Gardeners of Salonika*. New York: Simon and Schuster, 1965.

Perry, Duncan. *The Politics of Terror: The Macedonian Revolutionary Movements 1893–1903*. Durham, N.C.: Duke University Press, 1988.

Petsalis-Diomidis, N. *Greece at the Paris Peace Conference of 1919*. Thessaloniki: Institute for Balkan Studies, 1978.

Radev, Simeon. *Konferentsiyata v Bukyresht i Bukureshtkiyat mir ot 1913 g*. Sofia: Tinapres, 1992.

Revol, J. *La Victorie de Macédoine*. Paris: Charles-Lavauzelle, 1931.

Sheehan, James J. *Where Have All the Soldiers Gone?* Boston: Houghton Mifflin, 2008.

Silberstein, Gerard. *The Troubled Alliance: German-Austrian Relations 1914–1917*. Lexington: University Press of Kentucky, 1970.

Skoko, Savo, and Petar Opachich. *Vojvoda Stepa Stepanovich u ratovima Srbije 1876–1918*. 2 vols. Belgrade: Beogradski izdavachko-grafichki zavod, 1984.

Stanchev, Stancho, Ignat Krivorov, and Todor Petrov, eds. *Bŭlgarskata armiya v Pŭrvata svetovna voina (1915–1918)*. Sofia: Voenno izdatelstvo, n.d.

Stankovich, Djordje Dj. *Nikola Pashich i Jugoslovensko pitanje*. Belgrade: Beogradski izdavachko-grafichkkizavod, 1985.

Toshev, S. *Pobedeni bez da bŭden biti*. Sofia: Armeiskiya voen-izdatelski fond, 1924.

Tunstall, Graydon A. *Planning for War against Russia and Serbia*. Boulder, Colo.: Social Science Monographs, 1993.

Villari, Luigi. *The Macedonian Campaign*. London: T. Fisher Unwin, 1922.

Vlahov, Tushe. *Otnosheniyata mezhdu Bŭlgariya i tsentralnite sili po vreme na voinite 1912–1918 g*. Sofia: Bŭlgarskata komunisticheska partiya, 1957.

Wakefield, Alan, and Simon Moody. *Under the Devil's Eye*. Stroud, Glouchester-shire, U.K.: Sutton, 2004.

Weber, F. G. *Eagles on the Crescent*. Ithaca, N.Y.: Cornell University Press, 1970.

ARTICLES

Avramov, Iordan "Voennostrategicheski prichini za Solunsoto primirie ot 1918 godina." *Voennoistoricheski sbornik* 7, no. 2 (1999): 112–19.

Burgwyn, H. James. "Italy's Balkan Policy 1915–1917: Albania, Greece and the Epirus Question." *Storia delle Relazioni Intermazionoli* 2, no. 1 (1986): 3–61.

Crampton, Richard. "Deprivation, Desperation and Degradation: Bulgaria in Defeat." In *At the Eleventh Hour: Reflections, Hopes and Anxieties at the Closing of the Great War, 1918*, ed. Hugh Cecil and Peter Liddle, 255–77. Barnsley, South Yorkshire, U.K.: Leo Cooper, 1998.

Dimitrova, Elisavata. "Voennoplennicheskata sluzhba v bŭlgarskite lageri prez Pŭrvata svetovna voina." *Voennoistoricheski sbornikник,* 2003–2004, 25–58.

Dimitrova, Snezhana. "'My War Is Not Your War': The Bulgarian Debate on the Great War." *Rethinking History* 6, no. 1 (2002): 15–34.

Drenikov, Georgi. "'S zhelezni ili dŭrveni krŭstivi no ne inache . . .' Spomeni za Shturmovo napadenie sreshtu pozitsiya 'Sezar III' 13. XII. 1917 g." *Voennoistoricheski sbornik* 3 (2005): 32–36.

Galunov, Todor. "La Bulgarie d'après-guerre à recherché des responsables de la deuxième catastrophe nationale." *Bulgarian Historical Review* 3–4 (2002): 177–87.

Goranov, Petŭr. "Tŭrnovskiyat akt ot 5 oktomvri 1908 g." In *Obyavyavane na nezavisimostta na Bŭlgariya prez 1908 g.,* ed. Mito Isusov, et al., 9–22. Sofia: Bŭlgarskata akadmeiya na naukite, 1989.

Hamard, Bruno. "Quand la victoire s'est gagnée dans les Balkans: L'assaut de l'Armée d'Orient de septembre à novembre 1918." *Guerres mondiales et conflits contemporains* 184 (1996): 29–42.

Helmreich, E. C., and C. E. Black. "The Russo-Bulgarian Military Convention of 1902." *Journal of Modern History* 9 (1937): 471–82.

Hristov, Dimitŭr. "Mobilizatsiyata na Bŭlgarskata voiska prez 1915." *Voennoistoricheski sbornik* no. 1 (1972): 199–213.

———. "Osnovni voennostrategicheski problemi na Bŭlgarskoto komandyvane prez Pŭrvata svetovna voina 1915–1918 г." *Izvestiya na Voennoistoricheskoto nauchno dryzhestvo* 17–18, no. 3–4 (1974): 3–56.

———. "Otbranata na Doiranskata pozitsiya, (16–19. 9. 1918 г.)" *Izvestiya na Voennoistoricheskoto nauchno druzhestvo* 6, no. 5 (1968): 3–43.

Iliev, Iliya. "Voinite deistviya na 1 (11) armiya na yuzhniya front prez lyatoto i ecenta na 1916 godina." *Izvestiya na Voennoistoricheskoto nauchno dryzhestvo* 6, no. 5 (1968): 19–107.

Kamburov, Gencho. "Voennopoliticheskite otnosheniya mezhdu Bŭlgariya i Germaniya prez Pŭrvata svetovna voina." In Bŭlgarska akademiya na naukite, *Bŭlgarsko-Germanski otnozheniya i vŭzki,* 245–277. Sofia: Bŭlgarska akademiya na naukite, 1972.

Karaivanov, Asen. "Otbranata na Doiranskata pozitsiya prez Septemvi 1918 godina." *Voennoistoricheski sbornik* 2 (1988): 117–39.

Krivorov, Ignat. "Taktikata na Bŭlgarskite voiski prez Pŭrvata svetna voina." *Voennoistoricheski sbornik* 7, no. 2 (1999): 93–111.

Lilić, Borislava. "The Soldiers from Pirot at the Salonika Front." *Serbian Studies* 12, no. 2 (1998): 54–73.

Lyon, J. "'A Peasant Mob': The Serbian Army on the Eve of the Great War." *Journal of Military History* 11 (1997): 481–502.

Milanov, Iordan. "Bŭlgarskata armiya prez Pŭrvata svetovna voina (1915–1918)." *Voennoistoricheski sbornik* 59, no. 4 (1990): 88–118.

Mitev, Iono. "Voinishkoto vŭstanie v Bŭlgariya prez Septembri 1918 g. i uchastieto na germanski voisk v negovoto poushavane." In Bŭlgarska akademiya na naukite, *Bŭlgarsko-Germanski otnozheniya i vŭzki,* 279–93. Sofia: Bŭlgarska akademiya na naukite, 1972.

Noikov, Stiliyan [Noykov, Stilyan]. "The Bulgarian Army in World War I, 1915–1918." In *East Central European Society in World War I,* ed. Béla K. Király and Nándor F. Dreisziger, 403–15. Boulder, Colo.: Social Science Monographs, 1985.

———. "Probivŭt pri Dobro Pole prez 1918 godina." *Izvestiya na Voennostoricheskoto nauchno druzhestvo* 6, no. 5 (1968): 44–78.

Ognyanov, Lyubomir. "The 1918 Soldier's Insurrection in Bulgaria." *Revue Internationale d'Histoire Militaire* 60 (1984): 135–47.

Opačić, Petar. "Evakuacija Srpske vojske na Krf i diplomatska borba za opstanak Solunskog front krajem 1915 i početkom 1916. godine." *Vojnoistoijski glasnik* 25, no. 2–3 (1974): 79–103.

———. "Pedeset godina od proboja Solunskog fronta." *Vojnoistorijski glasnik* 19, no. 3 (1968): 7–68.

Petkov, Petko M. "SASHT i Bŭlgariya 1917–1918." *Godishnik na Sofiiskiya universitet, Istoricheski fakultet* 73 (1979): 63–105.

Pinguad, Albert. "Le second ministère Venizelos (24 août–5 octobre 1915) et les origines de l'expédition de Salonique." *Revue d'histoire de la guerre mondiale* 12 (1934): 127–47.

Potts, James M. "The Loss of Bulgaria." In *Russian Diplomacy and Eastern Europe 1914–1917,* ed. Alexander Dallin et al., 194–234. New York: King's Crown, 1963.

Prokpiev, Anatolii. "Belomorski chast na Bŭlgaski flot prez Pŭrvata svetovna voina." *Voennoistoricheski sbornik* 4 (2004): 27–31.

Rappaport, Alfred. "Abaniens Werdegang." *Die Kriegsschuldfrage* 5 (September 1927): 815–44.

Schindler, John R. "Disaster on the Drina: The Austro-Hungarian Army in Serbia 1914." *War in History* 9, no. 2 (2002): 159–95.

Sfika-Theodosiou, Aneliki. "The Italian Presence on the Balkan Front (1915–1918)." *Balkan Studies* 36, no. 1 (1995): 69–82.

Showalter, Dennis E. "Salonika." In *The Great War,* ed. Robert Cowley, 235–53. New York: Random House, 2003.

BIBLIOGRAPHY

Spence, Richard B. "Lost to the Revolution: The Russian Expeditionary Force in Macedonia, 1916–1918." *East European Quarterly* 19, no. 4 (January 1986): 417–37.

Stojanov, Petar. "Antiratno raspoloženje na frontu u Makedoniji krajem 1917 i tokim 1918 godine." *Vojnoistorijski glasnik* 18, no. 3 (1967): 35–48.

Tezich, Generalpukovnik Velimir. "Uloga Srpske vojske u Solunskoj ofanzivi." *Istoriski chasopis* 9/10 (1959): 509–48.

Torrey, Glenn E. "Romania and the Belligerents, 1914–1918." In *Romania and World War I*, 9–28. Iași: Center for Romanian Studies, 1998.

Veleva, Mariya. "Voinishkite buntove prez 1913 g." *Istoricheski pregled* 14 (1958): 14–24.

Yavashchev, Sevo. "Moralnoto sŭstoyanie na Bŭlgarskata armiya v zaklyuochitelniya period na Pŭrvata svetovna voina." *Voennoistoricheski sbornik* 7, no. 2 (1999): 120–26.

# Index

RICHARD C. HALL is Professor of History at Georgia Southwestern State University in Americus, Georgia. He is author of *Bulgaria's Road to the First World War* and *The Balkan Wars 1912–1913: Prelude to the First World War.*